CREATIVE HOMEOWNER PRESS®

WALLS, FLOORS & CEILINGS

W9-BBL-822

CREATIVE HOMEOWNER PRESS®, Upper Saddle River, New Jersey

Editorial Director: Timothy O. Bakke
Art Director: Annie Jeon

Editors: Neil Soderstrom, Richard Ziegner
Copy Editor: Marilyn Gilbert
Editorial Assistant: Georgette Blau

Graphic Designers: Melisa DelSordo
                   Heidi Garner
                   Michael James Allegra
Illustrators: Jim Randolph, Craig Franklin

Cover Design: Paul M. Schumm
Cover Photography: Freeze Frame Studio

Decorative tile shown on cover
courtesy of Artistic Bath & Tile

Manufactured in the United States of America
Electronic Prepress: TBC Color Imaging, Inc.
Printed at: Webcrafters, Inc.

Current Printing (last digit)
10 9 8 7 6 5 4 3 2

Library of Congress Catalog Card Number: 97-66399
ISBN: 1-880029-48-0

CREATIVE HOMEOWNER PRESS®
A Division of Federal Marketing Corp.
24 Park Way, Upper Saddle River, NJ 07458

Photo Credits

p.1: Elizabeth Whiting Associates, London, UK
p.6: Philip Thompson, Portland, OR
p.7: Curren Design Associates/Melabee M Miller, Hillside, NJ
p.13: Elizabeth Whiting Associates, London, UK
p.14 (top): Elizabeth Whiting Associates, London, UK
p.14 (bot.): Fashon "Kids Homeplaces", Hackensack, NJ
p.15 (top l): Philip Thompson, Portland, OR
p.15 (top r): Georgia-Pacific, Atlanta, GA
p.15 (bot.): Georgia-Pacific, Atlanta, GA
p.16: Georgia-Pacific, Atlanta, GA
p.17 (top): Georgia-Pacific, Atlanta, GA
p.17 (mid.): Elizabeth Whiting Associates, London, UK
p.17 (bot.): Elizabeth Whiting Associates, London, UK
p.18 (top): J.B. Grant, West New York, NJ
p.18 (bot.): Georgia-Pacific, Atlanta, GA
p.19: Marvin Windows & Doors, St. Paul, MN
p.20 (top): Wood-Mode Fine Custom Cabinetry, Kreamer, PA
p.20 (mid.): Georgia-Pacific, Atlanta, GA
p.20 (bot.): Bradley Olman, New York, NY
p.21: Congoleum Corporation, Mercerville, NJ
p.87: Bruce Hardwood Floors, Dallas, TX
p.88 (top): Philip Thompson, Portland, OR
p.88 (bot.): Kitchens by Deane/Nancy Hill, Mount Kisco, NY
p.89: Armstrong World Industries, Lancaster, PA
p.90 (top): Furniture Classics/Bob Braun, Orlando, FL
p.90 (bot.): Bruce Floors, Dallas, TX
p.91: Congoleum Corporation, Mercerville, NJ
p.92 (top): Congoleum Corporation, Mercerville, NJ
p.92 (bot.): Armstrong World Industries, Lancaster, PA
p.93 (top): Bruce Hardwood Floors, Dallas, TX
p.93 (bot.): Congoleum Corporation, Mercerville, NJ
p.94 (top l): J.B. Grant, West New York, NJ
p.94 (top r): Nancy Hill, Mount Kisco, NY
p.94 (bot.): Philip Thompson, Portland, OR
p.95: Halbeib/Beggs, Inc., Louisville, KY
p.137: Armstrong World Industries, Inc., Lancaster, PA
p.138 (top): Andersen, Bayport, MN
p.138 (bot. l): Velux-America Inc., Greenwood, SC
p.138 (bot. r): Velux-America Inc., Greenwood, SC
p.139 (bot. l): Georgia-Pacific, Atlanta, GA
p.139 (bot. r): Bufalini Design Assoc./Melabee M Miller, Hillside, NJ
p.140: Beth Mellina/Melabee M Miller, Hillside, NJ
p.141 (top): Georgia-Pacific, Atlanta, GA
p.141 (bot): Velux-America Inc., Greenwood, SC
p.142 (top): Elizabeth Whiting Associates, London, UK
p.142 (bot.): Nancy Hill, Mount Kisco, NY
p.143 (top): Bradley Olman, N.Y., NY
p.143 (bot. l): Armstrong World Industries, Inc., Lancaster, PA
p.143 (bot. r): Velux-America Inc., Greenwood, SC
p.144 (top l): Armstrong World Industries, Inc., Lancaster, PA
p.144 (top r): Armstrong World Industries, Inc., Lancaster, PA
p.144 (bot.): Mikel Patti/Melabee M Miller, Hillside, NJ
p.145: Philip Thompson, Portland, OR

SAFETY FIRST

Though all the designs and methods in this book have been tested for safety, it is not possible to overstate the importance of using the safest construction methods possible. What follows are reminders—some do's and don'ts of work safety. They are not substitutes for your own common sense.

- *Always* use caution, care, and good judgment when following the procedures described in this book.

- *Always* be sure that the electrical setup is safe; be sure that no circuit is overloaded and that all power tools and electrical outlets are properly grounded. Do not use power tools in wet locations.

- *Always* read container labels on paints, solvents, and other products; provide ventilation, and observe all other warnings.

- *Always* read the manufacturer's instructions for using a tool, especially the warnings.

- *Always* use hold-downs and push sticks whenever possible when working on a table saw. Avoid working short pieces if you can.

- *Always* remove the key from any drill chuck (portable or press) before starting the drill.

- *Always* pay deliberate attention to how a tool works so that you can avoid being injured.

- *Always* know the limitations of your tools. Do not try to force them to do what they were not designed to do.

- *Always* make sure that any adjustment is locked before proceeding. For example, always check the rip fence on a table saw or the bevel adjustment on a portable saw before starting to work.

- *Always* clamp small pieces firmly to a bench or other work surface when using a power tool on them.

- *Always* wear the appropriate rubber or work gloves when handling chemicals, moving or stacking lumber, or doing heavy construction.

- *Always* wear a disposable face mask when you create dust by sawing or sanding. Use a special filtering respirator when working with toxic substances and solvents.

- *Always* wear eye protection, especially when using power tools or striking metal on metal or concrete; a chip can fly off, for example, when chiseling concrete.

- *Always* be aware that there is seldom enough time for your body's reflexes to save you from injury from a power tool in a dangerous situation; everything happens too fast. Be *alert!*

- *Always* keep your hands away from the business ends of blades, cutters, and bits.

- *Always* hold a circular saw firmly, usually with both hands so that you know where they are.

- *Always* use a drill with an auxiliary handle to control the torque when large-size bits are used.

- *Always* check your local building codes when planning new construction. The codes are intended to protect public safety and should be observed to the letter.

- *Never* work with power tools when you are tired or under the influence of alcohol or drugs.

- *Never* cut tiny pieces of wood or pipe using a power saw. Cut small pieces off larger pieces.

- *Never* change a saw blade or a drill or router bit unless the power cord is unplugged. Do not depend on the switch being off; you might accidentally hit it.

- *Never* work in insufficient lighting.

- *Never* work while wearing loose clothing, hanging hair, open cuffs, or jewelry.

- *Never* work with dull tools. Have them sharpened, or learn how to sharpen them yourself.

- *Never* use a power tool on a workpiece—large or small—that is not firmly supported.

- *Never* saw a workpiece that spans a large distance between horses without close support on each side of the cut; the piece can bend, closing on and jamming the blade, causing saw kickback.

- *Never* support a workpiece from underneath with your leg or other part of your body when sawing.

- *Never* carry sharp or pointed tools, such as utility knives, awls, or chisels, in your pocket. If you want to carry such tools, use a special-purpose tool belt with leather pockets and holders.

CONTENTS

FLOORS

CEILINGS

GLOSSARY

INDEX

INTRODUCTION

Walls, Floors & Ceilings deals with repairing and beautifying the interior surfaces of your home, and you won't find another book that deals so comprehensively with home repair and improvement. Written for the homeowner with rudimentary carpentry and masonry skills and a set of basic tools, Walls, Floors & Ceilings is packed with informative, clearly illustrated, step-by-step projects. Some of these projects are complex and require making structural changes to your living areas. Other projects are simple descriptions of how to repair minor damage or replace worn-out materials. The introduction to each project tells you how to plan the job, what to anticipate, and which tools and materials you need. The instructions give you the fundamental techniques and helpful hints that you'll need to do the job right without a lot of wasted time wondering what to do next.

And to inspire your creativity, there are dozens of color photographs of finished rooms featuring many of the construction details described in the step-by-step projects.

Here's a sample of some of the things you'll learn from Walls, Floors & Ceilings: how to remove a bearing wall safely; what the most efficient sequence is for painting a room; what to do about squeaky stair treads; how to lay ceramic tile; how to hang a suspended ceiling; how to cut ceiling molding.

From hanging drywall to hanging a painting, Walls, Floors & Ceilings will provide every do-it-yourselfer with the information and inspiration to create the ultimate home.

The floor and ceiling above can be installed by a beginning do-it-yourselfer with a modest array of tools. The same is true of the interior on the next page.

TOOLS

The following pages show many of the tools that will save you time and effort when repairing or renovating your home. Some of the tools are indispensable, such as a taping knife for finishing drywall or a spirit level for checking that your work is perfectly horizontal or vertical. Other tools, especially power tools, might be considered luxuries. However, they'll do the work faster and more accurately than hand tools, so if you plan to work on your house regularly, a collection of basic power tools is a good investment. These include a circular saw, a variable-speed drill and, for renovations, a reciprocating saw. But you might consider renting more specialized tools, such as a power miter saw or a rotary drill, instead of buying them.

Essential hand tools include a hammer, a 25-foot tape measure, a hand saw, assorted screwdrivers, and (for concrete work) a shovel and rake. With a few exceptions, such as the wallpaper brush shown here, tools that are used only for a particular project are shown on pages accompanying that project. For example, a knee-kicker and power stretcher are shown in "Installing Wall-to-Wall Carpet," page 123, because you'll probably need them only for that particular job.

Finishing Tools

Caulking gun has a trigger-operated plunger that forces caulk from its tube.

Paint scraper has a curved blade that shaves paint from surfaces.

Respirator has filter cartridges that remove harmful pollutants from the air.

Taping knife has a wide, rectangular blade for spreading joint compound on drywall seams.

J-roller has a plastic wheel that presses edges of sheet materials into adhesive.

Wallpaper brush has short, soft bristles and a large wood base.

Working on your home can be fun and rewarding, but it can also pose hazards. Always observe all of the safety precautions for any tool. When you use a tool, you shouldn't need to be stepping over clutter underfoot. Keep your work area clean. If you're tearing out a wall, for example, get rid of the plaster or drywall and old framing lumber, and bend over or pull out all nails. If you use portable power tools, be sure the cords are safely out of your way and clear of the tool's action.

Use a tool only for its intended purpose. For example, not all hammers are intended for all types of striking. If the instructions in a project call for a rubber mallet, do not use a framing hammer. And don't use a screwdriver where the project calls for a chisel. If you don't have the right tool, find a means of getting it.

Keep cutting tools sharp. A sharp tool is actually safer than a dull one. A dull tool is much more likely to slip off the work and mar the surface or injure the user. And sharp blades put less strain on power tools.

Masonry Tools

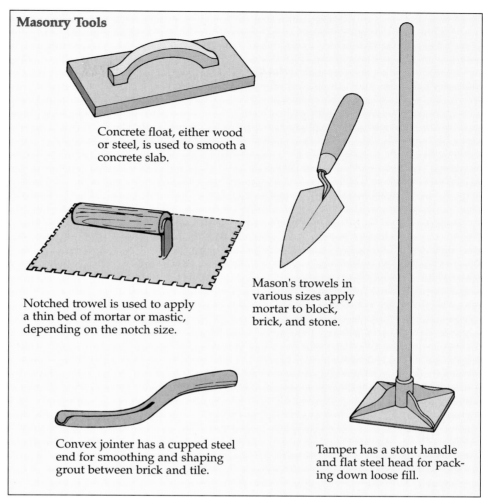

Concrete float, either wood or steel, is used to smooth a concrete slab.

Notched trowel is used to apply a thin bed of mortar or mastic, depending on the notch size.

Mason's trowels in various sizes apply mortar to block, brick, and stone.

Convex jointer has a cupped steel end for smoothing and shaping grout between brick and tile.

Tamper has a stout handle and flat steel head for packing down loose fill.

Power Tools

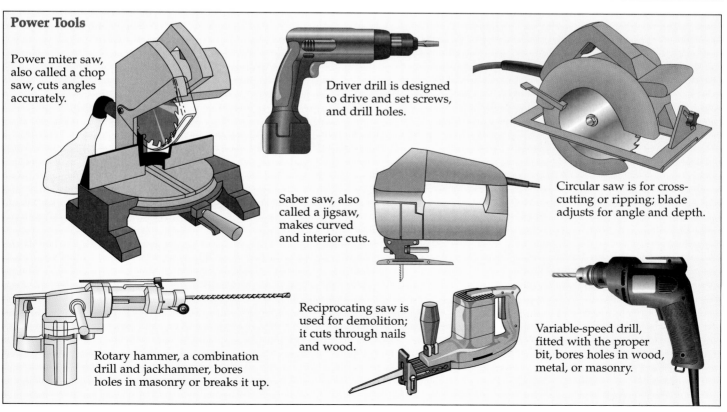

Power miter saw, also called a chop saw, cuts angles accurately.

Driver drill is designed to drive and set screws, and drill holes.

Saber saw, also called a jigsaw, makes curved and interior cuts.

Circular saw is for crosscutting or ripping; blade adjusts for angle and depth.

Rotary hammer, a combination drill and jackhammer, bores holes in masonry or breaks it up.

Reciprocating saw is used for demolition; it cuts through nails and wood.

Variable-speed drill, fitted with the proper bit, bores holes in wood, metal, or masonry.

Never use damaged tools. A cracked pry bar will soon snap; this could ruin a perfectly good piece of molding or, even worse, chew up your hand. Discard tools that can't be repaired. And if you make repairs, try to use new parts.

Watch out for other people in the work area, especially children. If children want to learn, determine ways to let them watch from a safe distance. And because you need your concentration for your projects, avoid being distracted by conversation.

Dress for the job. Avoid loose-fitting clothing that might get caught in power tools. Wear safety goggles whenever the operation will produce flying chips or debris. Also, wear a dust mask or respirator to avoid breathing dust or fumes, and wear ear protection when running power tools.

Struck Tools

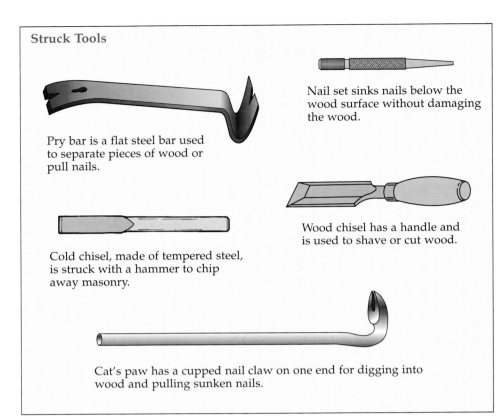

Pry bar is a flat steel bar used to separate pieces of wood or pull nails.

Nail set sinks nails below the wood surface without damaging the wood.

Cold chisel, made of tempered steel, is struck with a hammer to chip away masonry.

Wood chisel has a handle and is used to shave or cut wood.

Cat's paw has a cupped nail claw on one end for digging into wood and pulling sunken nails.

Cutting Tools

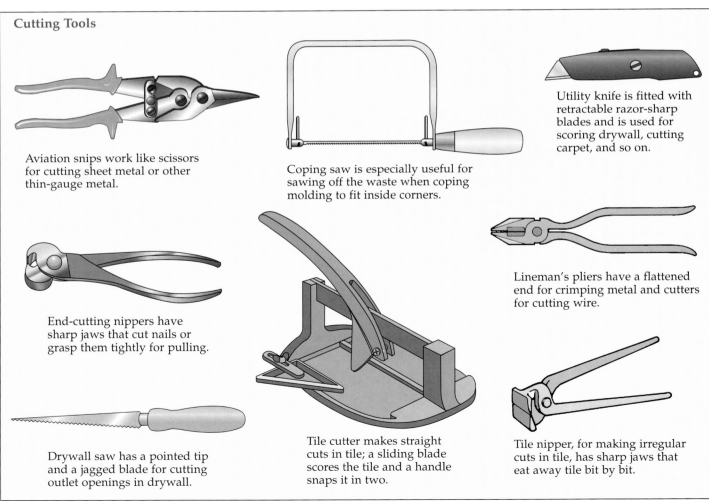

Aviation snips work like scissors for cutting sheet metal or other thin-gauge metal.

Coping saw is especially useful for sawing off the waste when coping molding to fit inside corners.

Utility knife is fitted with retractable razor-sharp blades and is used for scoring drywall, cutting carpet, and so on.

End-cutting nippers have sharp jaws that cut nails or grasp them tightly for pulling.

Lineman's pliers have a flattened end for crimping metal and cutters for cutting wire.

Drywall saw has a pointed tip and a jagged blade for cutting outlet openings in drywall.

Tile cutter makes straight cuts in tile; a sliding blade scores the tile and a handle snaps it in two.

Tile nipper, for making irregular cuts in tile, has sharp jaws that eat away tile bit by bit.

Even tools unintended for cutting, boring, or delivering blows can cause injury. Some squares, for example, don't fit into every toolbox, with the result that they can become tripping hazards. To avoid puncture wounds, be sure to tuck pointed markers, such as compasses and scratch awls, safely into tool boxes or pouches after use. And a plumb bob carelessly released from ceiling height onto a worker below has spoiled many a good relationship.

Layout Tools

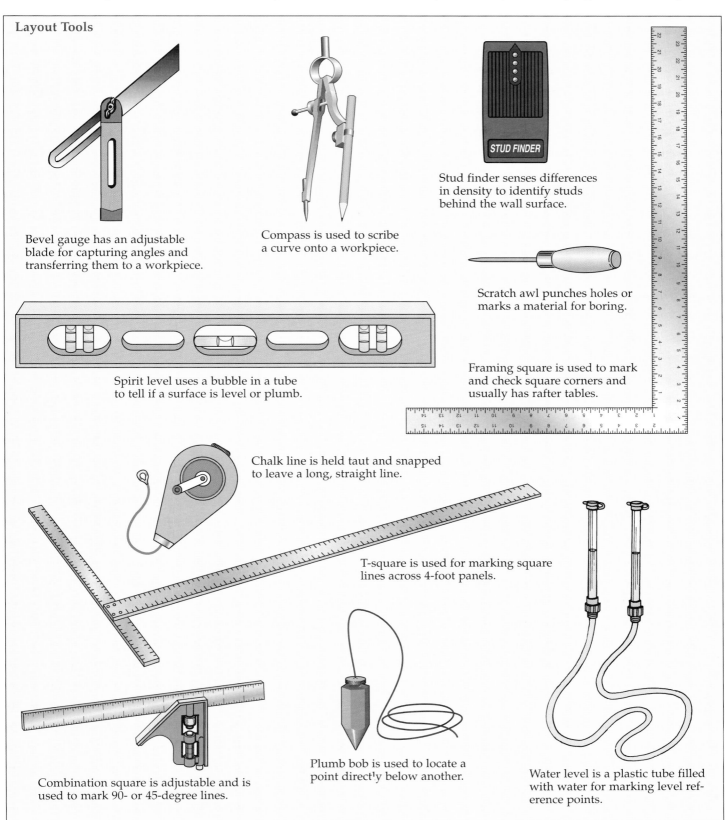

Bevel gauge has an adjustable blade for capturing angles and transferring them to a workpiece.

Compass is used to scribe a curve onto a workpiece.

Stud finder senses differences in density to identify studs behind the wall surface.

Scratch awl punches holes or marks a material for boring.

Spirit level uses a bubble in a tube to tell if a surface is level or plumb.

Framing square is used to mark and check square corners and usually has rafter tables.

Chalk line is held taut and snapped to leave a long, straight line.

T-square is used for marking square lines across 4-foot panels.

Combination square is adjustable and is used to mark 90- or 45-degree lines.

Plumb bob is used to locate a point directly below another.

Water level is a plastic tube filled with water for marking level reference points.

WALLS

The most common kind of wall in residential construction is the wood-framed wall, also called a stud wall. Most projects in this section concern stud walls. If you have a basement, its walls may be built of concrete blocks or poured concrete. These can be finished with many of the same surface materials as stud walls, so most procedures on upcoming pages apply to both.

Structure

A stud wall consists of vertical members called *studs* attached at the top and bottom to horizontal members called *plates*. The plates in a wall are attached to the floor and ceiling. At corners and where adjacent walls meet, walls are secured to each other at the studs. In most houses, these studs and plates are 2x4s. Newer homes may have exterior walls built with 2x6s, which offer more space for insulation, or even lightweight steel studs and plates instead of wood. The framework of studs provides space for wiring and outlets, plumbing, ducts, and insulation. Studs also support a surface of some kind, usually either plaster or drywall. This surface may in turn be covered by another, such as paneling or tile.

Wall moldings figure strongly in this room's success. At chair-back height, chair-rail molding atop the wainscoting allows the use of two wallpaper patterns. Tying the woodwork together, light-gray paint was applied to all moldings and to door casings.

Molding in this kids' bath defines the tile wainscoting, as well as the lively wallpaper trim. In the trim at upper right, tight 45-degree miters are harder to accomplish than the 90-degree butts at window casings, but come easily with practice. Incidentally, Webster's recognizes two spellings, but only one pronunciation, for wainscoting *and* wainscotting *(both pronounced wain-SCOTT-ing).*

Interior walls are either bearing walls or nonbearing walls, depending on their structural function. Nonbearing walls are simply partitions, dividing open space into rooms, while bearing walls hold up the roof or the floor above. "Removing Nonbearing Walls," page 23, outlines the steps for taking out a wall so that you can make two small rooms into one large open living space. "Removing Bearing Walls," page 25, describes how to use a beam to replace a wall that carries weight.

If you want to build a closet or finish a basement or attic, you'll need to build walls. "Framing Walls," page 29, gives the basics of wall-building, from stud layout to building corners and intersections. "Framing-in an Attic," page 34, explains how to construct walls that conform to sloping roofs. "Installing Prehung Doors," page 37, shows how to hang interior doors in rough openings. "Framing with Steel Studs," page 38, offers an economical option to framing with wood and may be required by local building codes for fire protection.

When you are dividing space, you should consider whether the procedures for "Soundproofing Walls," page 48, will be necessary. There are several options for noise contr ol that are most easily worked into new construction, but they can be applied to old walls, too.

Surface

Most walls in houses built since the 1940s are surfaced with drywall, also known as plasterboard, or wallboard, or by the trade name Sheetrock. Drywall may be used as the wall surface or serve as a foundation for some other surface material. "Hanging Drywall," page 40, shows how to work with the material and how to cover walls with it. "Taping and Finishing Drywall," page 44, offers advice on applying joint compound to cover

When installing wainscoting in a room with a slanted ceiling, such as this one, it's often advisable to position the wainscot cap at the intersection of wall and ceiling. Note also how the simple wide-plank baseboard with quarter-round shoe molding contributes to the desired old-time look.

The vertical beaded wood in this wainscoting is available in boards and in 4x8 panels. There are also special wainscoting panels precut to 32-inch height.

seams between drywall sheets and in corners.

One way to change the appearance of existing walls is to bond a new surface to the old. "Installing Sheet Paneling," page 50, gives a wall the warm glow of wood in a great variety of finishes. It is quick and easy to put up, and it can hide a damaged wall surface. "Installing Board Paneling," page 55, takes a little more labor, but most people feel that the depth of the real wood tones makes the effort worthwhile. In both cases, you can install the paneling so that the planks (or grooves in the sheets) are in a vertical, horizontal, diagonal, or herringbone pattern.

Sometimes, a wall may be too badly deteriorated to take a new surface without some modification. "Repairing Drywall and Plaster," page 58, offers remedies for common wall defects, such as cracks, gouges, and holes, as well as pointers for making cosmetic improvements. These projects also may be required before you apply wallpaper. "Preparing Walls for New Surfaces," page 62, includes a range of

Good wallpapers require less maintenance than paint and are available in washable materials other than paper. Some wallcoverings can be purchased prepasted; others must be pasted at home. With patterned wallpapers, as shown, you need to match patterns at the vertical seams.

procedures, from covering a wall with a framework of wood strips shimmed to be plumb, to erecting a new stud wall over one that cannot accept a new surface. Both wood-frame and masonry walls are presented.

"Working with Trim," page 66, is essential for unifying the elements in a room and hiding gaps between walls, floors, and ceilings. Some of the projects include putting trim around doors and installing base trim. "Hanging Things on Walls to Stay," page 70, catalogs the kinds of fasteners you'll need when decorating walls with pictures, shelves, or cabinets.

The most common kind of wallcovering is presented in "Painting Basics," page 72. It explains the types of brushes and other tools required, and also outlines the procedure to follow for the best results. Any room in the house, especially bathroom and kitchen, can look good with a surface of ceramic tile. "Tiling Walls," page 75, explains that tiling walls is easy, requiring more patience than expertise. "Wallpapering Basics," page 80, shows how to apply this wallcovering using time-tested techniques of the experts. Once you have made the walls sound, wallpaper can give a room a new look with only a moderate effort.

Simulated wood boards are available in 4x8-foot sheet paneling, which is among the easiest of wall materials to install, if mounted directly to studs. However, for improved fire-resistance, it's usually safer to first install a layer of drywall; in fact, local code may require it.

Cut and installed diagonally, as shown, sheet paneling is more likely to be mistaken for true board paneling, although this technique creates goodly amounts of waste cuts.

In this all-wood motif, tongue-and-groove pine boards on walls and in the flooring show differing responses to drying. Uneven spacing between wall boards suggests shrinkage after installation. To avoid this phenomenon, season finish lumber in a well-ventilated stack at normal room temperature and humidity before installation.

Paneling boards are available in a wide variety of softwoods and hardwoods, which are milled to interlock. Nails don't show because they are hidden in the "tongue" portion of one edge. To avoid uneven shrinkage and possible warping, you should coat fronts, backs, and edges with a sealer before installation.

An arch over a doorway can create relief from dominating rectilinear lines. As shown, the arch also eliminates the need for door casings, which on this wall might otherwise have competed with the artwork and shelf.

This elaborate woodwork may at first appear to be a daunting do-it-yourself project. Yet it was created with standard moldings available at home centers. For example, the wide matching patterns of the fireplace mantel and the ceiling cornice were created simply by overlapping several types of molding. The keys here were good planning and skillful cuts.

Although heavy to transport and position, double doors are available prehung. That is, they come mounted on hinges within a prefabricated door jamb that is fairly easy to level and install, aside from the heavy lifting. Prehung doors eliminate the fussier tasks of hanging doors precisely within a framework. Such assemblies still allow your selection of door moldings, called casings, to harmonize with other woodwork.

In kitchens, ceramic tile provides an attractive easy-wipe wall surface. When installing ceramic tiles on a small area, it's usually best to use small tiles and place them so that full, or nearly full, tiles reach the outside edges, as shown. In this case, the angled ceiling required tile cutting; note the nearly full tile at top left. The bottom edge is concealed by molding.

Above, the old-time look is achieved with beaded boards, like the beaded boards commonly used in the late 19th and early 20th centuries. You can also buy 4x8-foot panels that simulate beaded boards.

Besides being easy to install, drywall is easy to patch smoothly and easy to repaint after accidental damage or after removal of picture-hanging hardware. Drywall is sometimes called gypsum board, plaster board, or wallboard.

In this showroom, colors in the wallcovering (not always wallpaper these days) complement those of the tile-look sheet vinyl flooring. Installation of both surfaces is within the abilities of most beginning do-it-yourselfers.

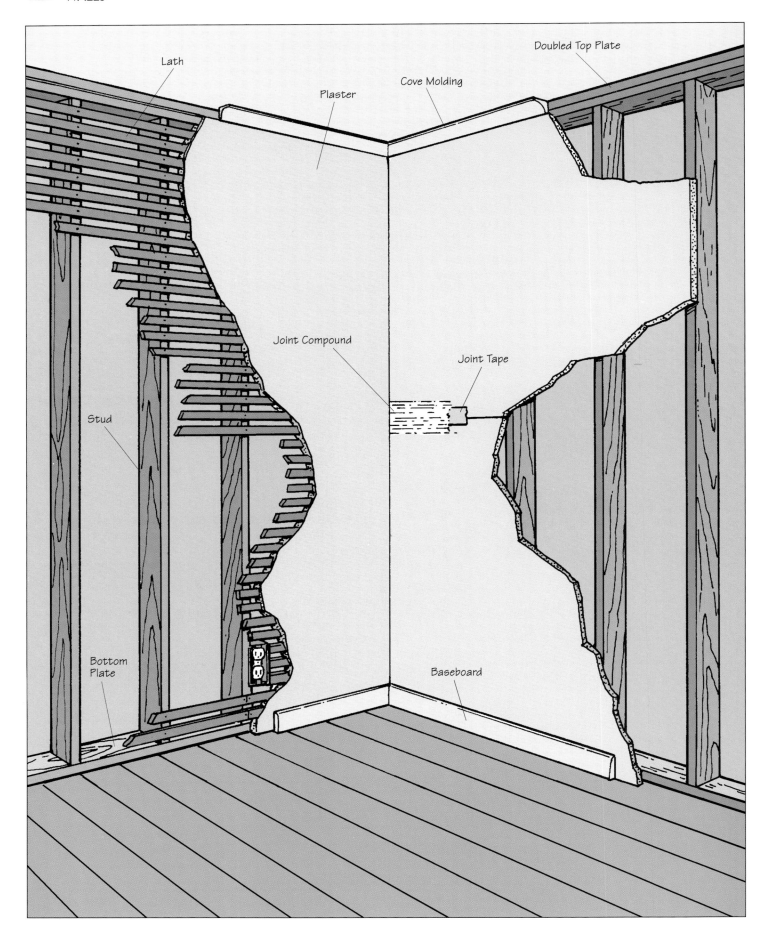

Lath

Plaster

Cove Molding

Doubled Top Plate

Joint Compound

Joint Tape

Stud

Bottom Plate

Baseboard

REMOVING NONBEARING WALLS

Taking out a wall changes interior space dramatically. With the removal of a partition, two small bedrooms side by side become a comfortable master bedroom, and a cramped living room adjoining a small dining room becomes a contemporary open living space. If you are considering such a change, make a scale drawing of the new space to be sure it will have agreeable proportions.

Every house has two kinds of interior walls, and their difference is extremely important. Bearing walls are structural supports carrying some of the weight of the structure above. Nonbearing walls are simply room dividers with no structural role at all. When a bearing wall is removed, it must be replaced by a beam (see page 25), but a nonbearing wall can be removed easily without structural considerations. You can repair the gaps left in ceilings, floors, and abutting walls by following the directions in "Taping and Finishing Drywall," page 44.

Tearing out a wall is messy, so move furniture out of the room and cover the floor with drop cloths. Because of the dust this job will create, the space should be well ventilated to the outside and sealed off from the rest of the house. Use sheets of plastic and masking tape to cover heat registers, doorways, and other interior openings. And always wear a dust mask and goggles when you tear out a wall.

Identifying Bearing Walls

Checking the Joists. One clue that will help you determine whether a wall is bearing or nonbearing is the direction of the joists running on top of the wall. If the joists run parallel to the wall, you can be certain that it is a nonbearing wall; if the joists run perpendicular, the wall may or may not bear weight. If joists are lapped above a wall, it is a bearing wall. Joists that aren't lapped are probably supported by a bearing wall that is near the middle of the distance they span. If a wall occurs near one end of the span, it is probably nonbearing, but you should consider what is above. For example, the wall may be bearing the weight of a tiled bathroom floor. In the basement, a beam or a wall running directly beneath an upstairs wall is another indication that the wall bears weight.

Using a Stud Finder. If you don't have access to the attic to inspect the joists, use a stud finder, available at home centers, to determine which way the joists run. You also can use the stud finder to determine the location and spacing of the studs in the wall. Studs set closer together than the standard 16 inches on center may indicate that a wall bears weight. If you have any doubts, assume that the wall bears weight, or else consult a builder.

Removing a Nonbearing Wall

1. Probe Interior Wall Spaces. Before you begin tearing out a wall, find out what's inside it. The presence of pipes, ducts, and wires could change your remodeling plans or affect your budget. Of course, electrical outlets and switches indicate wiring in the wall, but wires may still exist even without outlets and switches. Check in the basement or attic for pipes and ducts passing into or emerging from the wall. If no access is available, shut off power to the area of the house where you are

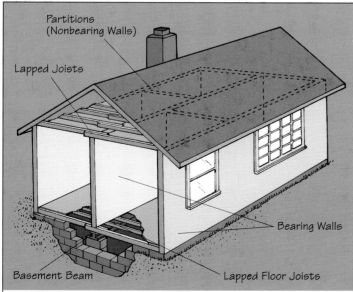

Checking the Joists. Joists running perpendicular to the wall usually indicate that it bears weight; lapped joists always do. Parallel joists mean that the wall is nonbearing.

Labels: Partitions (Nonbearing Walls); Lapped Joists; Basement Beam; Lapped Floor Joists; Bearing Walls

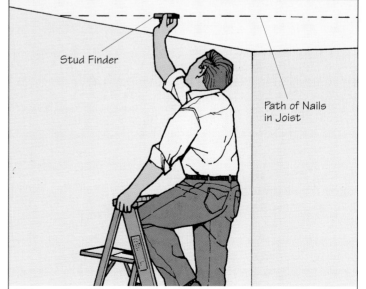

Using a Stud Finder. To use an electronic stud finder, press a button and slowly drag the device across the ceiling to determine the location of nails and thus the direction of the joists.

Labels: Stud Finder; Path of Nails in Joist

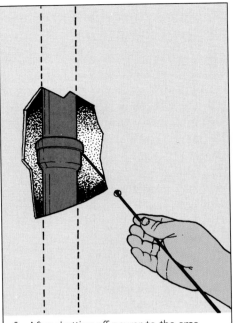

1. After shutting off power to the area where you are working, drill a small hole and probe through it with a stiff wire.

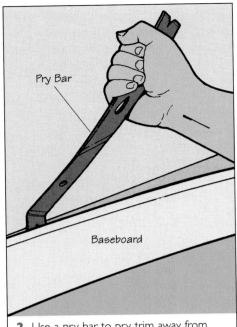

2. Use a pry bar to pry trim away from the wall, and use end nippers to pull finishing nails through the back of the trim.

3. Drywall pulls off in large sections. After scoring the surface down to the framework, use a hammer to knock away the drywall chunk by chunk.

working, and use a heavy-gauge extension cord to bring power from another part of the house to the work area. Drill a peephole in the wall between studs, insert a wire, and probe the wall cavity for any obstructions. If you don't have the expertise to move pipes and wires, consider hiring a plumber or electrician.

2. Pry Off the Trim. After covering the floor with drop cloths, use a pry bar to pry off all the trim from the wall. Tap the curved end of the pry bar behind the trim; then gently pry it off of the wall. Use pliers or end-cutting nippers to pull the nails through the back of the trim. Try not to damage it, since you may be able to use it again. Remove all outlet and switch plates.

3. Cut the Wall Material. Drywall can often be pulled off by hand in large sections. To avoid damaging surrounding areas, cut out old plaster or drywall using a utility knife. Keep scoring the material down to the lath or studs; then use a hammer to knock out the plaster chunk by chunk. Pry off any wooden lath with the claw of a hammer.

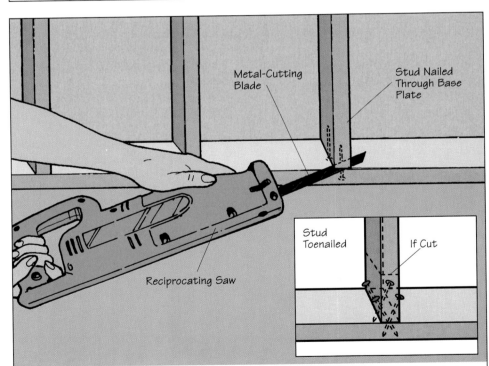

4. To remove studs when no nail heads are visible, assume that nails were driven through the base plate before the wall was raised into position. In this case, use a reciprocating saw with metal-cutting blade to sever the nails or use a wood-cutting blade to sever the stud above the nails before hammering and twisting the stud sections free. If toenails are visible, cut above them as marked, or, to save lumber, pull the nails.

4. Remove the Studs. If there is no wiring in the wall, use a reciprocating saw with a metal-cutting blade to cut the studs at the bottom plate; then twist them away from the nails in the top plate. If there is wiring, shut off power and then disconnect wiring and remove it.

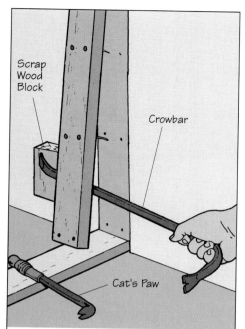

Scrap
Wood
Block

Crowbar

Cat's Paw

5. Remove the nails at the bottom of the end stud, and pry it away from the wall with a crowbar. Put a piece of scrap behind the crowbar to protect the good wall.

5. Pry Off the End Studs. Usually, the end stud is face-nailed to a stud in the adjoining wall. Use a cat's paw to pull out the nails at the bottom of the end stud; and once the stud is loose, insert a crowbar and pull the stud away from the wall.

6. Pry Out the Top and Bottom Plates. In most cases, the top plate will be two 2x4s nailed together. The top 2x4 will overlap the adjoining walls. The bottom 2x4 will butt into the adjoining walls. Drive a pry bar between the 2x4s and pry off the bottom one. Put a piece of scrap wood behind the pry bar to protect the ceiling. With a reciprocating saw, cut the remaining 2x4 flush with the adjoining walls, then pry the 2x4 away from the ceiling joists. To remove the bottom plate, cut out a small section from the middle of the bottom plate, and pry up the two halves from the cut.

REMOVING BEARING WALLS

If you have determined that a wall you wish to remove is a bearing wall, you must replace its load-carrying function with a beam. (See "Removing Nonbearing Walls," page 23.) The beam must be strong enough to carry the weight above it, and the posts that will carry the beam must be strong and adequately supported. City or county building departments and most lumberyards have charts that specify which size wood or steel beam is required to span the opening and carry the weight. But many variables affect the load a bearing wall can support. So before doing any removal work yourself, consult a structural engineer to find out the exact size of posts and beam required and obtain approval from your local building department.

This section describes general techniques for replacing a bearing wall with a beam that protrudes below the ceiling. The beam may be wood or may need to be steel, depending on the span and the weight supported. You can later mask the beam's presence by covering it with drywall finished to match the ceiling, or you can add a false exterior, as described in "Making and Installing False Beams," page 164.

To replace all of a bearing wall, set the beam on posts fastened to studs in the adjoining walls. To replace part of the wall, set the beam on posts hidden within the remaining portion of the wall. Before removing any portion of a bearing wall, you must frame temporary walls, called shoring, on both sides of the wall to support the structure above it.

Defining Types of Beams. A typical wood beam is made by sandwiching pieces of $\frac{1}{2}$-inch plywood between 2-by boards and nailing or bolting them together. This is called a built-up beam, and generally it can span about 8 feet before it becomes

6. With a reciprocating saw, cut the double top plate at each end, and pry it off the ceiling joists. Cut out a small section of the bottom plate, and pry both halves away from the floor.

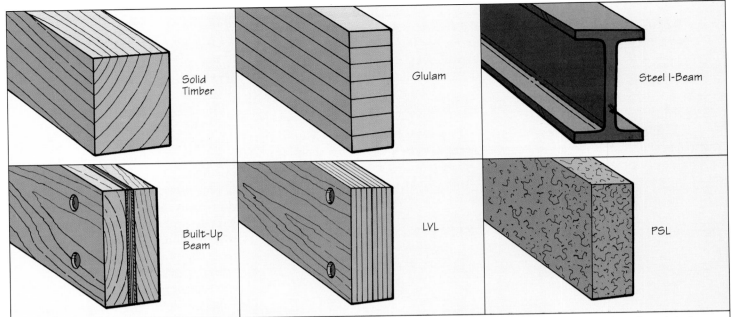

Defining Types of Beams. Solid-wood timbers are milled from logs, built-up beams consist of plywood fastened between boards, and steel I-beams can span great distances. The three types of engineered lumber include a glue-laminated timber (glulam), laminated-veneer lumber (LVL), and parallel-strand lumber (PSL)

too massive to be practical. Beams made from engineered lumber, such as laminated-veneer lumber and parallel-strand lumber, can span longer distances and support greater loads than built-up beams. Usually, both engineered lumber and built-up beams are covered with drywall and finished to match the ceiling. If you want an exposed wood beam, you can choose a solid timber or a glue-laminated beam, both of which cost more than a built-up beam. Glue-laminated beams (glulams) consist of dimensional lumber glued face to face. Glulams come in three appearance grades; best to worst, they are premium, architectural, and industrial. Finally, steel is used where a wood beam wouldn't be strong enough to carry the weight.

Removing a Bearing Wall

1. Ensure Post Support. Posts supporting a beam must transfer the weight from the beam to the structure below. Again, as a general rule, get approval of your local building department before you begin removing a bearing wall.

If you are working above a basement with an unfinished ceiling that gives access to the floor joists, check to be sure that the posts will stand directly over a point where a floor joist crosses the basement girder. As close as possible to the post location, drive a nail through the floor, and locate where the nail emerges below from the subfloor. If the post will stand over a beam but between joists, add

blocking under the post between the subfloor and the beam, as shown. Make sure the blocking is both totally dry and wide enough to provide support for the entire post. If you can't determine exactly what a post will stand on, or if there is no beam below, consult a structural engineer.

2. Build the Beam and Posts. Order or cut a beam the size of the

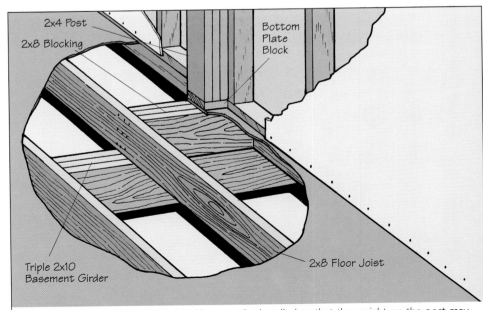

1. If a post rests between joists, blocking must be installed so that the weight on the post may be transferred directly to a main building support, such as a basement girder.

2. After removing drywall from the bearing wall, measure the distance between plates at each end. Subtract the width of the beam, and the result is the height of the posts.

Position of Shoring Wall

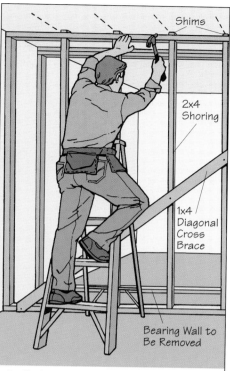

Shims

2x4 Shoring

1x4 Diagonal Cross Brace

Bearing Wall to Be Removed

3. On both sides of the wall, set up temporary walls, or shoring, for support when the wall is removed. Use shims to tighten.

opening plus the thickness of the posts. For ease of handling later, place the beam beside the length of wall it will replace. Tear off the wall surface material to expose the studs. Measure the distance between the floor plate and the top plate, and subtract the width of the beam. Cut 2x4s to this length; these 2x4s will be the trimmer posts. The number of 2x4s you will need depends on the length of the beam, but usually two 2x4 posts on each side are enough.

3. Set up the Shoring. On both sides of the wall, set up two stud walls, called shoring, the length of the beam. You can follow the directions in "Framing Walls," page 29. Lay out the studs in the shoring so that they will be directly below the ceiling joists. Nail the studs to the top plate, and position the bottom plates within 2½ feet of the bearing wall. Then, with a helper, set the top plates and studs on the bottom plates and toenail the ends of the studs to the bottom plates. After making sure the shoring is plumb and square, nail a

1x4 brace diagonally across the shoring, attaching it to every stud. You don't need to nail the shoring in place; instead, drive wood shims between the top plates and each joist above, as shown. The shims will hold the shoring tight.

4. Dismantle the Bearing Wall. When the shoring is securely in place, dismantle the bearing wall. Cut and remove all the studs except the "posts" at the ends of the wall. Because the beam will project below the ceiling, you don't need to remove the top plate; the beam simply butts under it. You can also leave the bottom plate in place for now.

5. Lift the Beam into Place. You'll need at least two people to lift the beam. Mount steel connectors as shown to receive the beam. Set up a sturdy platform and walk the beam into position directly under the top plate. A third person should then wedge a 2x4 trimmer post under each end of the beam, and nail the trimmer to the end post. If sagging joists prevent the beam from seating tightly

Old Bearing Wall

End Stud "Post"

Second Shoring Wall

Shoring Wall   Beam

4. Once the drywall is removed, use a reciprocating saw to sever nails at stud bottoms. Then twist the studs away from the top plate. Leave the end studs intact. (Note position of shoring in the foreground too.)

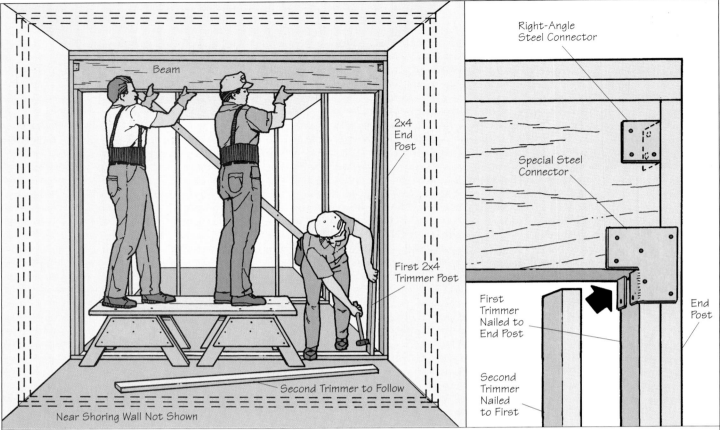

5. After installing right-angle steel connectors to receive the top portion of the beam, have strong helpers walk the beam into position. Another helper sets a trimmer post under each end of the beam to set it firmly in place. Then he fastens the trimmer post to the old stud.

under the top plate, raise the joists by driving extra wedges between them and the shoring walls. Then add another trimmer at each end, and use a hand saw or a reciprocating saw to cut the bottom plate flush with the posts.

Removing a Portion of a Bearing Wall. To remove part of a bearing wall, find the stud at the end of the portion of wall you will remove, and score the wall surface material along the edge of the stud. Remove the wall surface and the studs, but leave the top and bottom plates intact. Cut a beam the length of the open portion of the wall. Measure the distance between the top and bottom plate, subtract the width of the beam, and cut 2x4 trimmer posts to this length. With a few helpers working on step ladders, lift the beam into position while another person installs 2x4 posts under each end of the post, using 2½-inch deck screws to fasten the posts to the end studs.

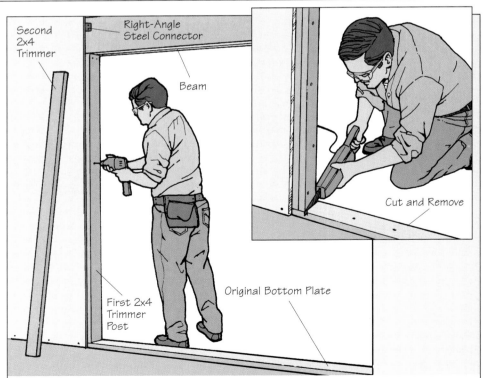

Removing a Portion of a Bearing Wall. If you're removing only part of a bearing wall, strip the wall up to a stud. After positioning the beam, install steel connectors as shown at top of page, or toenail the beam to the end post. Then fasten the second trimmer post to each side. After the posts are installed, cut the bottom plate with a hand saw or reciprocating saw.

Installing a Steel Beam. When installing a heavy steel I-beam, be sure to have plenty of help. First, rest the beam atop sturdy platforms, and then lift it into position while installing the trimmer posts. At the ends of the I-beam, fasten plywood cleats or angle iron to further stabilize it.

Installing a Steel Beam. Installing a steel beam is not much different from putting up a wooden one, but steel beams are heavier and require more help. Plan to have one assistant for each 3 feet of beam when you raise it. The beam bears under the top plate of the wall it replaces. When the wall is removed, rest the beam atop sturdy platforms and lift it to shoulder height. Then walk the beam into position, and install trimmer posts under both ends, as shown. Cut the bottom plate flush with the trimmer posts.

Creating a Nailing Surface. Since you can't nail into steel, you'll have to cover an I-beam with nailing surfaces for drywall or paneling. Fill in above the beam with blocking to bring out a nailing surface flush with the edge of the beam. Rip a 1-by board to fit under the beam; then measure the thickness of this board plus the distance from the bottom of the I-beam to the ceiling, and cut 1x2s to this length. Drill pilot holes, and use 6d resin-coated box nails to fasten the 1x2s to the edge of the board every 16 inches.

Lift this assembly under the beam; after drilling pilot holes, nail the tops of the vertical 1x2s to the blocking along the top of the beam. Cover the beam with drywall or paneling.

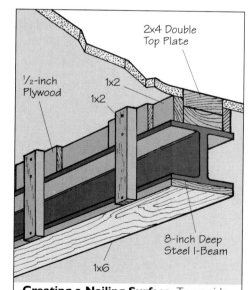

Creating a Nailing Surface. To provide backing for drywall or paneling over an I-beam, build out the top plate flush with the edge of the beam; then rip a plank as wide as the beam and screw 1x2 furring strips every 16 inches to the edge of the plank. Lift this assembly into place under the beam and screw it to the top plate.

FRAMING WALLS

Putting up a wall involves three separate activities: building the frame, covering it, and finishing the surface. The frame is a rigid skeleton of studs providing space for wiring and pipes and a foundation for wall surfaces. Unfinished basements are the easiest places to frame walls because the walls, floors, and ceilings already in place are usually exposed and ready for the attachment of new framing. Adding walls to rooms on the ground floor and above often means breaking into finished walls or ceilings or both. (An unfinished attic presents special problems; see "Framing-in an Attic," page 34.) When the space you are framing is level and square, you can build most of the wall on the floor and tilt it into position. Where the angles are off or where obstacles such as pipes prevent you from tilting walls into place, you must put up the wall stud by stud. The two methods are treated separately in the directions that follow.

Framing an Interior Partition.

Most interior walls are framed using 2x4s. (You might consider using light-weight-steel framing, which won't rot and won't burn. See "Framing with Steel Studs," page 38.) You will need one stud at each end of the wall, and studs every 24 inches between. Doorways require double studs—a king stud and a trimmer stud—at each side of the opening, and a horizontal header and a small cripple stud over the door. You will also need 2x4s for the top and bottom plates.

Fastening Walls to Ceilings.

The first stage in building a frame wall is to determine how it will be attached to the ceiling and adjoining walls. If the ceiling joists run perpendicular to the new wall, simply nail the wall through the ceiling surface into the joists.

If your new wall will run parallel to the ceiling joists, you can nail the top plate to a joist. First make sure the joist will provide nailing along the entire wall. Find the edge of the joist, and snap a chalk line on the ceiling square to an abutting wall. Probe along the line with a hammer and nail to be sure of the joist's location. Install the wall so that it aligns with the chalkline.

If you place a new wall so that it runs between two joists, you must add blocks between the joists and nail the wall to the blocks. First, find the two joists between which the wall will run. Then score the ceiling along the middle of the joists, and knock out the ceiling surface with a hammer. Cut 2x6s to fit between the joists at 24-inch intervals, and use 8d common nails to toenail them flush with the bottom of the joists. Repair the ceiling with a piece of drywall cut to span across the joists; then install the new wall.

Attaching Walls to Existing Walls.

If a new wall meets an adjoining wall at a stud, remove sections of trim above and below, and after checking with a 4-foot level to be sure the new wall is plumb, use

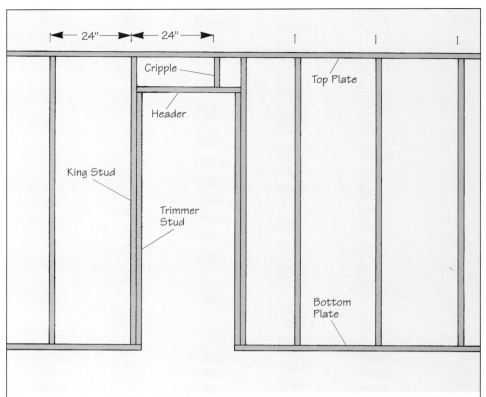

Framing an Interior Partition. An interior partition wall is built using 2x4s spaced 24 inches apart. The plates are single 2x4s. Studs around doors are doubled, and the top of the door has a header and short cripple studs.

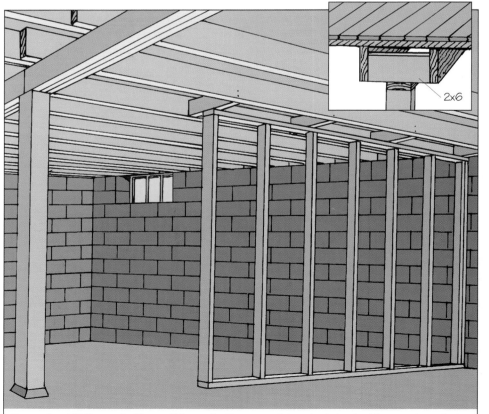

Fastening Walls to Ceilings. If the wall will run parallel to the joists, it either can be nailed to a single joist or nailed to 2x6 blocks between two joists. If a new wall runs perpendicular to the joists above, it can be nailed to each joist.

Attaching Walls to Existing Walls

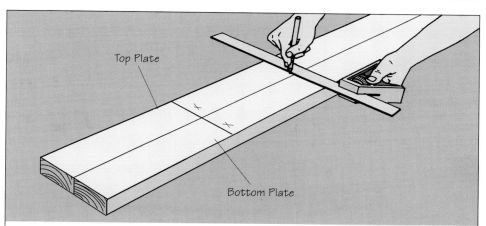

Attaching Walls to Existing Walls.
A new wall can be attached directly to an existing stud (top drawing), or to 2x4 blocking between two studs. Patch the wall before attaching the new wall.

16d nails to nail the end stud through the adjoining wall surface and into the existing stud.

If the new wall meets an adjoining wall between studs, strip the wall surface back to the two studs. Cut three 2x4 blocks to fit between the studs, and toenail the blocks horizontally every 24 inches. Repair the wall with a piece of drywall cut to span across the studs. The blocks allow you to fasten the new wall securely to the old wall.

Framing a Tilt-Up Wall

1. Mark the Wall Location.
Mark the exact location of the wall on the floor. With a helper, stretch a chalk line across the floor, and use a framing square to check that the line is square to an abutting wall. Snap the line. If you are working alone, wedge one end of the chalk line under a weight to hold it as the other end is snapped.

2. Lay Out the Plates. Cut two 2x4 plates to the length of the wall. Align the plates; and measuring from one end, mark the first stud at 23¼ inches and the rest at 24-inch intervals on center. This spacing allows a full length of drywall to end halfway over the fifth stud, eliminating the need to cut the drywall. Be sure to mark the end stud; it doesn't matter if the space between the last two studs is less than 24 inches.

3. Lay Out the Rough Openings.
If your wall will have a doorway, you will need to frame a rough opening.

1. Decide where you want the wall, and mark it at both ends. Then stretch a chalk-line, check it for square, and snap the line.

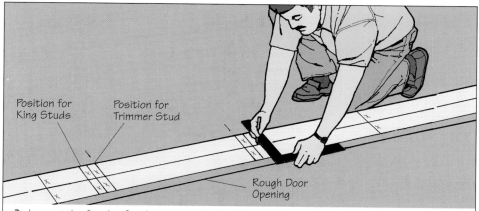

2. Align top and bottom plates. Hook a tape measure on one end, and mark 23¼ inches. Then move the tape to that mark and lay out the rest of the studs every 24 inches. Use a square to mark both plates at once, putting an "X" on the side of the mark where the stud will be.

3. Lay out the framing for doorways using double studs on each side: a full-length king stud and a door-height trimmer stud. The space between the studs should be 2½ inches wider than the door.

Traditionally, a rough opening is 2½ inches wider than the door, with double studs on both sides. So, if you are installing a 32-inch door, for example, lay out the plates by marking two studs next to each other; then measure 32½ inches and mark two more studs next to each other.

4. Cut the Studs. Wall studs are the height of the wall minus the thickness of the plates. Subtract an additional ¼ inch from this figure to provide enough clearance to tilt the wall into place. Cut all the studs that are needed. (To come up with this number, simply count the number of layout marks on the plates.) For the wall to fit properly, the cuts must be square.

5. Build the Frame. Separate the plates by the length of a stud and set them on edge with layout marks facing inward. Lay all the studs in the approximate position, and then drive a pair of 16d nails through each plate and into the ends of each stud. Use the marks as guides to align the studs.

6. Tilt Up the Frame. First slide the bottom plate into position along the chalk line on the floor. Then, with a helper, tilt the wall upright. Make sure the bottom plate is aligned with the chalk line, and then nail the bottom plate to the floor. If the floor is concrete, use 8d concrete nails set every 18 inches or so. If a wood subfloor is already in place, use the longest possible common nails to nail into the subfloor without hitting the concrete. Nail into underlying sleepers wherever possible. Space the nails in pairs every 24 inches or so.

7. Plumb the Wall. Use a 4-foot level to ensure that the wall is plumb, and then add shims between the top plate and each intersecting joist to take up the ¼-inch clearance. Do not overshim; otherwise you may raise the joists or bend the top plate. Just make sure the wall is wedged snugly in place and square. Then nail

4. Measure the height of the ceiling, subtract the thickness of both plates plus ¼ inch (3¼ inches total), and cut to this length the number of studs needed. (Reminder: 2x4's actual size is 1½ x 3½ inches.)

Distance: Floor to Ceiling
Wall Height ¼" Less

5. Align each stud with its layout marks, and drive a pair of 16d nails through the plates into the ends of the studs. End studs are installed flush with the plates. At doorways, install only the full-length king studs.

6. Slide the bottom plate into position along the chalk line, and tilt the wall upright. Even though the wall is ¼ inch shorter than the ceiling height, you may have to hammer the wall into place. Nail the bottom plate along the chalk line.

Shim as needed.

7. Use a 4-foot level to check that the wall is standing straight up. Shim the gap between the wall and the ceiling. Nail through the top plate into the ceiling framing or blocks. Nail the end studs to the existing walls, using shims where necessary.

through the top plate and shims and into the ceiling framing (or blocking if the wall runs parallel to the ceiling joists). Finally, use 16d nails to attach the end studs to the existing walls. Use shims to fill any gaps.

Framing Corners and Intersections. Where walls meet, you must add studs to provide a nailing surface for wall covering. One method of turning a corner is to build a post using 2x4 blocks nailed between two

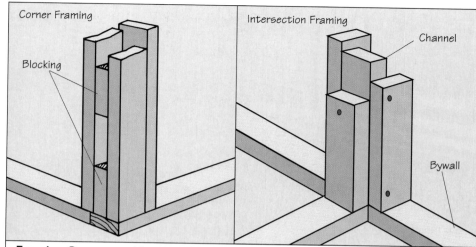

Framing Corners and Intersections. Frame a corner so that it provides backing for drywall on both sides. At intersections, frame a channel in the bywall, as shown, and nail the end stud to the channel.

studs, and then butt the end stud of the adjacent wall to this post. At intersections, build a channel post by nailing two studs to both edges of a third stud. The intersecting wall butts into the channel and is nailed to it.

Framing a Wall in Place

It is not always possible to tilt a partition wall into place. For example, pipes or ducts may be in the way, the room may be out of square, or the wall may be unusually long. Instead, walls can be built in place by slipping each stud between plates that have been nailed to the ceiling joists and floor.

1. Install the Top Plate. First mark the position of the wall on the ceiling, and then cut the top and bottom plates to fit. Mark the stud layout on the top plate ($23\frac{1}{4}$ inches for the second stud, and 24 inches on center for the rest). Position the top plate on the ceiling, and use a 16d nail to attach the top plate to each intersecting joist (or to blocking between the joists). Be sure the stud layout faces down.

2. Install the Bottom Plate. Hang a plumb bob from the edge of the top plate, transferring the position of the top plate to at least two points on the floor, as shown. Align the bottom plate with these layout marks, and nail it to the floor. Use a single concrete nail every 18 inches or so if you're nailing into a concrete slab, or pairs of common nails every 24 inches if you're nailing to a wood subfloor. Use a plumb bob to transfer the stud layout from the top plate to the bottom plate as shown.

3. Nail Studs to the Top Plate. Measure between the plates at each stud location and cut studs to fit. (They may be different lengths if the floor or the ceiling is not level.) Put a stud in position, align it with the layout marks, and use a pair of 12d nails to toenail it to the top plate. To make toenailing easier, use a backup block to keep the stud from shifting as it is toenailed. Cut the block to fit exactly between studs. (If the stud spacing is 24 inches on center, and the studs are exactly $1\frac{1}{2}$ inches thick, the block will be $22\frac{1}{2}$ inches long.) Remove the spacer as successive studs are toenailed.

4. Nail the Studs to the Bottom Plate. Plumb each stud and toenail it

1. Install the Top Plate. After marking the stud layout on the top plate, nail it to the ceiling frame with the layout marks facing down.

2. Install the Bottom Plate. Use a plumb bob to mark the floor. Nail the bottom plate. Then transfer the stud layout from the top plate to the bottom plate.

3. Nail the Studs to the Top Plate. Measure and cut each stud individually. Align the top of the stud with its layout mark, and toenail it to the top plate.

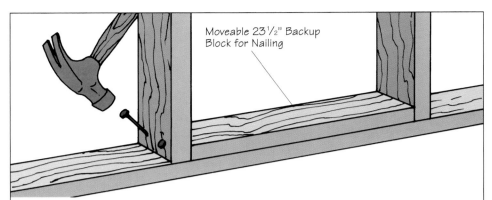

Moveable 23¹/₂" Backup Block for Nailing

4. Nail the Studs to the Bottom Plate. Move the bottom of the stud into position and check it for plumb with a 4-foot level. Toenail the stud to the bottom plate, using a backup block to hold the stud in position. If the floor is concrete, use 8d nails; these will not reach through the plate into the concrete.

to the bottom plate; the same spacer block can be used. If you are installing the wall directly over a concrete floor, make sure the toenails do not hit the concrete. Use three 8d nails and start the toenailing high enough on the stud so that the end of the nail stops short of the concrete.

FRAMING-IN AN ATTIC

In an attic, partition walls are used to enclose a bathroom or to divide the space into separate rooms. Since the walls used in an attic typically are not very large, they can be built one at a time on the subfloor and then tipped into place. If space is limited, however, you may need to piece the wall together in place.

Types of Walls

Often, an attic renovation requires the building of knee walls to seal off the unusable low space along the roof eaves. Knee walls run perpendicular to the rafters and have an angled top plate to match the roof slope. The height of knee walls varies, but you can save some work by building 4-foot-high knee walls to match the width of drywall panels. It's a good idea to frame an access door so that you can use the space behind a knee wall for storage.

Partition walls running parallel to the rafters are built with a series of progressively shorter studs cut to fit between plates nailed to the floor and roof. If you frame a flat ceiling, you

can attach partition walls to the ceiling joists. These walls will have horizontal top plates, and framing them is no different from framing a conventional stud wall. Be sure to provide a nailing surface for the ceiling drywall where it meets the wall.

Framing Sloping Walls in Place

1. Install the Plates. If the wall is situated between rafters, install 2x4 blocking 24 inches on center between the rafters to provide a nailing surface for the top plate of the wall. If blocking is installed, snap a chalk line across the blocks to mark the position of the top plate. Nail the top plate to the blocks or to the bottom of a rafter. Drop a plumb line at both ends of the top plate to mark the position of the bottom plate. Nail the bottom plate to the floor.

2. Mark Stud Locations. Lay out the stud locations 24 inches on center across the bottom plate. Then use a plumb bob to transfer these locations to the top plate. Do not try to lay out the positions by measuring along the angled top plate; if you do, the studs will not be 24 inches on center.

3. Capture the Angle. The tops of the studs are cut at an angle to fit under the sloping top plate. To replicate the angle of the top plate, place

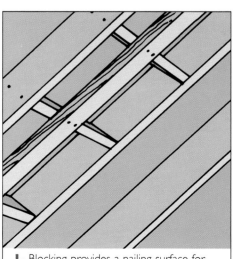

1. Blocking provides a nailing surface for top plates located between rafters.

2. Use a plumb bob to transfer the stud layout on the bottom plate to the top plate.

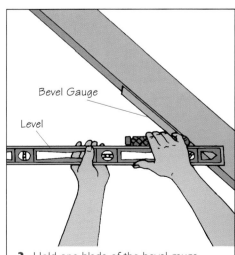

Bevel Gauge

Level

3. Hold one blade of the bevel gauge against the rafter and level the other blade. Transfer this angle to the circular saw blade.

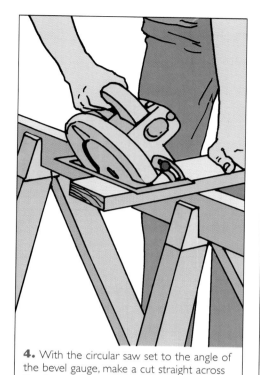

4. With the circular saw set to the angle of the bevel gauge, make a cut straight across the face of the stud.

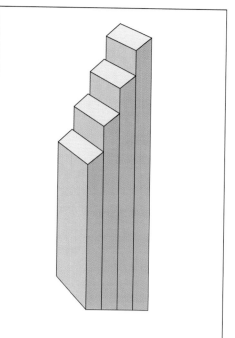

5. Use the difference in length between the first two studs to determine the other stud lengths.

6. Nail the top of a stud to the top plate with 12d nails. With 8d nails, toenail the bottom of the stud to the bottom plate.

one blade of a bevel gauge against the top plate while holding the other blade level.

4. Cut the First Stud. Measure the distance between plates to get the length of the first stud (measure to the "high" side of the angle). Then use the bevel gauge to set the angle on a circular saw, and cut across the face of the stud.

5. Cut Successive Studs. Measure and cut the second stud just as you did the first. Then hold the two against each other and measure the difference in length between them. You can use this measurement, called the common difference, to determine the length of all remaining studs spaced the same distance apart. Each one is shorter (by the amount of the common difference) than the one before it.

6. Install the Studs. Use a pair of 10d nails at the top and three 10d or 12d nails at the bottom of each stud to toenail it into place. Use a backup block (see top drawing on page 34) or your foot to keep the stud bottoms from shifting.

Installing Knee Walls

1. Mark the Plate Locations. Mark and cut a 2x4 the height of the knee wall; holding the 2x4 plumb at

each end of the knee-wall location, mark the height of the knee wall on the rafters. Snap a chalk line to mark all the rafters; this mark indicates the location of the top plate of the knee

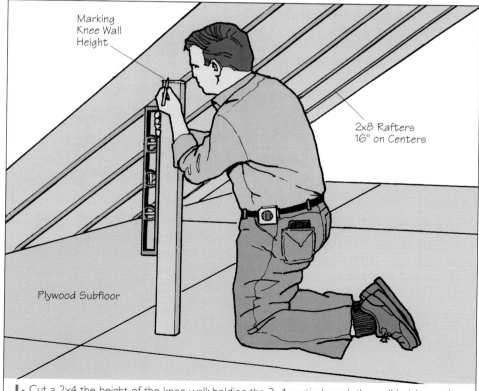

Marking Knee Wall Height

2x8 Rafters 16" on Centers

Plywood Subfloor

1. Cut a 2x4 the height of the knee wall; holding the 2x4 vertical, mark the wall height on the rafters at each end of the wall.

wall. Use a plumb bob to transfer both ends of the top plate to the floor, and then snap a chalk line to mark the location of the bottom plate.

2. Lay Out the Plates. Measure the length of the knee wall and cut a 2x4 bottom plate and a 2x6 top plate. Place one plate alongside the other and mark the stud layout on the plates, positioning one stud at the end, the next stud 23¼ inches from the end, and the remaining studs 24 inches on center.

3. Mark the Studs. Stack the plates one atop the other along the bottom-plate chalk line, and set a piece of 2x4 on the plates with the top end resting against a rafter and aligned with the top-plate mark. Mark the angle of the rafter along the side of the 2x4, and then cut it along the line. Use this 2x4 as a template to mark and cut the rest of the knee-wall studs.

4. Bevel the Top Plate. Rip the edge of the 2x6 top plate so that it will be plumb when nailed to the rafters. This beveled edge provides support for the drywall. To determine the bevel angle, hold one blade of a bevel gauge against a roof rafter and the other blade level. The angle is best cut on a table saw, although you can use a circular saw and a rip fence.

5. Assemble the Wall. Align the front of the top plate with the studs, and drive two 12d nails through the plate into the studs. Nail the bottom plate to the studs, and then tip the wall into place and fasten it with 16d nails to the rafters and the floor joists.

6. Install Nailers. Provide blocking to support the ceiling edges. Cut 2x4 blocks to fit between the rafters. (Measure each space between rafters to account for small differences in the spacing.) Attach one end of each block by face-nailing through a rafter into the block with 16d nails. The other end will be inaccessible to face-nailing, so toenail it to the rafter with 8d nails.

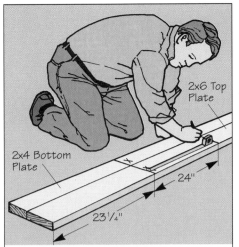

2. Align the 2x4 bottom plate and the 2x6 top plate next to each other, and mark the stud layout. The first two studs are 23¼ inches on center; the rest of the studs are 24 inches on center.

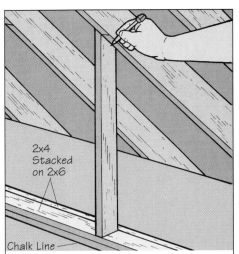

3. Stack the bottom and top plates along the chalk line on the floor, aligned with the top-plate chalk line, and mark the angle of the rafter on the vertical 2x4.

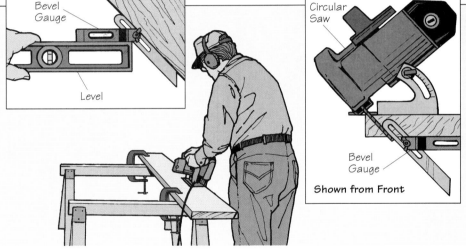

4. Bevel the edge of the 2x6 top plate so that it will be plumb when installed under the rafters. Use a bevel gauge and a level to transfer the roof angle to the circular saw.

5. After assembling the wall with 12d nails, tilt it into place along the chalk lines; fasten it to the floor joists and rafters with 16d nails.

6. The ceiling drywall must be supported where it meets the top of the knee wall. Use 2x4 blocks nailed between the rafters to "back" the drywall.

Installing Prehung Doors

The easiest interior door to install is a prehung door, which is a pre-assembled unit including the door, 4 9/16-inch-wide jambs, door-stop molding, and hinges. Because the size of the framed opening depends on the size of the door, purchase the door before you start framing so that you will know how large to build the doorway or rough opening. You can install the prehung door after hanging the drywall.

Framing the Rough Opening

When marking the wall plates with the stud layout, use the rough-opening width of the door to establish the location of the studs on either side. Generally, a rough opening is framed 3/8 inch higher than the door jambs, and 3/4 inch wider than the prehung door unit. To frame a rough opening, install doubled studs—one full-length king stud and one door-length trimmer—at each side of the doorway; place a short beam, called a header, across the opening. Short studs, called cripples, are cut to fit between the header and the top plate.

Install the king studs with the other studs in the wall; and after the wall is in place, cut the trimmers to size (the height of the door jamb plus 3/8 inch) and face-nail them to the king studs with 10d nails. Cut the header to fit between the king studs and attach it with 16d nails. With 8d nails, nail the cripple studs above the header, spacing them to maintain the 24-inch on-center spacing of the rest of the studs. Use a handsaw to cut the bottom plate between the trimmers.

Installing the Door

1. Check the Opening. Use a level to check that the header is horizontal, and that the trimmers are plumb in both directions. Also check that the floor is level. If you framed the rough opening with the proper dimensions, you can use shims to compensate for floors or walls that are slightly out of level or plumb.

2. Shim the Door Jambs. You will need a 4-foot level, 10d finishing nails, and tapered shingle shims to install the door. After removing the stretcher brace from the bottom of the door jambs and extracting any duplex nails holding the door shut, insert the door assembly in the opening so that the jambs are flush with the drywall surfaces. Wedge shims between the framing and the jambs to hold the door in place. Use three pairs of shims on each jamb: one pair at the level of the top door hinge, one pair in the middle of the jamb, and one pair near the bottom door hinge. Also put shims under the door to support it. Push the pairs of shims in or out so that there is an 1/8-inch gap between the door and the jambs all the way around.

3. Fasten the Hinge Jamb. After checking that the edge of the hinge jamb is flush with the wall surface, nail the top of the hinge jamb first and then the middle and bottom with one 10d finishing nail positioned just under the shims. Drive the nails about halfway in, and check the jamb

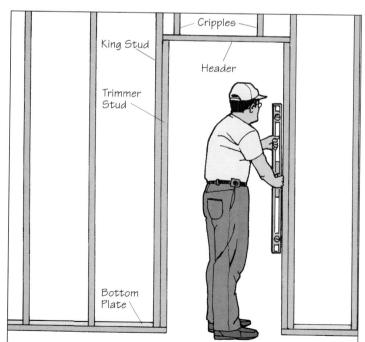

1. A rough opening is framed 3/4 inch wider and 3/8 inch higher than the prehung door. Be sure to check the trimmers, header, and floor for plumb and for level.

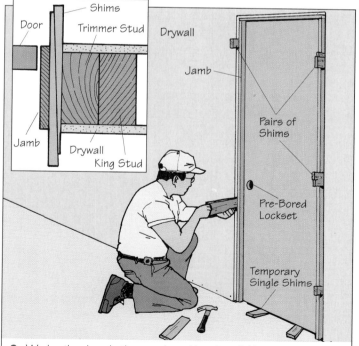

2. Wedge the door in the opening with pairs of shims near the top and bottom hinges, and also in the middle. Shim under the door so that it's level. The pairs of shims face each other so that pushing one in or out adjusts the clearance between the door and the jamb.

for plumb. Adjust the shims as necessary, and then drive the nails the rest of the way. Open the door and drive three 10d finishing nails next to the first three nails.

3. When the clearance between the door and jamb is ⅛ inch, nail the hinge jamb to the frame with two 10d finishing nails driven just below the shims.

4. Close the door and check the clearance. Tap the shims in or out as necessary; then nail the latch jamb with a second 10d finishing nail just below the shims.

4. Fasten the Latch Jamb. Close the door and check that the clearance between the door edge and the latch jamb is ⅛ inch. Also check that the latch jamb is flush with the wall surface. Then nail the jamb just under the shims, sending the nails halfway in. Check the clearance, adjust the shims if necessary, and send the nails home. Add another nail at the top, middle, and bottom; then set all the nails slightly below the jamb surface with a nailset. Finally, cut off the shims flush with the jambs.

FRAMING WITH STEEL STUDS

Light-gauge steel framing is less expensive than wood framing, yet it provides a wall just as sturdy. Steel framing is ideal for basement renovations because it won't rot or warp, and it won't burn. Some building codes, especially those governing city loft conversions, require metal framing for fire protection.

Steel wall framing consists of studs and tracks, both of which are C-shaped when viewed from the end. Studs have extra crimps on the open ends, however, making them stiffer than tracks. Studs fit inside tracks, which are used for top and bottom plates in walls. Steel framing members for interior nonbearing walls are 24-gauge steel; they can be purchased at large home centers and drywall supply outlets, where you may have them cut to a specified length, or you can cut them yourself with straight tin snips.

Studs are fastened to tracks with pan-head sheet-metal screws, and drywall is attached to the steel frame with bugle-head screws. For attaching wood, such as a prehung door jamb, use square-drive trim screws. All of these screws should be self-drilling, to eliminate the need to drill pilot holes. You will need a variable-speed power drill or power screwdriver to drive the screws efficiently.

Building Corners and Doorways. Steel-frame walls are built in place with studs 24 inches on center. One trick to ease corner construction is to leave a gap between all intersecting tracks. The gap should be wide enough to slip drywall between the tracks, as shown. At door openings, stop the bottom track at the rough opening and continue on the other side. Studs around door openings are doubled for heavy, solid doors, and single studs are used for hollow-core doors. Headers are made by trimming the flanges on

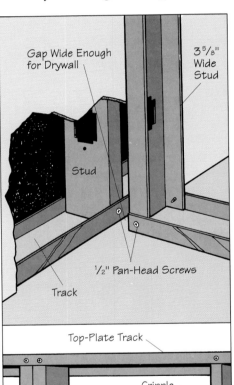

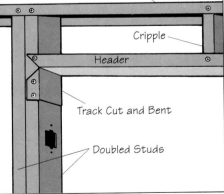

Building Corners and Doorways. Intersections, such as corners, are made by attaching the tracks so that the gap between them is wide enough to slip in a sheet of drywall. Headers over door frames are made from a track cut at the flanges, bent at right angles, and screwed in place with #8, ½-inch pan-head screws.

a track so that the ends may be bent at right angles and screwed to the trimmer studs, as shown.

Framing a Wall

1. Install the Bottom Track. Cut the tracks to length with tin snips. You can attach the bottom track with adhesive, nails, or screws. When using adhesive, make sure the floor is level and clean, and that it provides a sound surface for the adhesive to grip; that is, don't attempt to use adhesive on loose linoleum or on a floor with gaps. Run a $\frac{3}{8}$-inch bead of panel adhesive in a 1-inch-wide squiggle along the chalk line you have snapped for the track. Seat the track on the line and press firmly into the adhesive; allow to dry according to manufacturer's instructions. To attach without adhesive, use masonry nails into a concrete floor, or spiral nails, or sheet metal screws into wood.

2. Install the Top Track. Use a plumb bob to mark the position for the top track, and install it across joists or along one joist. Or use toggle bolts to affix the track to a finished ceiling. Once the top and bottom tracks are installed, you can mark the stud layout with a pencil.

3. Snap the Studs into Place. Cut the studs to length if necessary, and insert them into the tracks. Check to be sure they are plumb. The tension applied by the track flanges should hold the studs snugly in place until you attach them with two #8, $\frac{1}{2}$-inch pan-head sheet-metal screws at the top and bottom tracks.

4. Attach the Drywall. The frame will not be completely rigid until you put on the wall surface. When you attach drywall to the metal studs, use a power drill or a power drywall screwdriver to drive $1\frac{1}{4}$-inch bugle-head drywall screws with self-drilling points, just below the drywall surface.

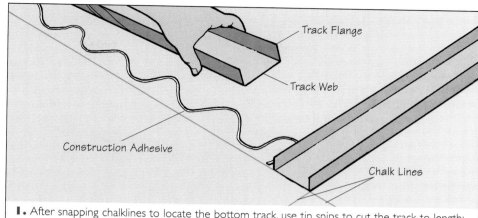

1. After snapping chalklines to locate the bottom track, use tin snips to cut the track to length; then set it into a bead of construction adhesive, or fasten it with screws or nails.

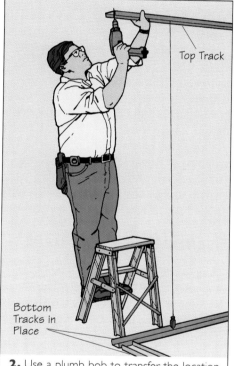

2. Use a plumb bob to transfer the location of the bottom track to the ceiling, and screw the top track to the ceiling framing. Or use toggle bolts.

3. Cut the studs to length, insert them between the tracks, and turn them so that they snap in tight. Screw the studs to the tracks with $\frac{1}{2}$-inch pan-head screws.

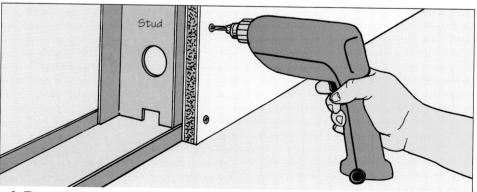

4. The most efficient way to attach drywall to metal studs is with a power screwdriver and self-drilling bugle-head screws. Be sure to set the screws slightly below the drywall surface.

HANGING DRYWALL

Drywall (also known as plasterboard, gypsum board, wallboard, or by the trade name Sheetrock) is a popular option for finishing walls. It is readily available, easy to work with, and inexpensive. Drywall may be paneled or tiled as it is; or it may be finished with tape and joint compound, and then painted or wallpapered.

Drywall comes in many varieties. Standard drywall has a smooth, off-white surface that takes paint well. Specialty drywall products include moisture resistance (MR), usually blue or green in color; it is for use in damp areas, such as bathrooms, or as a base for ceramic tile. Fire-code drywall contains chemical additives for fire resistance. Type X, the most-common fire-code drywall, sometimes is required by building codes for fire-prone places, such as around a furnace. Foil-backed drywall can be used in lieu of a vapor barrier on the inside surfaces of exterior walls. Prefinished drywall is faced on one side with a durable finish that needs no paint, and patterned drywall is available with an embossed wood-paneling texture.

Drywall is available in $\frac{1}{4}$-inch, $\frac{3}{8}$-inch, $\frac{1}{2}$-inch, and $\frac{5}{8}$-inch thick-nesses. For walls with studs on 24-inch centers, use $\frac{5}{8}$-inch drywall. For ceilings, $\frac{5}{8}$-inch drywall is prefer-able because it will not sag between joists as easily as $\frac{1}{2}$-inch drywall. For walls with studs on 16-inch cen-ters, $\frac{1}{2}$-inch drywall is fine. When resurfacing old walls, use $\frac{3}{8}$-inch drywall; if you are building a curved wall, use two layers of $\frac{1}{4}$-inch dry-wall, which is flexible. Although most do-it-yourselfers work with 4x8 sheets, 4-foot-wide panels up to 16 feet long are available. Regardless of panel length, the long edges are sealed and slightly tapered to accept tape and joint compound.

Hanging drywall is easy if you observe a few basic cautions. Most

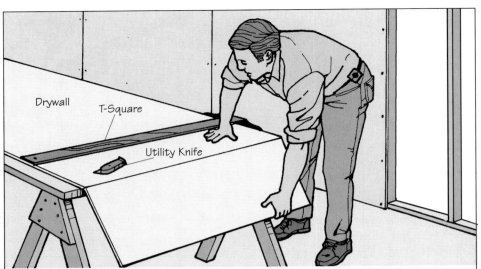

Cutting Pieces to Fit. Mark the cutting line with a straightedge and use a utility knife to score the drywall through the paper into the plaster. Break the sheet downward, and run the blade through the paper backing to remove the piece.

important, remember that drywall is delicate. It crushes if stood on one corner, and treat it gently, because it breaks easily if dropped or hit. Dry-wall should be stacked flat to prevent warping if it is not used right away. Also, a sheet of drywall is heavy (a $\frac{1}{2}$-inch 4x8 panel weighs 65 pounds), so it's best to work with a helper.

Estimating Materials.

To figure out how many sheets of drywall your job requires, calculate the square footage of each wall you will cover, and then add 10 percent to the total for waste. Divide by the number of square feet per drywall panel (32 square feet per 4x8 sheet), and the result is the number of panels to order. Drywall is fastened to wood studs with $1\frac{5}{8}$-inch drywall screws. Metal corner beads are positioned on all outside corners.

Cutting Pieces to Fit. Measure the size of the piece you need; and using a T-square, draw the out-line on a sheet of drywall laid on a flat work surface. Use a utility knife guided by the T-square to score the face paper. Shift the drywall so that the score line overhangs a straight-edged surface, and snap the drywall. Slice through the back side to remove the piece.

Hanging Drywall Vertically

1. Mark the Stud Locations. Because the drywall will cover the wall framing, it's important to mark

1. Before installing drywall, mark the stud locations on the floor and ceiling so that you will know where to drive the drywall screws.

the exact location of the wall studs along the floor and ceiling so that you will know where to drive drywall screws.

2. Trim the Bottom Edges.
Cut the sheets of drywall about ³⁄₄ inch shorter than the height of the wall. The sheets will be installed vertically, and the ³⁄₄-inch gap at the bottom will be covered with baseboard molding.

3. Lever the Panel into Position.
Install the drywall vertically so that the tapered edges of each sheet reach over a stud (or over a wood cleat). Set the bottom of the sheet on the pry bar, and then step on it to lift the panel tightly against the ceiling.

4. Secure the Panel.
Push the drywall against the studs with your hand, and drive a few 1½-inch drywall screws through the panel into the frame at the top and along a side. Although you can use a variable-speed cordless drill, the best tool for driving drywall screws is a drywall screwdriver. It is a variable-speed electric drill fitted with a Phillips-head bit. The tool's clutch automatically sets the screw below the surface while preventing the driver from driving screws too deep.

5. Complete the Driving.
Release the pry bar and drive panel screws into the framing. Standard procedure calls for screws at intervals of 6 inches along both edges and 16 inches along studs in the middle. Should you miss a stud, be sure to back out the screw and reposition it so that it's driven securely into the stud. Drive all screws slightly below the drywall surface as shown, but be careful not to break the paper. The dimple

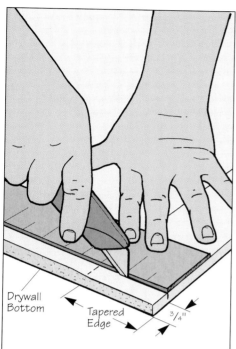

Drywall Bottom — Tapered Edge — ³⁄₄"

2. Cut the drywall panels ³⁄₄ inch shorter than the wall height. Guide the utility knife with a straightedge, such as a T-square.

Pry Bar

3. Step on the pry bar to raise the panel, then drive a few 1½-inch drywall screws near the top and along the edge to hold the sheet in position.

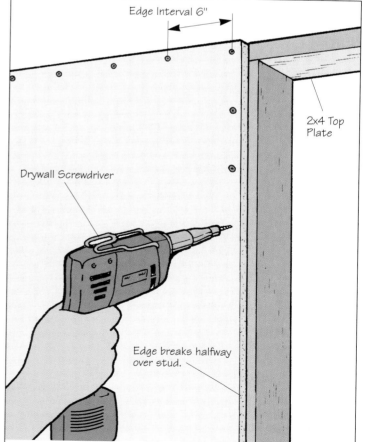

Edge Interval 6"

2x4 Top Plate

Drywall Screwdriver

Edge breaks halfway over stud.

4. Drive the screws with a variable-speed drill or a drywall screwdriver, which automatically sets the screws about ¹⁄₁₆ inch below the wall surface. If you miss a stud, back out the screw and try again.

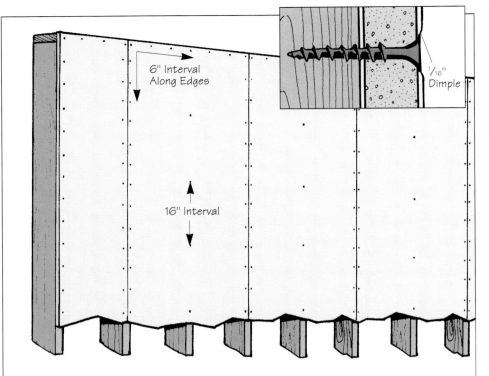

5. Screws are placed every 6 inches along drywall edges and every 16 inches in the middle of a panel. Set the screws slightly below the drywall, but not so deep that they tear through the paper facing. Drive screws 1/16-inch below the surface.

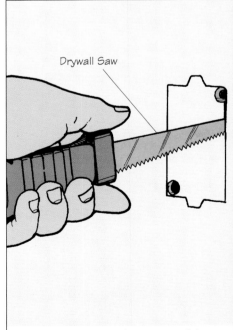

6. At outside corners, cut metal corner bead about 3/4 inch shorter than the wall and nail it in place, starting at the middle.

left by this countersinking will be filled in with joint compound.

6. Install Corner Bead. If there are any outside corners, cap them with metal corner bead. Use tin snips to cut a length of metal corner bead about 3/4 inch less than the height of the wall. Angle the ends inward slightly to ensure a better fit, and use 1 5/8-inch drywall nails, not screws, to attach the bead to the wall. Nail the bead at the middle first on both sides, and then work your way up and down. Be sure to set the nails about 1/16 inch below the surface.

Cutting Holes for Outlets, Switches, and Lights.

1. Mark the Outline. Cut holes in the drywall to accommodate electrical boxes. Use lipstick to mark the outside edges of the box; then set a sheet of drywall into position, pressing it firmly against the box. The lipstick leaves marks showing where to make the hole.

2. Cut Out the Opening. With an awl, make a hole in one corner of the lipstick outline, carefully punching through the drywall so that you

won't damage it. Rotate the awl until the hole is wide enough to insert the tip of a drywall saw, and then cut out the opening from the front.

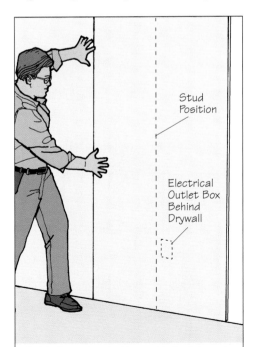

1. Mark an electrical box with lipstick, and set the drywall into position, pressing it against the box to mark the drywall with the outline of the box.

2. Drill holes in opposite corners of the electrical-box layout, and use a drywall saw to cut out the opening. For a cleaner cut, saw from the front of the panel.

Cutting Corners, Doorways, and Windows.

1. Install a Full Panel. Put up the entire sheet, even if it completely covers a doorway or overhangs a

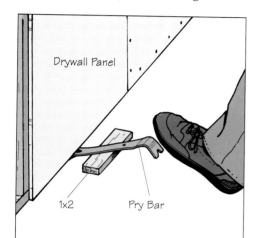

Drywall Panel

1x2   Pry Bar

1. After trimming the drywall ¾ inch shorter than the wall height, set the sheet against the framing and raise it off the floor, using a pry bar over a piece of 1×2.

corner. It is important to hang the sheet so that it will clear the floor when you cut it, so be sure to trim the sheet about ¾ inch shorter than the ceiling height. When you install the sheet, set it on a lever made from resting a pry bar on a scrap of 1x2. Step on the pry bar to raise the sheet a bit, but don't let it hit the ceiling. Secure the edges of the drywall with screws.

2. Cut along a Corner Stud. At outside corners, score the back of the drywall along the stud and snap the drywall; then slice the opposite face to remove the waste.

3. Cut Doorways with a Saw and Knife. At doorway or window openings, use a drywall saw to cut the horizontal lines along the headers or sills. Be careful around door and window trimmers. Score the drywall vertically with a utility knife. Snap it, and cut the other side to remove the waste.

Hanging Drywall Horizontally

If the wall you are building is less than the length of a drywall sheet, you can reduce the number of seams you have to finish—and perhaps improve the look of the finished wall—by hanging panels horizontally. For this you will need helpers, or you can do it yourself using a drywall lift from a rental dealer.

To hang drywall horizontally, mark the stud locations on the floor and ceiling and drive 10d nails halfway into the studs 4 feet down from the ceiling. With a helper, lift a panel into position onto the nails and push it against the wall. Screw the panel to a few of the studs to hold it, and complete the screw driving as in "Hanging Drywall Vertically," beginning on page 40. If the wall is 8 feet high, install the panel below using a lever to hold it snug against the one above. If the wall is higher than

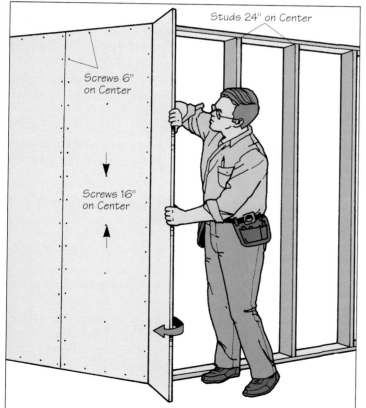

Studs 24" on Center

Screws 6" on Center

Screws 16" on Center

2. Drywall sheets that overhang corners are scored along the framing and then snapped. Hanging the sheet off the floor allows you to swing and snap it; the facing is then cut and the waste piece removed.

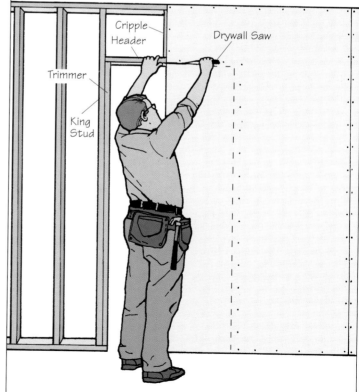

Cripple Header

Trimmer

King Stud

Drywall Saw

3. After installing a sheet directly over a doorway, use a drywall saw to cut along the bottom of the header. Then score the drywall vertically along the trimmer; snap it and cut the face to remove the waste.

Hanging Drywall Horizontally For horizontal installation, hang the top half of the wall first. Set the sheet on 10d nails driven partway into the studs 4 feet below the ceiling, and then screw the sheet to the framing.

8 feet, repeat the procedure given here and fill in between the bottom panel and the floor with lengths cut to fit. Measure the distance between the floor and the bottom panel in several places in case the floor and ceiling are not square. Cut the bottom panels about ³⁄₄ inch shorter than absolutely necessary, and then use the pry bar to raise them into position.

Installing Drywall with Adhesive

1. Apply the Adhesive. You can reduce the amount of screw or nail driving by using construction adhesive to attach drywall to center studs. Use an adhesive that meets ASTM standard C557, and apply it to the studs in a ³⁄₈-inch bead as shown. Start and stop your application of

adhesive 3 inches from the top and bottom of the studs. Because the edges of the drywall must be screwed to the edge studs, there's no need to apply glue to the edge studs.

2. Fasten the Panel to the Studs. Fit the panel against the studs and screw it along the perimeter every 6 inches. In the middle of the panel, screw only the top, middle, and bottom of the panel.

TAPING AND FINISHING DRYWALL

After the drywall is in place, the seams and screw-head dimples, as well as imperfections such as accidental gouges, are concealed in a three-step process called finishing. Finishing work must be done meticulously, because even the smallest dents and ridges show through paint and wallpaper.

Tools and Materials

A thick paste-like material called joint compound is the main ingredient for drywall finishing. Several layers of compound are spread over imperfections, and each layer is either dry- or wet-sanded smooth after it dries. Compound is available in several formulations, but "all-purpose compound" is generally suitable. It's sold in 5-gallon buckets.

Several taping knives of different sizes are necessary to spread and smooth the compound. Each knife has a thin, flexible-steel blade. Even though knife size is partly a matter of personal preference, 10-inch, 12-inch, and 14-inch rectangular taping knives are good for smoothing joints; and a 4- or 5-inch crescent-shaped broad knife is good for applying the first coat and for filling screw-head dimples. If you find the inside corners difficult to finish, you can use a right-angle corner trowel, which allows you to smooth both sides of the corner simultaneously.

1. Apply adhesive to the center stud (or studs) only, stopping the bead about 3 inches from the top and bottom.

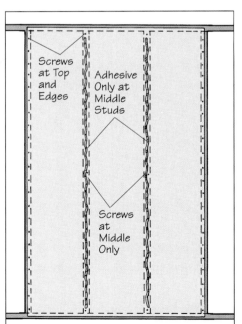

2. Drive screws along the drywall edges at 6-inch intervals; panels are screwed to the center studs at the top, middle, and bottom only.

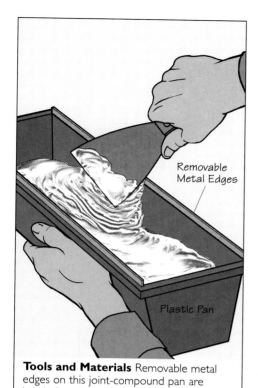

Tools and Materials Removable metal edges on this joint-compound pan are handy for wiping the knife clean.

Instead of scooping the compound out of the bucket onto your knife over and over again, use a plastic pan to carry a big dollop of compound with you to the work area. This hand-held pan also has removable metal edges for scraping compound off the finishing knife. Another advantage of a pan is that you'll be going to the bucket less often, allow-

ing you to keep it sealed. This is important because you don't want the compound to dry out. As you deplete the bucket, be sure to use the side of a broad knife to scrape the bucket walls clean. Also make sure no compound is on the inside of the lid. When this dries, it crumbles into the bucket and ends up on the wall, where it gouges the wet compound you are spreading.

After applying each coat of compound, wet-sand it with a dampened sponge or dry-sand it with 100-grit sandpaper on the first coat and 150-grit on subsequent coats. Because conventional sandpaper tends to clog with joint compound, consider using open-weave silicon-carbide paper or nylon sanding screens. Both are available at paint stores, and neither will become clogged with sanding dust.

The disadvantage of dry-sanding is that it creates lots of fine white dust. Wear goggles and a dust mask (or respirator) when sanding, and close off the work area from the rest of the house. Leave windows open for ventilation.

Joint and Corner Reinforcement. To reinforce seams and prevent cracks from appearing at these locations, use 2-inch-wide seaming tape, sold by the

roll where you buy joint compound. Seaming tape may be paper or fiberglass mesh. Paper tape is set into a bed coat of compound, but mesh is self-adhering, so you don't need to set it into a bed coat. Mesh tape, however, can be used only on flat seams; you'll need paper tape to finish inside-corner seams, such as the joint between a wall and ceiling.

Outside corners are protected with corner bead, which are thin pieces of sheet metal bent at a right angle. The bend is reinforced with a rounded "bead." Corner bead is nailed in place over the corner, and then covered with several coats of joint compound. See "Hanging Drywall," page 40, for instructions on installing corner bead.

Taping Flat Joints

There are two types of flat joints: butt joints and tapered joints. Butt joints occur where the short sides of drywall panels meet; tapered joints occur where the long sides meet.

1. Fill and Tape the Butt Joints.
If you're working with paper tape, use the broad knife to apply joint compound to the butt joints first, creating a slight hump. Cut a length of joint tape long enough to run into any

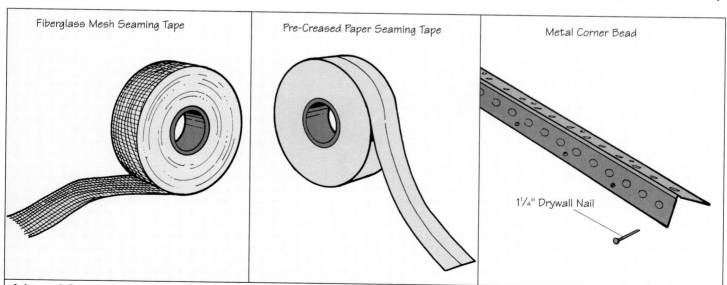

Fiberglass Mesh Seaming Tape

Pre-Creased Paper Seaming Tape

Metal Corner Bead

1¼" Drywall Nail

Joint and Corner Reinforcement. Two types of tape are used to prevent flat seams from cracking when finished. Paper tape is used for inside corners. Fiberglass mesh adheres without a bed coat of joint compound, but it cannot be used in inside corners. Metal corner bead is nailed to outside corners and filled with joint compound.

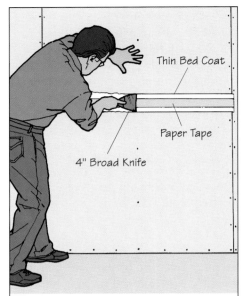

1. Starting with the butt joints (where short edges of drywall sheets meet), apply a thin bed coat of compound with a broad knife; then cut the tape to fit and smooth it with the knife.

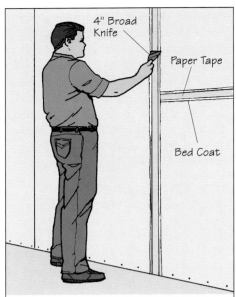

2. Next, apply a bed coat to the tapered joints (where the long edges of drywall meet); cut tape to fit, and smooth it over the joint with a broad knife.

3. Embed the tape with a thin coat of joint compound applied with a 10-inch taping knife. Tapered joints are coated first, then the butt joints.

seams on both sides of the butt joint. Center one end of the tape over the joint, and then embed the tape by using the broad knife to smooth it into the compound. If you're using mesh tape, simply cut it to length and adhere it along the joint.

2. Fill and Tape the Tapered Joints. With the broad knife, force the compound into the tapered drywall joints until they are filled and level. Then cut a piece of paper tape to length, center it over the joint, and embed the tape into the compound with the broad knife. Be sure this tape covers the ends of butt-joint tape. Again, mesh tape can be adhered over the tapered joint without compound.

3. Coat the Tape with Compound. With a 10-inch taping knife held at a 45-degree angle, spread a $\frac{1}{8}$-inch-thick layer of compound over the tapered joints. Then go back over the joint, scraping away the excess compound, smoothing the joint and blending, or feathering, the edges so that they taper evenly onto the drywall. Allow the compound to dry, and then coat the butt joints as you did the tapered joints.

Finishing Corners

1. Tape the Inside Corners.
With the broad knife, fill both sides of the inside corner joints with compound. Fold a length of paper tape along its centerline (the tape is pre-creased for this purpose), and press it lightly into the joint every few inches. Then use the same knife to smooth

the paper one side at a time, making sure it covers any tape ends running into the joint.

2. Fill the Outside Corners.
At outside corners, load a broad knife with joint compound, and run the knife along the edge of the corner bead as you cover it with compound. Apply pressure on the drywall to feather the edge of the compound.

1. Spread a bed coat of compound on both sides of inside corners. Fold a length of paper tape along its crease and press it lightly into the compound. Smooth the tape one side at a time with a broad knife.

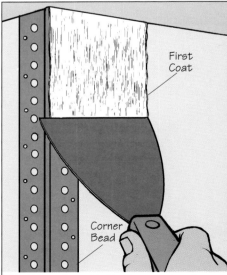

2. Using a broad knife, fill corner beads with compound. Let the knife ride along the rounded corner of the corner bead as you apply light pressure on the drywall, creating a tapered effect.

Finishing and Sanding

1. Clean Up the First Coat. After the first coat is dry, inspect the seams and remove all ridges that might interfere with the smoothness of subsequent joints. Ridges can be scraped off with taping knives, or they can be lightly wet- or dry-sanded.

2. Apply the Second Coat. Use the 10-inch taping knife to apply a thin coat of compound to the joints.

Finish the joints in this order: butt joints first, followed by tapered joints, outside corners, and finally screw-head dimples. Inside corners require only one finish coat, so coat one side of each corner while doing the second coat on the flat (butt and tapered) joints, and complete the corners while doing the third coat on the flat joints.

3. Fill Screw-Head Dimples. Use the broad knife to fill all the screw-head dimples and other minor imperfections with compound. No tape is required.

4. Apply the Third Coat. After the second coat dries, use a 12-inch taping knife to spread a thin layer of compound over the joints; then make long, smooth runs over them with your knife while applying plenty of pressure. Don't forget to finish the second coat on the inside corners. Use the 4-inch knife to "spot" the dimples again.

5. Sand the Compound. After 24 hours, or when the third coat of compound is completely dry, sand all joints and dimples until smooth. To dry-sand, fold a sheet of 150-grit sandpaper into quarters and go over the compound lightly. Be careful not to sand through the face paper.

A univeral pole sander makes dry-sanding easier. This tool has a pad with clamps to hold sandpaper or drywall mesh. The pad is swivel-mounted to a pole. This tool is particularly handy for reaching ceilings, but you may find yourself using it almost everywhere because it extends your sanding stroke. Brush or vacuum away all traces of sanding dust before painting or papering the walls.

Tape Still Visible Under Compound

1. Before applying the second coat of joint compound, clean up the first coat, knocking down any ridges either with a broad knife, a damp sponge, or 100-grit sandpaper.

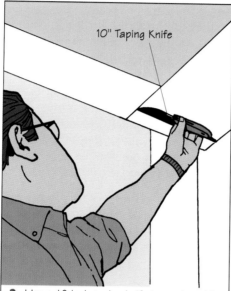

10" Taping Knife

2. Use a 10-inch taping knife to apply a thin coat of joint compound over the flat joints and outside corners, and on one side of the inside corners.

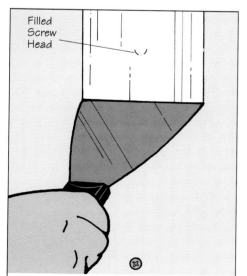

Filled Screw Head

3. Use a 4-inch broad knife to swipe a coat of joint compound over the screw-head dimples and other imperfections, such as gouges in the drywall.

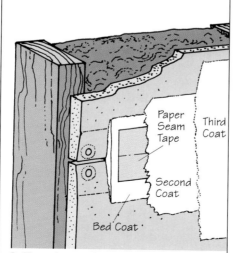

Paper Seam Tape

Third Coat

Second Coat

Bed Coat

4. Three layers of joint compound spread in successively wider swaths make a finished joint. Note the tapered edges on the drywall.

Pole Sander

5. If you dry-sand ceiling joints, wear a dust mask. Wet-sanding with a damp sponge works well too. Shine a bright light across the walls to check your work.

SOUNDPROOFING WALLS

Ordinary frame walls and ceilings stop some sound, but this may not be enough for a quiet bedroom in a busy house, for instance, or to contain the sound of power tools in a home workshop, or music in a practice room. You can take several steps to reduce the amount of sound passing between rooms in your house or apartment. Options range from sealing cracks to building new walls and ceilings. (See "Soundproofing Ceilings," page 153.)

Sound enters or leaves a room in two ways: airborne through openings and transmitted by the vibrations it causes in walls, floors, and ceilings. To stop sound, you must seal openings and deaden vibration in walls and ceilings.

A surprising amount of sound can leak into a room under doors and through unsealed outlet and switch plates, cracks, open joints, and seams. These leaks will render any amount of structural soundproofing ineffective, but they can be sealed up easily.

The only way to reduce the direct transmission of sound through walls and ceilings is to alter their structure. Methods can range from hanging new drywall on special metal channels that hold it away from the old surface to building a double wall stuffed with fiberglass batt insulation.

If you are adding a wall, plan any soundproofing carefully. If you want to make a room quieter, you must consider all the possible routes by which sound enters it, as shown in the diagram. For effective soundproofing, you must block these routes. Expensive renovations for soundproofing lose value if they stop bothersome noise from one direction and do nothing to stop it from another.

Planning for Soundproofing. When you are planning soundproofing, you must consider every possible pathway, because any amount of intervention that does not completely seal a room will usually be a waste of time. It would be like building a dam only partway across a river. You may find that the level of soundproofing you desire is simply not possible without an impractical amount of reconstruction. You would be better off abandoning your plans than spending time and money on halfway measures. Of course, stopping sound at its source is the most efficient way to soundproof.

Sealing Acoustic Leaks. Use paintable caulk to fill any cracks at the top and bottom of a wall, and around outlet and switch plates. If noise is entering through duct work, you should line as much of the duct as you can reach with neoprene duct liner held in place with adhesive. The duct liner should be sealed with a coating of the same adhesive recommended for use with the liner along any edges that are cut so that small glass fibers from the liner are not carried out of the duct on the streams of forced air.

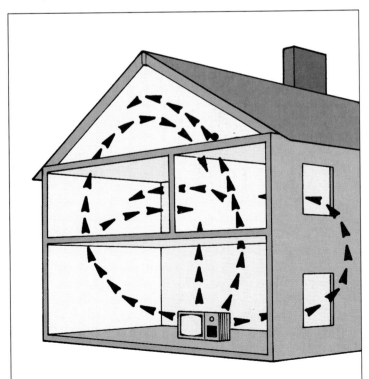

Planning for Soundproofing. Try to locate all possible pathways that sound can take to the room you want quieter, and make provisions for each.

Sealing Acoustic Leaks. Block pathways for airborne sound waves with paintable caulk. Seal the top and bottom of the walls, and around outlets and switches. Smooth with an old spoon.

Sealing Doors with Gaskets.

Use neoprene gaskets that you cut to fit around the top and sides of doors. The door should squeeze the gasket slightly when it is closed, but not so much that the gasket prevents the door from latching easily. At the bottom, install an aluminum sill, plane the door to fit, and attach a gasket to the bottom so that it just meets the sill. Check for proper fit by slipping a thin tool, such as a putty-knife blade, under the door. There should be some resistance.

Using Resilient Channels.

Resilient channels are metal tracks that hold a wall surface in position away from the surface to which it is attached; these channels are designed to isolate the two surfaces so that the outer surface will not pick up the vibrations of the inner surface. To enhance the sound-stopping qualities of an existing wall, strip off the old surface and fill the wall cavity with 3½-inch insulation. Attach resilient channels across the studs with channels located 6 inches below the ceiling and 2 inches above the floor. Space them evenly for the attachment of drywall, but intervals should not exceed 2 feet. Overlap the channel where you must in order to span the length of the wall. Attach drywall to channels with 1-inch drywall screws and seal at the top and bottom with caulking.

Staggered-Stud Walls.

You can improve soundproofing by building a staggered-stud wall, where 2x4 studs are placed alternately along either edge of 2x6 plates. Lay out the top and bottom plates for studs 12 inches on center, but build the wall so that every other stud is flush with one side of the plates. This will create a wall with nailing surfaces 24 inches on center. Erect the plates and studs, and staple 3½-inch fiberglass batt insulation between the studs on one side of the wall. Attach drywall as on any wall, and caulk at the top and bottom, before taping.

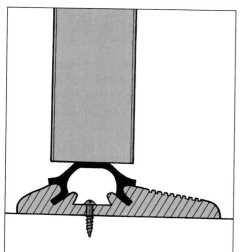

Sealing Doors with Gaskets. Install neoprene gaskets around doors to block sound leaks. Trim the door so that you can install a sill beneath.

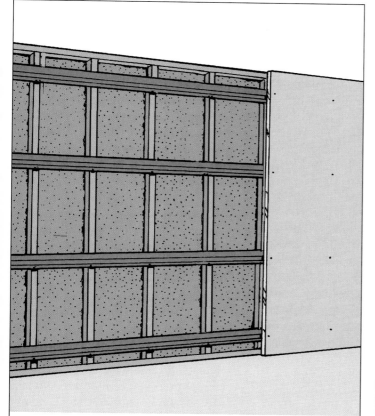

Using Resilient Channels. Resilient channels isolate a wall surface from some of the structural vibrations that transmit sound. The channels are attached to studs with 1¼-inch drywall screws. When installing drywall, leave a ⅛-inch gap at the top and bottom, and seal the gaps with caulking.

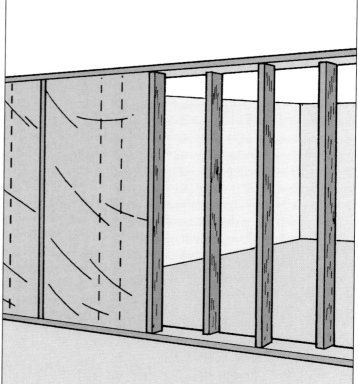

Staggered-Stud Walls. This wall is built with studs 12 inches on center. The plates are 2x6s and the studs are 2x4s. Every other stud is set flush with the outside edge of the plate so that one side of the wall has almost no contact with the other side.

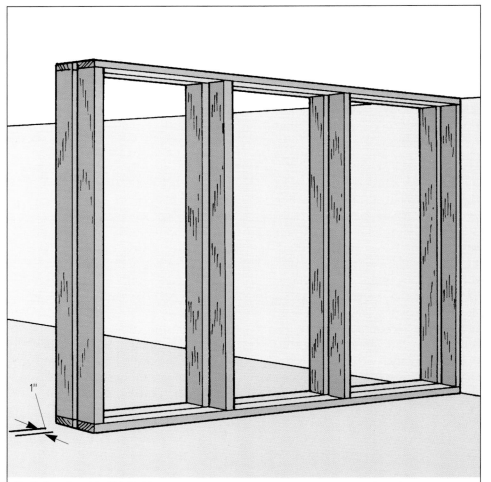

1"

Building Double Walls. Two walls are better than one because their surfaces have no communication at all. This wall will be stuffed with 6 inches of insulation and then covered with two layers of drywall on each side. When installing drywall, leave an ⅛-inch gap at top and bottom, and seal with caulking before taping.

Building Double Walls. For the most soundproof wall possible with drywall, build two stud walls that are set 1 inch apart. Cover one side of this double frame with two layers of drywall. Then fill the double wall with 6-inch-thick, fiberglass-batt insulation, and cover the other side with two layers of drywall, as you did on the other side. Caulk at the top and bottom on both sides.

Where you can afford the lost floor area in a room with existing walls, you can strip the surface facing into the room from the wall that requires additional soundproofing; then you can erect the second wall in front of the first, as described above. Stuff it with insulation and cover the new wall with drywall.

INSTALLING SHEET PANELING

Sheet paneling—of real or simulated wood—is one of the most popular wall surfaces for do-it-yourself installation. Paneling adds warmth to any room in the house and is particularly desirable in recreation rooms because it holds up to hard use. Paneling goes up quickly, too, without need for the time-consuming finishing steps required by drywall.

Building codes regulate whether paneling may be applied directly to studs. Sometimes, a layer of drywall must be installed beneath thin paneling to support it, as well as to add a measure of fire resistance. Check your local codes.

In general, though, plywood and hardboard paneling not less than $^{13}/_{64}$ inch thick ($^{1}/_{4}$-inch nominal thickness) can be applied directly to studs, or to furring strips spaced no more than 16 inches on center. If the paneling is thinner, however, it should be applied over drywall that's at least $^{3}/_{8}$ inch thick. Some thin panels ($^{5}/_{32}$-inch thick) are not recommended under any circumstances for use in a basement, so check with the paneling manufacturer.

Types of Sheet Paneling

Sheet paneling comes in a wide variety of prices and styles. Among the least expensive is prefinished hardboard paneling. Sometimes referred to by the trade name Masonite, hardboard paneling often has a top layer that is factory-finished with a wood-grain pattern. Made from wood fibers that have been mixed with adhesive and pressed together to form a dense sheet, hardboard panels typically measure 4 feet wide by 8 feet long and range in thickness from $^{1}/_{8}$ inch to $^{1}/_{4}$ inch. Longer panels may be available; check with your local paneling supplier.

Prefinished plywood paneling is available in the widest selection of patterns, colors, and thicknesses. Like any plywood, prefinished plywood paneling consists of layers of wood veneers bonded together with adhesive. The grain of each layer is perpendicular to adjoining layers, resulting in a cross-grain construction that's fairly stable. Sheets are typically 4x8, ranging from $^{5}/_{32}$-inch to $^{1}/_{2}$-inch thick ($^{1}/_{4}$ inch is common). The face of each panel is printed, embossed, or color-toned with wood grain or other decorative effects. Some are laminated with a paper overlay that offers even more variety. In addition, some types of prefinished paneling are grooved to simulate individual wood boards.

Hardwood plywood, unlike prefinished plywood paneling, is finished

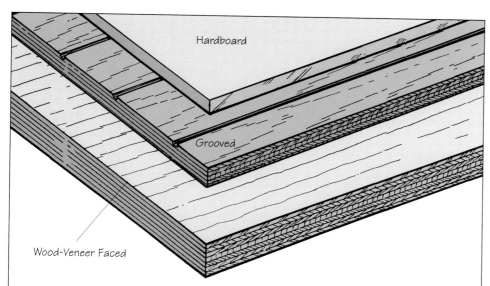

Hardboard

Grooved

Wood-Veneer Faced

Types of Sheet Paneling. Among the many types of sheet paneling, hardboard is inexpensive and usually has a simulated wood face. Plywood paneling often is grooved to mimic board paneling. Most expensive is hardwood plywood, with real wood face veneers available in many species from ash to Zambesi redwood.

after installation, typically with light stains or clear finish treatments, such as polyurethane, to enhance the natural beauty of the wood grain. The outer layer (called the face veneer) is a high-quality wood veneer, in species such as ash, cherry, walnut, and oak, as well as others; inner layers will be other, less valuable woods. The most common thickness of this costly product is $3/4$ inch, but $1/2$ inch and even $1/4$ inch are available.

Installing Prefinished Paneling

1. Condition the Paneling.
Like any wood product, paneling responds to changes in humidity by expanding and contracting. To bring new panels into balance with humidity levels in the room, stack them there for at least 48 hours before installing them. Stack the panels on the floor or lean them against a wall, and use scrap wood spacers (called stickers) between each sheet to promote air circulation.

2. Arrange the Paneling.
Panels with a finished surface of wood veneer will show natural variations in the pattern and color of the wood. You can avoid inadvertent groupings of like-colored panels in one area by lining them up side by side around the room, and then arranging them in whatever order you find pleasing. Before restacking the panels, number the back of each one so that you can keep track of where they should go.

3. Trim the Panels to Size.
Measure the height of the wall and subtract $1/2$ inch for the desired height of the panel. This will allow room for each panel to expand and contract, and it will also make it easier for you to maneuver the panel into place. Use a T-square to mark a straight line across the panel, and cut along the line. You can cut paneling on a table saw, or you can use a circular saw, saber saw, or even a handsaw. To minimize splintering when you cut a panel, make sure you orient it properly. If you are using either a table saw or a hand saw, you should cut the panels with the good side facing up.

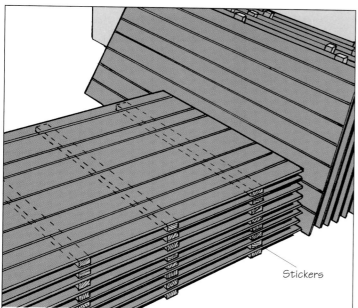

Stickers

1. At least 48 hours before the installation, stack the panels on the floor or against the walls so that they can adjust to room conditions. Provide spacers, called *stickers*, between each sheet.

2. Because real veneer plywood varies in color and grain pattern from sheet to sheet, arrange the panels to avoid grouping too many sheets of similar appearance in one spot.

If you are using a circular saw or saber saw, however, the good side should face down. You can improve the cut even further by using a plywood blade, which has numerous small teeth. It's best to clamp a straightedge to the panel to guide the circular saw. But where you'll be covering the edges with molding or baseboard, a reasonably straight freehand cut will suffice.

4. Scribe Irregular Cuts. Plan the job so that the vertical edges of every panel will fall over a stud. As you install panels, check one edge for plumb with a level. If the first panel has to fit against a corner that's not straight, or against an uneven surface, you'll have to scribe it. Hold the panel in place on the wall, with one edge against the surface you are fitting it to. Use a compass or scriber to transfer a layout line to the panel, and then cut along the line. If you are scribing to an irregular surface, such as brick, cut the panel with a saber saw. To minimize chipping, fit the saw with a special panel-cutting blade, which has teeth oriented to cut on the plunge instead of the upstroke.

5. Cut Openings for Electrical Boxes. After tucking the rough wiring into the boxes, mark the edge of an electrical outlet or switch box with lipstick or chalk. (See "Mark the Outline," page 42.) Now press the panel against the box to transfer the shape of the box to the back of the panel. Drill two $\frac{1}{2}$-inch holes just inside the layout, and cut along the lines with a keyhole saw or saber saw fitted with a metal-cutting blade.

6. Nail Up the Paneling. The easiest nailing option is to use 6d color-matched nails, usually available where you buy paneling. Most paneling has grooves simulating vertical boards; when you nail into the studs through these grooves, colored nails will be virtually invisible and needn't be countersunk. If you use standard finish nails, however, you should

countersink them lightly and fill the hole with a colored putty stick. In any case, you'll need to space nails 6 inches apart at the panel edges and 16 inches apart in the middle of the sheet. Lift each panel into place to ensure that the bottom edge will not be in contact with a concrete floor. If you are installing dark paneling over

an unfinished or light-color wall, you can conceal the seams between panels by painting a dark strip behind the seam on the wall before installing each panel.

7. Add Trim. To complete the job, you can add trim in a variety of profiles to the base and top of the

3. When cutting paneling with a circular saw, place the good side down and clamp a straight board to the panel to guide the saw.

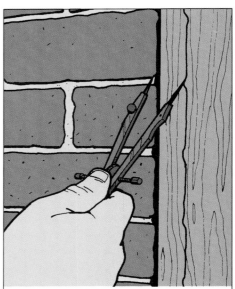

4. Use a compass or scriber to transfer the shape of an irregular surface, such as a brick chimney, onto the paneling. Then cut along the line with a saber saw fitted with a fine blade.

5. Make cutouts for electrical boxes with a saber saw. Drill holes at opposite corners of the box outline; then insert the saber-saw blade into the holes to make the cut.

6. Paneling should be nailed every 6 inches along the edges and every 16 inches in the middle of the sheet. When possible, use paneling nails of a color that matches your paneling, and nail them into grooves.

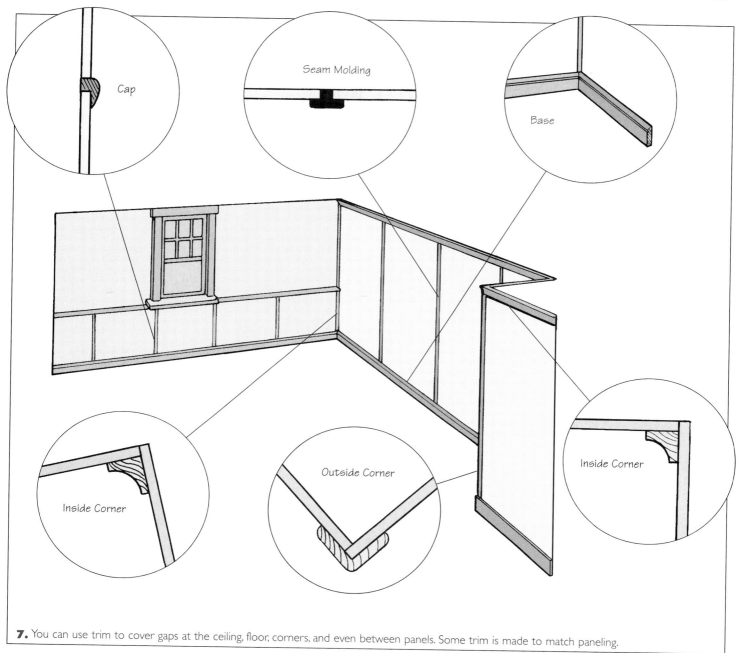

7. You can use trim to cover gaps at the ceiling, floor, corners, and even between panels. Some trim is made to match paneling.

wall and around any openings as well. In some cases, you can purchase prefinished trim that matches the paneling exactly. Trim is also available to cover inside and outside corners, giving you some leeway to conceal minor fitting errors.

Paneling High Walls. If you have an unusually high ceiling—something over 8 feet—check with several paneling suppliers to see whether they have 9-foot- or 10-foot-long paneling in stock. If not, they might be able to order it for you. If

the wall is only slightly over 8 feet, lift 8-foot panels off the floor several inches: You can cover the gap with base trim. And you can cover any remaining gap at the top of the wall with trim.

Installing the Extension Sheet. If you can't find long panels, and trim won't cover the gaps, you'll have to cut short panels to fill the gap between the top of the paneling and the ceiling. Use matching seam molding to cover the joint between an 8-foot panel and an extension panel. For the best-looking results, take care

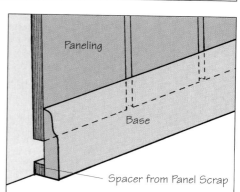

Paneling High Walls. For ceilings slightly higher than 8 feet, raise the sheet off of the floor and cover the gap with base trim. To support the base, put a strip of paneling at the bottom of the wall.

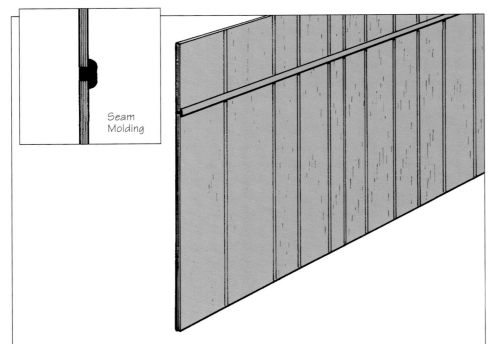

Seam
Molding

Installing the Extension Sheet. If you must install an extension sheet above a full sheet, try to align the grooves, and cover the seam with matching seam molding.

to match any vertical grooves in adjoining panels.

Installing Paneling over Furring Strips

Paneling manufacturers usually caution against the application of wood paneling directly against masonry, even if you are sure the wall doesn't have moisture problems. Sealing the walls with special paint and using rigid insulation beneath the paneling is an excellent way to keep moisture away from the panels. But if you live in a very mild climate, you might not want to go to the expense of insulating. Instead, you can nail the paneling to furring strips that keep the paneling away from the masonry.

1. Install the Furring Strips. The strips can be 1x2 lumber, or 1/2-inch plywood cut into lengths 1 1/2 inches wide. The strips are applied in horizontal bands running the length of the wall, and they can be attached with masonry nails or masonry screws. Install the strips every 16 inches on center, making sure they are level, and then add vertical strips every 4 feet on center to support the joints between panels.

2. Shim the Strips Plumb. To compensate for imperfections in the wall, you can shim behind the strips as needed, using wood shingles. (For more information, see "Preparing Walls for New Surfaces," page 62.) A dab of construction adhesive the size of a quarter will keep the shingles from sliding out of position over time.

3. Install a Vapor Barrier. Once all the furring strips are in place, staple a sheet of 4-mil plastic to the top of the wall, then drape it over the furring strips. This will prevent any small amounts of wall moisture from reaching the panels.

4. Nail Up the Paneling. Paneling can be installed normally once the

Furring Strips
48" On Center

Furring Strips
16" On Center

Wood-Shingle Shim

Shims

1. Furring strips nailed or screwed to masonry provide nailing surfaces for paneling. Install horizontal strips every 16 inches and vertical blocks every 48 inches.

2. You can create a flat wall by shimming any strips that aren't plumb. A dab of construction adhesive placed on the shim will hold it in place.

4-mil
Plastic

3. To help prevent moisture from damaging the paneling, staple 4-mil plastic sheets to the strips before installing the paneling.

4. Once the paneling is in place, go back around the room with a utility knife and cut off any plastic protruding from behind the paneling.

Excess Plastic

Utility Knife

vapor barrier is in place. When the paneling is complete, use a utility knife to trim off the excess strip of vapor barrier at the bottom of the wall, and complete the job with baseboard.

INSTALLING BOARD PANELING

No matter how good the simulation, sheet paneling cannot duplicate the richness of a room lined with real wood boards. Boards also allow you some flexibility in creating your own pattern, and they may be nailed up directly over studs, with no drywall necessary, unless fire codes prohibit this. Board paneling is generally more expensive than sheet paneling and can take more time to install and finish, but the results are well worth the extra effort.

Defining Types of Board Paneling.
Board paneling can be bought in a variety of hardwoods and softwoods milled specially for this use. It is 1 inch thick and comes in various widths up to 12 inches. The boards usually have either tongue-and-groove edges, or shiplapped edges, as shown. In

addition, the top surface of the board may be beveled or shaped for a decorative effect.

Estimating the Amount to Buy.
Boards for paneling are sold by the board foot; the price per board foot depends on the kind of wood and its grade. To keep costs down, you should spend some time estimating your needs carefully. Unlike estimating sheet paneling, you can't work simply with the square footage of the walls. Begin by deciding how you will apply the boards: vertically, horizontally, or diagonally. As an example, assume you will apply tongue-and-groove boards vertically.

First, measure the exposed face of a board (the width of the board minus the tongue), and then measure the length of the wall, in inches. Divide the width of a board into the length of the wall to get the number of courses, or rows, you will need. Now measure the height of the wall. Multiply this height by the number of courses to get the lineal feet of boarding. Finally, add 5 percent to this figure to account for waste. As an alternative method for figuring the number of boards required in a vertical installation, you can count the number of courses and order boards all one length.

If you want to install the boards diagonally, use the basic lineal footage figure (you're still covering the same amount of wall), but you should add about 15 percent for waste. In either case, the final figure will be the lineal footage of boarding that you'll need for the job.

For a horizontal installation, divide the wall height by the exposed face of a board to figure out how many courses of boards you will need. Then measure the length of the walls, and order boards at least 1 foot longer. If you can't get boards long enough to span the wall, order different lengths of boards—for example, 8-foot and 12-foot boards—so that you can stagger joints less conspicuously.

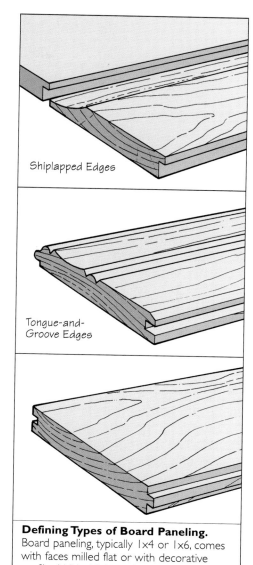

Shiplapped Edges

Tongue-and-Groove Edges

Defining Types of Board Paneling.
Board paneling, typically 1x4 or 1x6, comes with faces milled flat or with decorative profiles. With shiplapped or tongue-and-groove edges, you can hide nails and keep gaps from opening as the boards shrink.

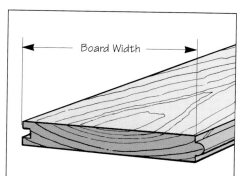

Board Width

Estimating the Amount to Buy.
When estimating the number of boards you'll need, be sure to measure only the section of board you'll see; don't include the tongue, which will be buried in the groove of the adjoining board.

Finishing the Boards. Before installation, stain or prime the boards, covering the front, back, and edges. If you are painting knotty boards, first prime them with a shellac-based primer.

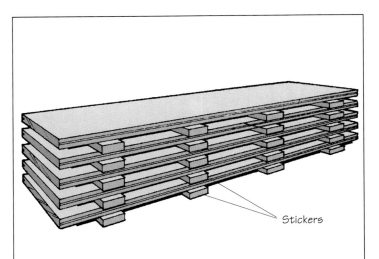

Installing Board Paneling Diagonally. Stack boards in the room for at least one week before installing them. Place 1x2 stickers between the boards to allow air circulation.

Stickers

Finishing the Boards. Solid wood expands and contracts with changes in humidity, especially across the grain. Whenever possible, put a finish on the boards before you install them. This ensures that you won't see strips of unfinished wood in the seams when slight gaps open up as the seasons change. Coat the edges, and don't forget to finish the back surfaces the same way as the fronts; this will prevent the boards from cupping because of uneven moisture changes. You can finish the boards with paint, stain, or a furniture-type finish, such as polyurethane or penetrating oil. If you paint, you should prime the boards first. For wood with knots—especially pine—use a shellac-based primer.

Installing Boards over Masonry Walls. Like other wood paneling, boards can be applied to a framed wall without special preparation. Correct application over a masonry wall, however, requires ensuring that the wall isn't plagued by moisture problems. You should put rigid insulation or a plastic vapor barrier in place before nailing the boards to furring strips. Your local building code may require that you cover rigid insulation with drywall before installing wood paneling; check with a building inspector.

Installing Board Paneling Diagonally

Let the boards become acclimatized to the humidity in the room for at least a week before installation. Stack the boards with wood spacers (called stickers) between them to ensure adequate air circulation. If you want to prime or prefinish the boards, do it after the boards have adjusted to the room conditions.

1. Cut the First Board. The first board is the base for all the others, so make sure it's correct. Start in the lower right-hand corner of the wall. Cut a short, triangular piece to fit into the corner, oriented so that the tongue faces up. Face-nail the board with 6d finishing nails to the end stud and to the plate.

2. Nail the Boards. Measure each subsequent board so that there will be about ¼ inch of clearance at each end

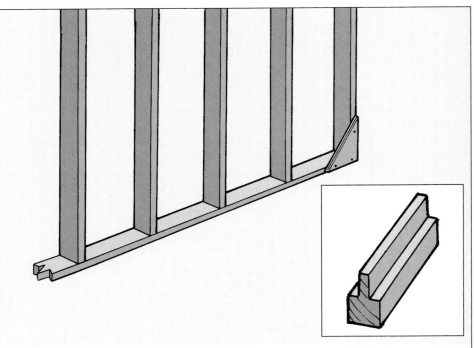

1. The first board in a diagonal installation is triangular and is installed with the tongue up. Drill pilot holes and use three 6d finishing nails to face-nail the board to the framing.

for fitting, and then cut the board to fit into place; a power miter saw is ideal for making accurate angle cuts repeatedly. At every stud, drive a 6d finish nail at an angle through the base of the tongue into every stud; this technique is called blind-nailing.

3. Cut Beveled Joints.
Once you reach the middle of the wall, you'll probably need to use more than one board to fill out each course. Cut a 45-degree bevel on the end of each joining board and lap them in a scarf joint; a butt joint would open up over time, revealing an unsightly gap between the boards. Tongue-and-groove boards don't require blocking under this joint, and the joint need not fall over a stud.

4. Install the Last Two Boards.
The last course of boards will be tucked into a corner, so you won't have room to fit tongues into their mating grooves. Instead, cut the tongue off the board in the second-to-last course to make room for the last board, which you should face-nail.

5. Complete the Wall.
Use a putty stick to fill any holes resulting from face-nailing and countersinking; then add baseboard and trim before applying a final finish to the wall.

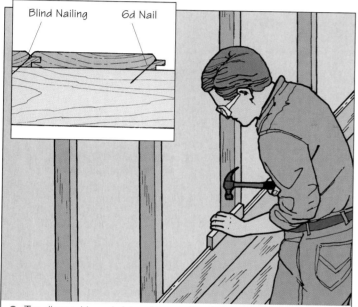

2. Tap diagonal boards into place so that the tongue engages the groove. Then drive a 6d finishing nail at an angle through the base of the tongue and into the stud.

3. When joining boards end to end, bevel the ends at 45° so that one board laps over the other, resulting in an inconspicuous scarf joint that won't show a noticeable gap over time.

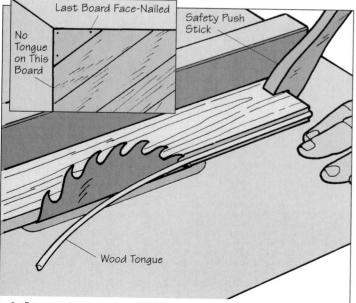

4. Because there won't be any room to slip the last board over the tongue of the adjoining board, remove this tongue before installing the board; then pop the last board into the corner and face-nail it.

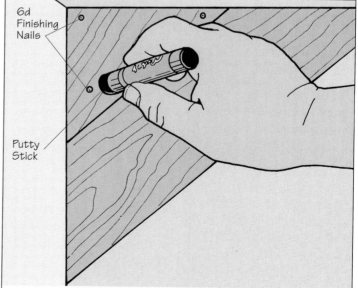

5. Fill any exposed nail heads using a putty stick or similar wood filler for stained boards. Or you could use glazing compound if you intend to paint the boards.

Vertical Installation

Installing Inside Corners. To panel a wall with solid wood boards that stand straight up and down, install horizontal furring strips on 24-inch centers. (See "Preparing Walls for New Surfaces," page 62, for more information.) Use 6d finishing nails to blind-nail the boards to the strips. If you have trouble fitting in the last board, rip one edge at a slight angle to get additional clearance so that you can slip it into place.

Mitering Outside Corners. Although you can use all sorts of trim to finish off outer corners, one advantage of solid wood is that you can miter the corners. Miter the boards, nail them together, and then nail the assembly to the wall. Leave a tongue on both edges of the assembly so that you can blind-nail subsequent boards, starting from this corner. After assembly, fill any gaps with wood putty and round over the corner's edge with sandpaper.

REPAIRING DRYWALL AND PLASTER

From impacts to gouges, cracks, and holes, walls can sustain plenty of damage, whether from people, from settling, or from faulty construction. This section deals with repairs to damaged drywall and the kinds of repairs to plaster that are possible for a do-it-yourselfer. For large areas that need to be re-plastered, it may be wiser to hire a professional because the techniques take years to learn.

Repairing Drywall. If a seam has come open, or the tape has come loose, remove all loose tape and bits of old joint compound and tape again, as shown in "Taping and Finishing Drywall," page 44. If the wall has an indentation with no fracturing of the drywall, simply apply vinyl spackling as if you were filling nail dimples. Also, you can use spackling to

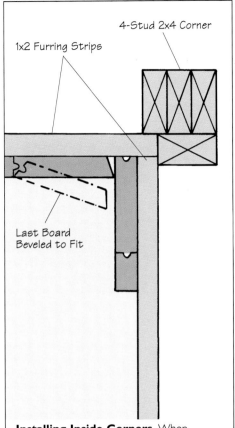

Installing Inside Corners. When boards are installed vertically, you can bevel the edge of the last board to make it easier to slip into place against the adjacent wall.

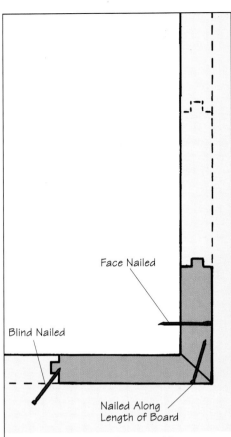

Mitering Outside Corners. You can make simple and elegant outside corners by mitering the grooved edges of two boards on a table saw, nailing them together, and fastening the assembly to the wall.

fill very small holes, such as those made by picture hooks that have been removed.

Sometimes, drywall nails pop out and show through the wall covering or paint. Most nail pops are due to wood shrinkage: Over time, the studs shrink, but the drywall nails stay put. As the drywall loosens from the nails, out pop the nail heads. To repair a popped nail, either remove it or pound it back into the wall so that you leave a dimple. Then drive another nail or a drywall screw about 2 inches above or below the one that popped. Push on the wall to make sure the drywall is now firmly pressed against the stud; you may have to install several nails or screws to bring the drywall tight. Apply joint compound over the new dimples, as described in "Taping and Finishing Drywall," page 44.

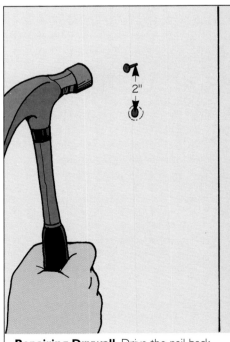

Repairing Drywall. Drive the nail back into the wall, dimpling the drywall; then drive another drywall nail about 2 inches above or below, dimpling it.

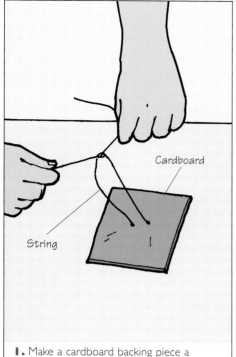

1. Make a cardboard backing piece a few inches larger than the hole, punch holes in the cardboard, and loop a string through them.

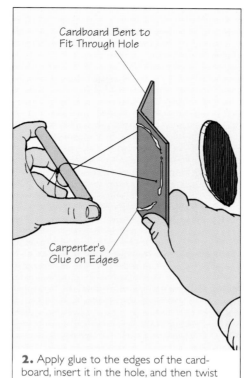

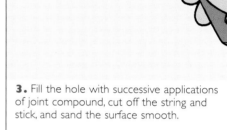

2. Apply glue to the edges of the cardboard, insert it in the hole, and then twist the string with a stick to pull the cardboard tight against the back of the drywall.

3. Fill the hole with successive applications of joint compound, cut off the string and stick, and sand the surface smooth.

Repairing a Hole in Drywall

1. Make a Cardboard Backing Piece. Begin by scraping away any loose debris from the hole. Cut out a piece of cardboard that is larger than the hole, but small enough to be bent easily and inserted through the hole. Punch two holes on each side of the cardboard. Then loop a piece of string through it, and tie the ends together, as shown.

2. Attach the Backing. Apply yellow carpenter's glue to the edges of the cardboard, push the bent cardboard through the hole, and then weave into the string a stick long enough to span the hole. Simply twist the stick to pull the cardboard tightly against the back of the drywall.

3. Fill the Hole. Fill the hole with applications of joint compound. Cut off the string and stick. Then finish the patch with one or two coats of joint compound, and sand or sponge smooth.

Repairing a Damaged Section of Drywall

1. Cut Out Damaged Drywall. To replace a piece of drywall that is damaged, draw a rectangle around it, using a framing square to keep the edges straight and the corners square. This will make it easier to get a good fit with the replacement piece. Drill

starter holes inside opposite corners, cut the piece with a drywall saw or a keyhole saw, and pull it out. If the damaged area is large, use a utility knife to cut back to the nearest studs on each side.

2. Install Patch Braces. Cut two patch braces, using either 1x4s or 1-inch-wide strips of $\frac{3}{4}$-inch ply-

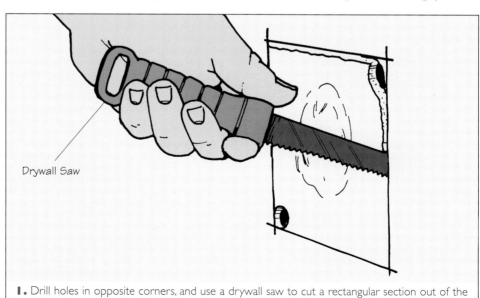

1. Drill holes in opposite corners, and use a drywall saw to cut a rectangular section out of the damaged wall.

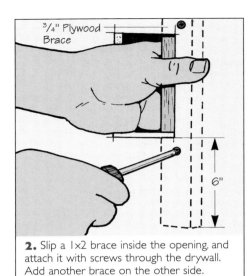

2. Slip a 1x2 brace inside the opening, and attach it with screws through the drywall. Add another brace on the other side.

Joint Compound

Drywall Patch

4" Broad Knife

Drywall Screws

Mesh Joint Tape

3. Cut a piece of drywall to fit, screw it to the braces, and finish the seams using mesh tape and joint compound.

wood. Plywood works best because it won't split as small pieces of solid wood might. Cut the braces 6 inches longer than the vertical sides of the hole. Insert a brace in the opening, and hold it tightly in place as you drive at least two screws (don't try it with nails) through the drywall and into the brace. Repeat with the second brace on the other side of the opening. If you had to cut back to studs, nail 1x2 strips flush to the front of the studs to provide a brace for the patch.

3. Patch and Tape. Cut a drywall patch the size of the hole, fit it in place, and drive drywall screws through the patch into the braces. Finish the seams with tape and joint compound, as shown in "Taping and

Finishing Drywall," page 44. Sand the successive applications of joint compound until the final coat is flush with the surrounding wall. Prime the patch and repaint to match the surrounding wall.

Repairing Plaster

Making small repairs to plaster is not much different from working with joint compound on drywall. A layer or two of joint compound applied with a broad knife will fill small holes. You can repair holes up to about 3 inches with a peel-and-stick repair patch, available at home centers. Cut a patch to the size of the hole and press the patch into place. Then apply two or more coats of vinyl spackle or joint compound. When dry, sand or sponge smooth.

Hairline cracks, as long as the plaster is solid, are only a cosmetic problem. A good primer paint followed by latex paint may hide hairline cracks for a while, or you can use a spray-on crack cover, available at paint stores, and paint over that. But hairline cracks can be stubborn, and sometimes you just have to accept them as part of the character of an old house.

Most holes larger than a nail hole or cracks larger than a hairline should be filled in several steps. You must first apply a foundation, or base, for the patch. Finish the patch with ready-mix joint compound. Or, to make your sanding job easier, use vinyl spackling.

Sometimes, plaster becomes dislodged from the lath (the wooden strips or the wire mesh that underlies it), resulting in a springiness or looseness as you push on the wall. Remove all dislodged plaster before patching, or your repairs soon will crack again.

Sealing a Crack in Plaster

1. Enlarge the Crack. Use a pointed can opener or a putty knife to enlarge the crack slightly. It is a good idea to undercut the channel a bit to

create a "key" for the patching material. Clear out any dust and debris. If the crack is longer than about 18 inches, gouge holes to anchor the plaster every foot or so along the length of the crack.

2. Fill the Crack. Fill the crack with a strong patching compound. Use patching plaster or powder-mix joint compound. Or, for a compound that can fill large cracks without sagging, mix one part perlited gypsum (sold by the bag at lumberyards) with one part powder-mix joint compound. When the patch is dry, apply a finish coat of joint compound or vinyl spackling, overlapping it onto the sound wall. Sand the patch smooth once it's dry.

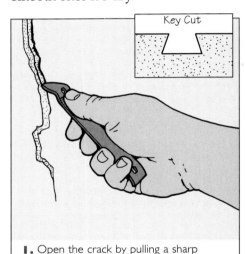

Key Cut

1. Open the crack by pulling a sharp object down its length. Create a key large enough to accept patching compound.

Patching Compound

4" Broad Knife

Key Cut

2. Fill the crack with patching plaster or other strong joint compound, feathering the edges. Apply two or three coats and match the texture of surrounding plaster.

Repairing a Hole in Plaster

1. Remove Loose Plaster. Using a putty knife, chip and scrape away all loose plaster around the edge of the hole down to the lath. Any loose plaster not cleared away will prevent the patch from anchoring to the wall at that point. Don't be afraid to enlarge the hole until you reach sound areas.

2. Undercut Plaster Edges. With a can opener or other implement with a hooked point, carve under the edge of the hole so that the bottom of the hole is wider than the top. This is called undercutting, and it provides a sound foundation for the patch.

3. Apply the Base Patch. Moisten the edge of the hole with a damp sponge. Fill the hole with a strong patching compound, covering the entire surface of the lath evenly, out to a level just below the surrounding wall. While the plaster is damp, score it with the corner of your taping knife to make it easier for the finishing coat to adhere.

4. Apply the Finish Coats. When the plaster is dry, use the taping knife to apply a coat of joint compound or vinyl spackle over the patch. Feather the edges into the surrounding wall; allow this coat to dry, and apply a second coat. Sand it smooth.

Repairing Plaster at an Outside Corner. If the damage is minor, you usually can repair it with joint compound and a taping knife, shaping the corner against a straightedge. If the damaged area is extensive, chip away all loose plaster, undercutting the edges toward the lath. Screw a straight-edged piece of scrap wood to one side of the corner and use it as a guide for filling one side of the damaged area with an undercoat of patching compound. Use drywall screws and pre-drill the holes. Move the guide and repeat on the other side. Finish with ready-mix joint compound or spackle.

1. Use a putty knife to remove broken and loose plaster from the damaged area.

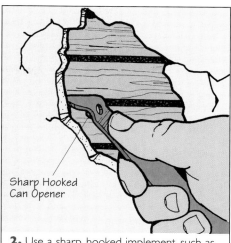

2. Use a sharp, hooked implement, such as a can opener, to carve the bottom of the hole wider than the top.

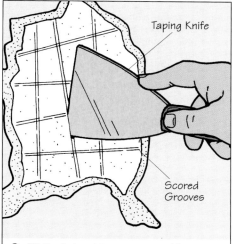

3. Fill the hole with a strong patching compound; while it's damp, score the surface with the edge of your taping knife.

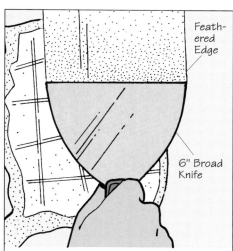

4. Spread ready-mix joint compound or vinyl spackle over the patch, feathering the edges out onto the sound wall.

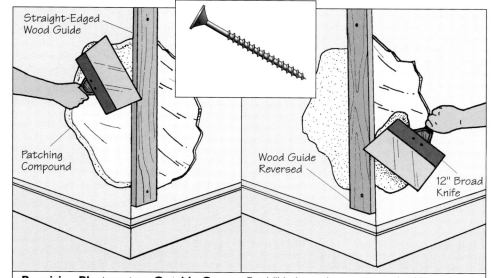

Repairing Plaster at an Outside Corner. Predrill holes and screw a wood guide to the damaged corner. Then fill the area with strong joint compound, moving your broad taping blade away from the guide toward the good part of the wall.

Skinning a Wall. If the framing is sound, you can cover old damaged walls with sheets of ³/₈-inch drywall. Fasten 2¹/₂-inch drywall screws to the studs.

Checking for Plumb and True. Hold a long, straight board on edge against the wall to identify high and low spots. Mark their locations with a pencil.

PREPARING WALLS FOR NEW SURFACES

Before installing a new surface—such as paneling, tile, or new drywall—on an old wall, you must make the wall ready to receive it. This preparation may be as simple as removing molding and cleaning the wall. But if it's out of plumb, crumbling apart, or otherwise badly damaged, you may need to rebuild the wall or replace it.

Just how straight and smooth a wall needs to be depends on what the new surface will be. For tiling, you need a nearly perfect wall; unless you are a very skilled tile setter, you will not be able to straighten out waves, although you can bridge small holes and gaps with the tile mastic. Sheet paneling and new drywall can bridge small holes but will not hide bulges. Out-of-plumb walls do not matter much if you are installing new drywall; if you install paneling or tile, however, you'll be able to see where corners are out of square.

Skinning a Wall. If the wall surface is badly deteriorated, it's a good idea to "skin" over it with new ³/₈-inch drywall; then tape and finish as described in "Taping and Finishing Drywall," page 44. Skinning will save you the trouble of demolition, but adding a layer of drywall means you'll have to widen window and door jambs and cut some moldings, such as baseboards and sills.

Checking for Plumb and True. On a frame wall, use a level to check for plumb at several places along the wall; then check it for bulges and depressions by setting a long, straight board against the wall. Shine a light under the board and mark the locations of low spots where the light peeps between the wall and the board. Also mark humps in the wall that cause the board to rock. If there are only a few low spots, they can be built out with joint compound. Better yet, mix perlited gypsum with powdered joint compound, which won't sag, and build out the surface layer by layer. High spots in plaster

should be banged out with a hammer and filled. You must correct widespread unevenness by attaching 1x2 furring strips or 1¹/₂-inch strips of ³/₄-inch plywood to studs and shimming them plumb. This process is called furring out a wall; if it's really important that the wall be flat, you will need to fur out the wall and then install new drywall or backer board.

Furring Out a Wood-Frame Wall

1. Mark a Grid. Use a chalkline or level and straightedge to make a grid on the wall where the furring will be nailed. The grid is laid out with horizontal and vertical lines 16 inches on center. The verticals must coincide with studs, so use a stud finder to locate all the studs and mark their positions on the wall.

2. Find the Highest Point. Snap a chalk line along the ceiling 2 inches out from the wall at each corner. Hang a plumb bob on the ceiling

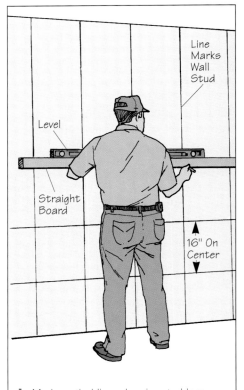

1. Mark vertical lines showing stud locations; then mark horizontal lines every 16 inches on center to show where each furring strip will go.

line at the first stud, and measure the distance from the plumb line to each intersection of lines. Repeat all along the grid to find the highest point on the wall.

3. Attach the First Furring Strip.
With an 8d nail or 2-inch drywall screw, attach a horizontal furring strip at the highest point on the grid. Cut the strip so that it stops 3 inches from the corners, which allows space for full-length vertical 1x3s at each end of the wall, plus ½-inch spaces

to allow air to circulate between the strips after the drywall or paneling is installed. If the wall is longer than the furring strips, butt them end to end over studs.

4. Shim the Furring Strip.
Hang the plumb bob from the ceiling line at the wall's high point, and measure from the line to the furring strip. Then hang the plumb bob from the ceiling line at the first stud, and shim behind the furring strip until it is the same distance from the plumb line as

at the highest point. Nail through the shims into the stud. Repeat at each stud.

5. Attach the Top Furring Strip.
Attach a 1x3 furring strip at the top of the wall by shimming at all points to bring it plumb with the strip below. Check with the straightedge and a level.

6. Attach and Shim the Remaining Strips.
Attach the rest of the horizontal furring strips, and use

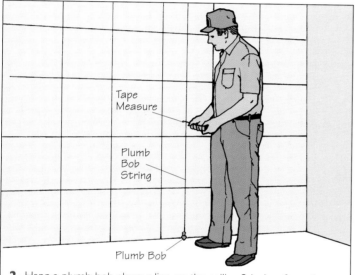

2. Hang a plumb bob along a line on the ceiling 2 inches from the wall, and measure out at each stud location to find the highest point on the entire wall.

3. Cut the first furring strip so that it stops 3 inches from the wall at each end, and then fasten the strip to the highest point, using an 8d nail or a 2-inch drywall screw.

4. Shim the furring to match the distance of the highest point of the plumb bob to the wall; then move the plumb bob to each stud location and shim to match that distance all along the wall.

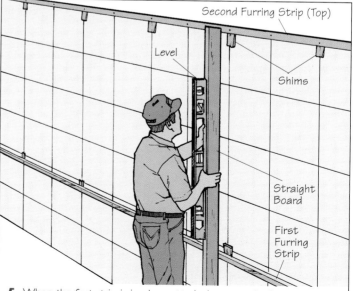

5. When the first strip is in place, attach the top strip the same distance from the plumb bob as the first strip.

6. Use a straightedge between the top and first strip as a guide for shimming the rest of the strips. Then attach vertical pieces in the corners and every 48 inches along the wall, shimming them as necessary.

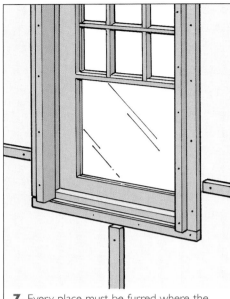

7. Every place must be furred where the new surface will have an edge. Door and window jambs must be brought out flush to the new surface, with jamb extenders nailed to the old jambs.

a long straightedge laid vertically over the original two furring strips to shim the other strips into the same plane. Attach vertical pieces in the corners and every 48 inches along the wall, shimming them as necessary. Be sure to leave 1/2-inch gaps between the strips (See "Furring Out a Masonry Wall" drawing below.)

7. Fur Out Doors and Windows. Remove moldings carefully so that you can re-use them later. Add furring strips around the window or door on all sides. Because the new surface adds to the wall thickness, you must install jamb extenders so that molding can be reinstalled on the new surface. Jamb extenders should be the same wood species as that of the window jambs. You fasten extenders with finish nails to the edge of the window jambs. The extenders should be the depth of the new surface plus the depth of the furring.

You may also need to cut a new windowsill or door threshold to fit the depth of the new surface. You can find all the dimensions of the new windowsill by tracing the old sill on new stock and adding the depth of the furring plus the new wall surface.

Covering Masonry Walls

Before installing paneling or drywall over concrete or masonry walls, as for example when finishing a base-

ment, you either must fur them out by attaching 2x2s directly to walls, or you can build new 2x4 stud walls, called false walls, and place them up against the old walls.

Furring Out Masonry Walls. To install 2x2s against masonry, rent a nail gun that uses gunpowder charges to drive special nails through the lumber and into the masonry. (These charges and nails are fairly expensive, one reason to opt for false walls.) Have the rental office explain in detail how the gun works. Wear safety glasses, and hold the tool very tightly against the 2x2 before you shoot each nail. Install the 2x2s horizontally every 16 inches on center and vertically every 48 inches on center.

Framing a False Wall. Furring may save some money, but if your masonry wall is not plumb and straight, it can be difficult and time-consuming to get each 2x2 plumb and aligned with the others. Also, 2x2s leave little room for insulation or plumbing. A false 2x4 wall, on

Furring Out a Masonry Wall. Before installing drywall or paneling, use powder-actuated fasteners to anchor 2x2 strips to a masonry wall. Horizontal strips are nailed every 16 inches on center, and verticals every 48 inches on center.

the other hand, can be made plumb and straight easily, and provides ample room for pipes and insulation.

Cut top and bottom plates the length of the wall (or walls), and mark the plates for studs located every 24 inches on center. (For more information, see "Framing Walls," page 29.) To determine how long the studs should be, measure from floor to ceiling at several points and subtract 3¼ inches (3 inches for the top and bottom plates, and ¼ inch to make sure they won't be too long). Measure carefully, or you may find that you must dismantle the framing because it's too tall. Build the wall on the floor, and raise it into position. Check for plumb, shimming the wall tightly at the top and bottom where necessary, and use 16d nails to attach the top plate to the ceiling joists; use 8d cut nails to fasten the end studs and bottom plate to masonry walls and floors.

Enclosing Pipes and Ducts.

Pipes and ducts that intrude into a room can be framed to receive paneling or drywall. Build two narrow stud walls (three where you wish to enclose something that is not in a corner), as shown. As in any framing, you must provide nailing surfaces along corners for drywall or paneling.

Applying Moisture Protection.

It is important that new surfaces on basement walls be well protected from moisture before you cover them up. If water sometimes seeps into your basement during a heavy rainfall, you may need foundation repairs; don't install a new wall surface until the problem is corrected. Slightly damp walls can be sealed with a waterproofing paint. For further protection from moisture damage, either paint the back side of the drywall or paneling, or staple 4-mil plastic sheeting to the studs before installing the surface material. When you install the sheets, leave a ¼-inch breathing space at the top and bottom.

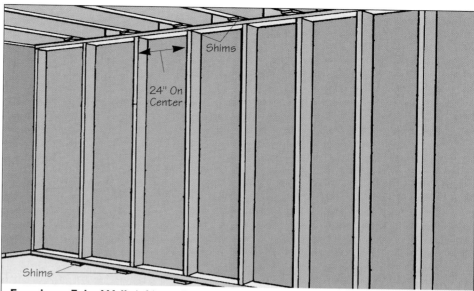

Framing a False Wall. A false wall made of 2x4s is built on the floor and tilted into position. False walls easily correct out-of-plumb or uneven walls, and they provide more space for insulation and pipes than 2x2 strips.

Enclosing Pipes and Ducts. To conceal a pipe in a corner, build the two short walls shown and attach the frame to floor, walls, and ceiling. Conceal horizontal pipes at the ceiling by building the 2x4 framing before attaching it.

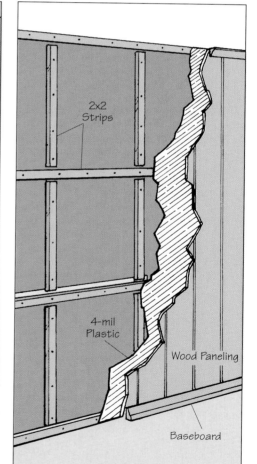

Applying Moisture Protection. Before installing drywall or paneling, staple 4-mil plastic sheets to the wood framing, and cut drywall or paneling short enough to provide breathing spaces at the top and bottom of the wall.

WORKING WITH TRIM

In building or renovating a room, trim installation is usually the last job. Trim unites floors, ceilings, and walls and gives doorways and windows a decorative highlight. It also hides the ragged junctions of a wall with the floor and the ceiling. Installing trim can be a rewarding job if you master the art of making various kinds of simple miter cuts to ensure a tight fit. To cut miters you need a good miter box and a saw, such as a backsaw, with enough teeth per inch to make fine cuts without splintering the trim. Power miter saws (chop saws) with sharp blades make quick work of cutting miters.

Trim is sold by the foot in lengths commonly ranging from 6 feet to 14 feet. Try to get lengths that will span walls from corner to corner, but if a wall is too long, you can splice pieces together. When measuring for a job, remember to take into account the extra few inches you may need for mitering to meet an adjoining piece at an outside corner.

When pricing trim, keep in mind that many softwood varieties come finger-jointed or clear. Finger-jointed is less expensive because it's made of shorter pieces spliced together with interlocking finger joints, but clear is a single length of lumber and is therefore more expensive. Ordinarily, finger-jointed trim is painted to cover joints, and clear trim is stained. It's a good idea to finish the trim before installation. The trim color may be different from that of the walls, or it may be painted the same color but in a shinier finish, such as semi-gloss or even gloss. You can even buy prefinished molding that matches sheet paneling.

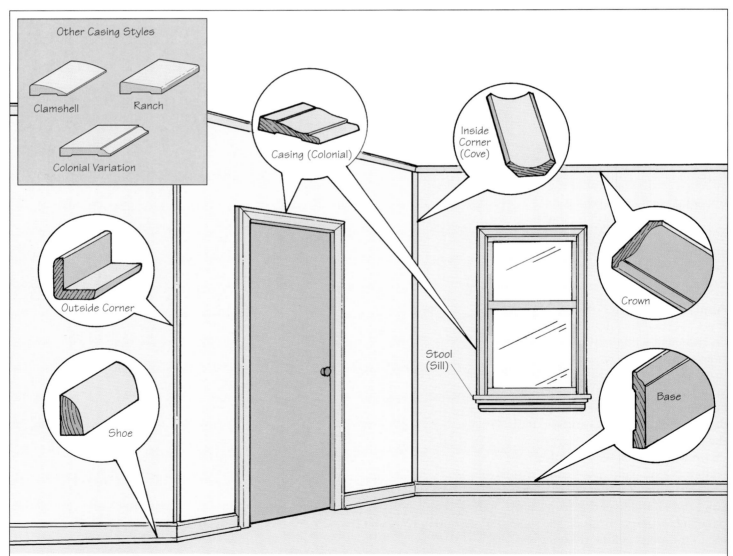

Considering Types of Trim. Trim is milled for different applications, such as casing for doors and windows, base and shoe molding for the bottom of walls, crown molding for the top of walls, and corner molding for outside corners. Door, window, and base trim is widely available in ranch, clamshell, and colonial styles.

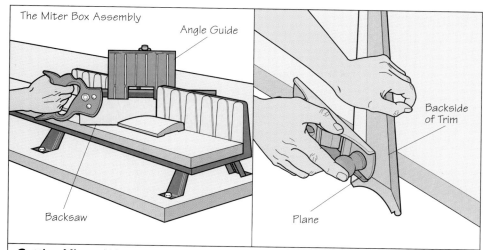

The Miter Box Assembly
Angle Guide
Backsaw
Backside of Trim
Plane

Cutting Miters. When cutting trim in a miter box, "sneak up " on the cut by trimming slightly away from the mark and then adjusting the cut as necessary. You can make minor adjustments by shaving off the excess with a sharp block plane.

Cutting Miters. There are two basic cuts in trim carpentry: a square cut, made at 90 degrees, and a mitered cut, made at an angle other than 90 degrees. Whether you use a miter box or a power miter saw to make these cuts, the best technique for making any cut is to follow the layout mark exactly, leaving just a trace of the pencil mark showing. Test-fit the trim before attaching it; if the joint doesn't quite come together, shave the back end with a plane.

Trimming Doorways

1. Mark the Reveal. The inside edge of the casing should be offset from the inside edge of the jambs by approximately $3/16$ inch. The small edge caused by offsetting the two is called a reveal. Set a combination square for $3/16$ inch, and use it to guide your pencil around the jamb, leaving a line $3/16$ inch from the edge.

2. Miter the Side Casing. Cut a length of casing square at one end. Place the casing against the reveal line, with the square cut on the floor. Mark the casing at the point where the vertical and horizontal reveal lines intersect, and cut a 45-degree angle at this point. Remember that the thick edge of casing is the outer edge.

Considering Types of Trim. Home centers carry pine, oak, and poplar trim in a great variety of shapes that are designed for specific locations and uses. The first trim to be installed is the casings that go around doorways and windows. Next to be installed are base and shoe moldings, which are used in conjunction to trim a wall at the floor. Cove or crown molding is used along the wall at the ceiling, and corner molding for both inside and outside corners is used to hide seams and protect corners. (For instructions on installing ceiling molding, see pages 150 and 167.)

Although trim is milled in dozens of different styles, the most common forms of base and casing are clamshell, ranch, and colonial. Ranch and clamshell have smooth, slightly curving surfaces; colonial molding is more ornate and will complement a traditional decor, such as Victorian. Usually, casing is $2 1/4$ inches wide, and base is $3 1/2$ inches wide. Because techniques for milling trim are not perfectly standardized, it's better to buy all pieces from the same milling lot if you can to avoid fractional differences in size. Check the trim piece by piece for damage when you buy it from stock.

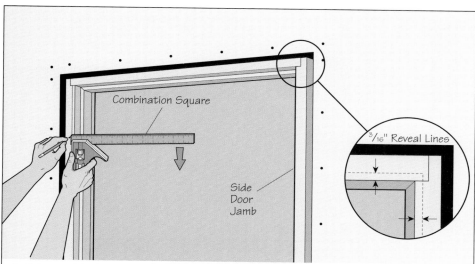

Combination Square
Side Door Jamb
$3/16$" Reveal Lines

1. Set a combination square for $3/16$ inch, and use it to guide a pencil to mark the reveal, which is the amount of door jamb that will be visible next to the casing.

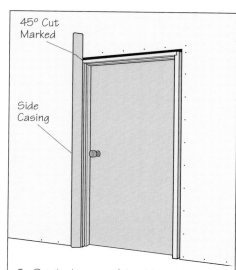

45° Cut Marked
Side Casing

2. Cut the bottom of the side casing square, and cut the top at 45 degrees where the side casing intersects the head-casing reveal.

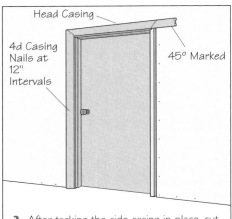

3. After tacking the side casing in place, cut a 45-degree miter on one end of the head casing; mark the other end and cut it. Nail with 4d casing nails.

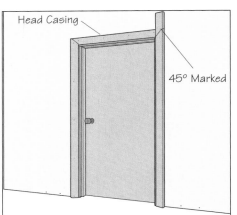

4. Square-cut the bottom of the other side casing, stand it along the reveal line, and mark and cut it even with the bottom of the head casing.

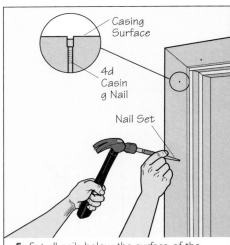

5. Set all nails below the surface of the casing with a nail set and a hammer.

3. Miter the Head Casing. Nail the side casing to the jamb with 4d casing nails spaced every 12 inches or so. Now cut a 45-degree angle on another piece of casing, fit it against the side casing over the top of the doorway, mark this head casing for the opposite 45-degree angle, and then cut and install it.

4. Complete the Trim. Square-cut the bottom end of the other side casing, hold it along the reveal line on the jamb, and mark it even with the bottom of the head casing. Make a 45-degree cut, check the fit and make

any adjustments, and nail the casing in place.

5. Set the Nails. Using a nail set and a lightweight hammer, set the nails just below the surface of the wood. Then fill the holes with wood putty, and sand them smooth when dry.

Casing a Window. Windows without stools (the technical name for the sill) can be framed like pictures with four pieces of casing mitered at all corners. Windows with stools are trimmed on the sides and top with casing, and a length of casing called

an apron is nailed below the sill. Return both ends of the apron so that they match the face profile of the molding. First, cut a 45-degree miter lengthwise through one end of the apron (A). Next, cut a mating 45-degree miter in the end of a scrap piece of apron material (B). Then, place the scrap piece face down on the miter box, and cut off the very end just mitered. This will sever a small triangular piece of the apron; set it aside for a moment (C). Lastly, nail the apron in place beneath the window stool, and glue the small return created in the previous step

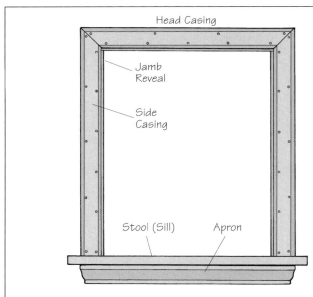

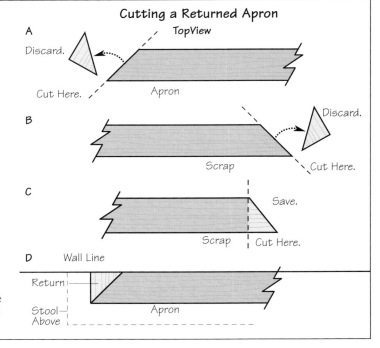

Casing a Window. Cut and install the head casing first, followed by side casings. Under the stool, install an apron with coped ends, called returned ends. Four drawings at right show the steps for making a returned apron.

into place at the end of the apron. Secure the return with small brads through pre-drilled holes (D). Sometimes, jamb extensions are required to build out window jambs flush with the wall surface before trim can be attached.

Installing Base Trim

1. Cut the Pieces to Length. Cut the base to rough lengths and distribute it around the room. Then measure all the pieces for their exact cuts, either by using a measureing tape or by holding a piece against the wall and marking where it should be cut.

2. Miter the Base. Start with an outside corner if there is one. Put the trim in the miter box right side up, with its back against the back of the box. When cutting an inside corner, angle the saw so that the back of the trim (the wall side) will be longer than the front side; for an outside corner, set the saw so that the front side will be longer than the back. Miter and fit the first piece, and then tack it temporarily in place.

3. Fit and Tack the Trim in Place. Work your way around the room, tacking each length of molding into place. Use pairs of 8d finishing nails driven into the studs and bottom plate. Drive the nails just far enough to hold the trim in place so you won't damage it if you have to pull the nails to adjust the trim positions.

4. Set the Nails. After all the trim is in place and you're sure it's where you want it, drive all the nails home, and set them with a nail set.

Joining Lengths of Trim. If you are working in a large room with long walls, you may have to use a scarf joint to join pieces of base end to end. Miter both pieces so that one laps over the other, making a smooth joint that can be tied together with a single nail as shown. Be sure that the scarf joint occurs over a stud.

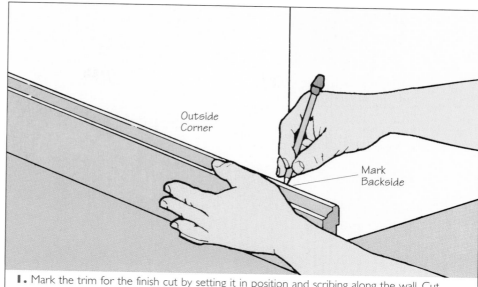

1. Mark the trim for the finish cut by setting it in position and scribing along the wall. Cut it slightly longer than needed.

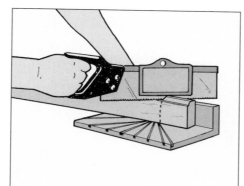

2. Position the base in the miter box, and adjust the saw for an outside corner or, as shown, an inside corner.

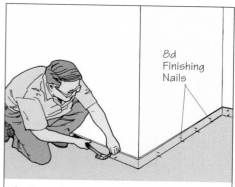

3. Base trim is tacked in place with two 8d nails driven into a stud and the bottom plate.

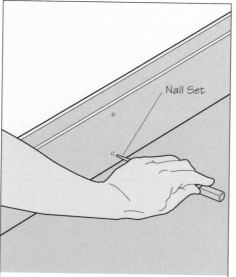

4. With all the trim tacked in place, send the nails home and set them. Hold the nail set as shown to make it easier to set nails close to the floor.

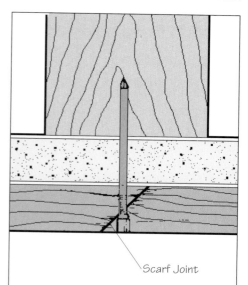

Joining Lengths of Trim. If a wall is very long, join pieces of trim end to end with a scarf joint. Make sure you cut the miters so that they occur over a stud.

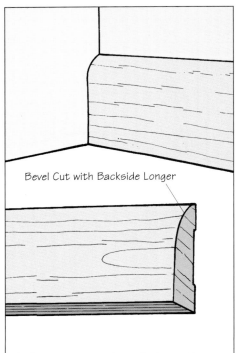

1. Square-cut one piece of trim, and butt it into the corner. Then bevel the end of the other piece so that the back is longer than the front.

Bevel Cut with Backside Longer

2. Transfer the contour of the face to the beveled piece. With a coping saw, cut off the beveled end, following the contour line you've drawn. The coped end interlocks with the first piece of trim, as shown at right.

Coping Saw

Line Follows Contour of Face

Coped Piece

Butted Piece

Coping Inside Corners

1. Cut the End. Instead of mitering inside corners, you can shape one piece to fit the contours of the other for a tight joint that won't open over time. This type of joinery is called a coped joint, and it requires three cuts. Cut the first piece with a square end that butts into the adjacent wall, and cut the next piece with a 45-degree mitered end (top to bottom) so that the back is longer than the front.

2. Cope the End. Mark a line along the face of the mitered end, and cut along this line, following the curve with a coping saw held vertically. In this way the cut shapes the piece to fit neatly over the face of the molding it abuts.

Installing Shoe Molding. At doors, where base trim butts against the casing, set the shoe molding in position, mark it for cutting, and shave off the protruding front corner with a block plane. Use 4d finishing nails to fasten shoe molding to the base trim, not the flooring.

Shoe Molding

Door Casing

Installing Shoe Molding. Cut the shoe molding to length with square ends, and bevel the end with a block plane to make a smooth junction with the door casing.

HANGING THINGS ON WALLS TO STAY

Many different kinds of fasteners are suitable for different jobs, from hanging a small picture to installing heavy kitchen cabinets. The fastener you choose depends on the construction of the wall and the weight and size of the object.

Using Hollow-Wall Fasteners. Walls are either hollow (drywall, plaster, or other surfaces over a stud frame) or solid (concrete block, brick, or plaster over masonry). You can hang very light objects on hollow walls, using only short nails driven into the wall surface, but it's always better to nail into a stud. If you're hanging a light object in a specific area but there's no stud, use plastic

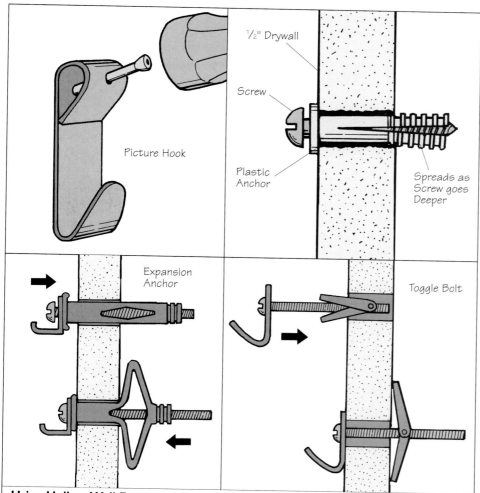

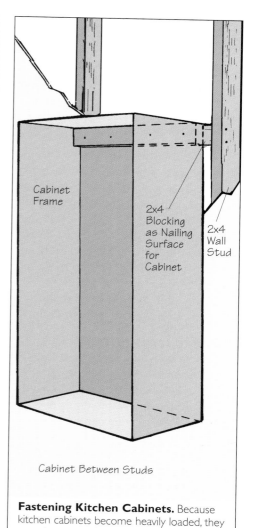

Using Hollow-Wall Fasteners. Picture hooks can be nailed between studs to support light items. Plastic anchors spread as the screw is driven, distributing weight better than nails do. Wallboard expansion anchors collapse against the back surface when the screw is driven. Toggle-bolt wings spring out after insertion; driving the bolt draws the wings tight.

Fastening Kitchen Cabinets. Because kitchen cabinets become heavily loaded, they must be screwed either directly into wall studs or into 2x4 blocking between studs.

anchors inserted into the wall surface and held tightly with a screw. Or for heavier objects, use metal expansion anchors or toggle bolts, which are inserted into a hollow wall and grip the wall surface from behind. One exception is a kitchen cabinet, which should be screwed into studs or, if no stud exists, into blocking.

Using Solid-Wall Fasteners. Attachments to solid walls are made either by driving a masonry nail into the wall or by inserting a plug or wall anchor of some kind into a drilled hole. The plug or anchor in turn accepts a screw. Also available are concrete screws, which are driven directly into the wall using a power screwdriver. The drawings show the most common wall attachments.

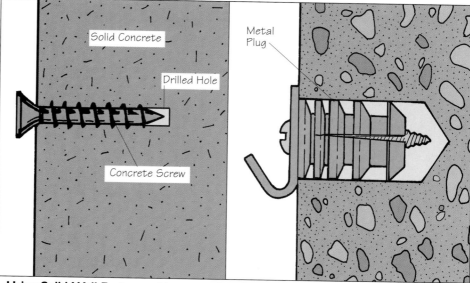

Using Solid-Wall Fasteners. Use screws for solid wall, moderate weights. Concrete screws are made from hardened steel and may be driven directly into a concrete wall with a power screwdriver. Use anchors and plugs for solid wall, heavy weights. Anchors and plugs should be seated in holes drilled to their diameter so that the fit is snug. A screw then spreads the plug inside the wall.

PAINTING BASICS

Painting is the fastest, least expensive way to redecorate a room. Painting a 15-foot by 15-foot room should take one weekend, with most of the time spent in surface preparation.

For paint to adhere properly, it must be applied to a clean, dry surface: free of dirt, dust, grease, and flaking paint or other wall covering. Paint only covers the surface. It does not fill in defects. Cracks, dents, popped nails, and any other surface defects will show through if they are not repaired. The care you invest in cleaning, scraping, and patching will make the rest of your efforts worthwhile.

Defining Types of Paint. The two most common kinds of paint for interior use are water-based (often called latex) and alkyd-based paints. Both are available in pre-mixed colors, or they can be custom-mixed to a specific hue. Traditional oil-based paint has been replaced for the most part by alkyd paint, a mixture of oil and synthetic resin that emits lower amounts of VOCs (volatile organic compounds) than oil-based paint.

Because of environmental concerns, paint companies have focused most of their research on latex paint. The technology is such that latex paint now spreads as easily, and has better color retention than traditional oil-based paints. Latex paint dries quickly, cleans up easily, and is available in a variety of sheens including flat, eggshell, and semi-gloss.

Alkyd paint is synthetic-based, will adhere to a variety of surfaces, and provides a durable finish that is best for areas such as baseboards and doors that get abuse and handling. Alkyd paint is both slower-drying and more expensive than latex paint, however, and alkyd paint must be cleaned with solvents. Provide ventilation while using alkyd paint.

Other special interior paints include texture and sand-finish paint, and fire-retardant paint for covering high-heat areas, such as kitchens and furnace rooms.

Choosing Brushes. Brushes are made with either natural or synthetic bristles. Natural bristles (often labeled "china bristle") should never be used with a water-based paint because the bristles absorb water and become

bloated. The tips of natural bristles are flagged to offer more brushing surface and hold more paint. Use natural bristles for alkyd-based paints. Synthetic (nylon) bristle brushes can be used for any paint.

Before buying a brush, check for thick, soft, resilient bristles held in place by a sturdy metal ferrule. Always buy the best brush you can afford. Cheap brushes lose bristles in the paint and will not provide a smooth finish.

Most interior paint jobs can be handled with two brushes: a 3-inch flat brush and an angled sash brush. The 3-inch flat brush is the brush you will use most often. Its tapered bottom will paint a fine line, but it is broad enough to cover large surfaces. The sash brush is angled for crisp lines on trim, molding, and window parts. Avoid buying brushes larger than 4 inches; use a roller instead.

Choosing Rollers and Pans. A roller consists of a cover and a frame. Covers come in several sizes and thicknesses. The most common length is 9 inches, and is available in short, medium, or long nap. Short

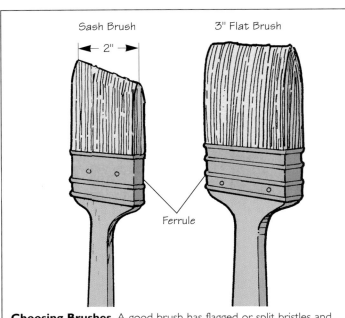

Choosing Brushes. A good brush has flagged or split bristles and a metal ferrule that holds them tightly. You'll need an angled sash brush and a 3-inch flat brush.

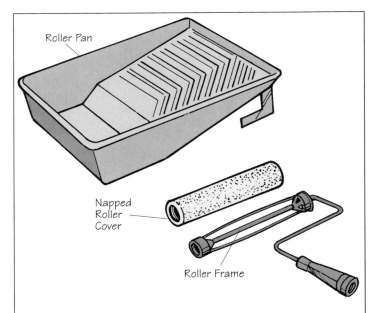

Choosing Rollers and Pans. Buy a deep, sturdy roller pan. Rollers consist of a frame and cover. Covers are designated by nap length: either long, medium, or short. Use long for rough surfaces, such as masonry, and short for smooth surfaces, such as new drywall.

nap, about ¼-inch thick, is used to apply paint to a smooth surface, such as drywall. Medium nap is used for semi-rough surfaces, such as plaster, and long nap is used for rough surfaces, such as concrete block, stucco, and brick.

Most roller frames have a threaded handle to accept an extension pole that allows your reaching high spots. You can use a standard size, screw-on mop handle or, better yet, a special extension pole.

Roller pans should be deep and sturdy with ribbed bottoms. The ribs help the roller cover pick up paint more evenly.

Removing Paint and Wallpaper

Old paint that is peeling, blistered, or alligatored (wrinkled) should be scraped smooth or stripped entirely. Loose paint must be removed with a paint scraper. If the paint removal leaves cracks and depressions, fill them with joint or spackling compound and sand smooth.

You can strip badly deteriorated paint, common on old woodwork and trim, by melting it with a heat gun or by applying a chemical paint remover with a brush. Wait at least 20 minutes to give the remover time to soften the old finish, and then scrape it off with a paint scraper. It may take several applications to remove the old finish completely.

You can paint over wallpaper if there is just one layer and the layer is firmly bonded. Seal the wallpaper surface first with a pigmented shellac sealer. The paper must not have an embossed finish, or the embossing will show through.

If there are several layers of paper on the wall, or if the paper is bubbled or loose, it must be removed. You can rent a wallpaper steamer, or buy glue-loosening chemicals made especially for paper removal. Both methods loosen the paper, which must be scraped off with a wallpaper shaver. When all the paper is off, scrub the wall with a solution of water and trisodium phosphate (TSP), available at paint stores and home centers.

Preparing a Room for Painting. Before painting, clean the walls, roughen any slick spots, and sand any patches; scrape and patch any old paint. The floor and anything else that you can't remove from the room should be completely covered. If moldings are finished wood, mask them off with painter's masking tape.

Remove the switch and outlet face plates, door knobs, picture hooks, and thermostat covers. Either remove or loosen the wall and ceiling lights so that you can enclose them in plastic bags.

When you paint a room, start with the ceiling; then do the walls, molding, doors, and, finally, the windows. All bare surfaces must be primed first. You can buy primers for latex, alkyd, and other finishes. New drywall and joint-compound patches should be primed with latex primer or an alkyd sealer. Some stains, such as water marks, will bleed through normal primer. For these stains, use a shellac-based primer.

Removing Paint and Wallpaper. After loosening glue with a steamer or chemical wallpaper stripper, use a wallpaper shaver to remove the wallpaper.

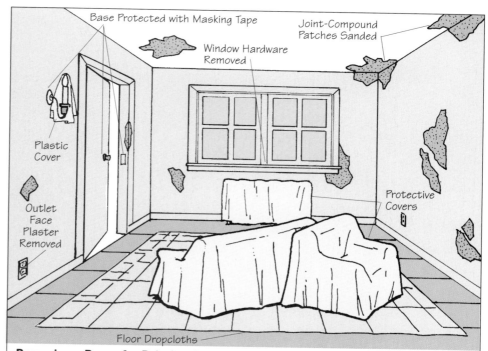

Preparing a Room for Painting. Before painting, prepare the room by scraping old chipped paint, patching damaged walls, and removing hardware, such as sash locks and switch-plate covers. Protect anything that can't be removed with plastic tarps or drop cloths.

- Base Protected with Masking Tape
- Joint-Compound Patches Sanded
- Window Hardware Removed
- Plastic Cover
- Outlet Face Plaster Removed
- Protective Covers
- Floor Dropcloths

Painting a Room

1. Roll the Ceiling. Start by rolling the ceiling, getting as close as you can to the walls. Roll the roller through the bottom of the paint pan, where the paint should be no more than ¾ inch deep. Distribute paint liberally over the entire roller. Apply the paint in a zigzag pattern, and then go back over the zigzag with strokes at a 90-degree angle to the original zigzag. Start and stop your strokes gently, so you don't leave roller marks on the wall surface.

2. Check the Paint Job. Without reloading the roller, finish the area by carefully rolling across the zigzag pattern. Overlap the strokes slightly, and then examine the area from several different angles as well as up close. Go back over any missed spots with a fairly dry roller cover.

3. Cut-In the Ceiling. With a 3-inch brush, paint the bare patch between the ceiling and walls. This is called "cutting-in." To deter drips, dip only one-third of the brush's bristle length into the paint.

When painting a wall and ceiling different colors, the standard approach is to let the lighter color overlap the edge, and cut in the darker color over it. Typically, ceiling color is lighter than wall color, so the ceiling color can overlap the wall. If the ceiling will be darker than the wall, use a painting edger to paint a straight, crisp edge between the ceiling and walls.

4. Roll the Walls. Roll the walls next, being careful not to hit the ceiling. Try to stop 3 or 4 inches from the ceiling. Apply the paint in the zigzag motion described above and, using a fairly dry roller, finish with up-and-down or side-to-side strokes.

1. Roll paint onto the ceiling first, generously loading the roller with paint and applying it in zigzags. Then lightly roll the area again, moving in zigzags in the opposite direction.

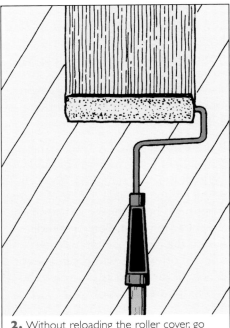

2. Without reloading the roller cover, go over the painted area with parallel up and down strokes.

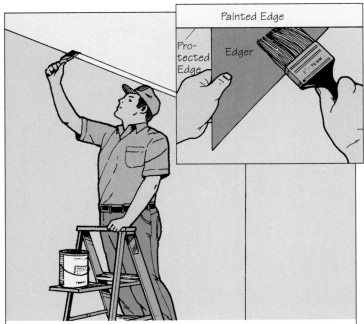

3. When the ceiling is completely rolled, use the flat brush to paint the bare spots along the walls. To avoid smearing paint onto other surfaces, use a painting edger.

Painted Edge

Protected Edge

Edger

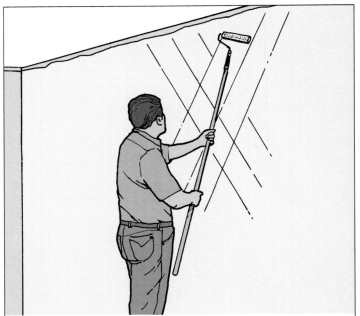

4. Roll the wall using zigzag strokes in two directions. Do not allow the roller to touch the ceiling.

5. Use the flat brush to cut in the bare patches in corners and at the top of the wall. Use a painting edger to keep from painting the ceiling (see Step 3).

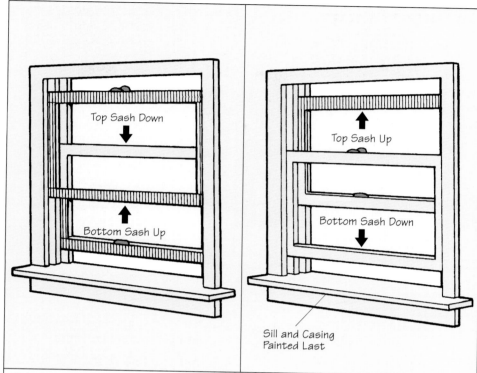

Painting Double-Hung Windows. Lower the top sash and raise the bottom sash, and paint all exposed areas of the window with a sash brush. Keep the brush loaded with paint. Reverse sash positions and finish painting. Don't close the window until it's dry. Then do the sill and casing.

5. Cut-In the Walls. With a 3-inch brush, cut-in along all edges where paint stops, such as in corners and above the baseboard. If the walls and ceiling are different colors, use a painting edger to cut-in at the top of the wall.

Painting Double-Hung Windows. The method for painting a double-hung window is to lower the top sash and raise the bottom sash in an established sequence. Paint the outside sash first as far as you can reach; then paint the inner sash, using a sash brush. You can make the job easier simply by keeping the brush well supplied with paint.

Reverse the position of the windows, but do not close either sash all the way. After the windows are painted, paint the sill and casing around them. You can use an edger at the casings to avoid spreading paint on the adjoining wall surface. Finally, use a razor-blade scraper to remove paint from the window panes.

TILING WALLS

Ceramic tile is an attractive wall surface anywhere and a practical one in bathrooms and kitchens because it is waterproof, durable, and easy to clean. It also works well on floors. (See "Laying Ceramic-Tile Floors," page 128.) The variety of tiles available makes it a decorating favorite.

Tile is clay that has been fired; it is produced in a variety of surfaces. The most important distinction between types of tile is whether they are glazed or unglazed. Glazed tile, available in matte or shiny finish, is impervious to stains, but it can be scratched; it is the standard tile around sinks and tubs. Unglazed tile, made only in matte finish, picks up stains from grease and oil but resists scratching; it is the choice for floors. Both kinds can be used on walls.

Flat tiles are called field tiles, and those shaped to fit around corners and edges are called trim tiles. Tiles larger than a few square inches are sold loose; smaller tiles can be purchased in sheet form with a few square feet of tile bonded to a thin webbing on the back.

To install ceramic tile, you need a clean surface that is sound and flat. You should strip wallpaper and other flexible coverings before tiling an old wall; unsound areas should be repaired. Both cement backer board and plywood make good surfaces for tiling in high-moisture areas. The wall surface is marked with guidelines to position the tile, and then covered with adhesive into which the tiles are pressed. The joints between tiles are then sealed with grout.

Tiling requires only a few special tools: a tile cutter to cut straight lines in tile and tile nippers to cut odd shapes (both can be rented), a notched trowel for spreading adhesive (check with your dealer to make sure the notches are the right size for the job), and a rubber float for

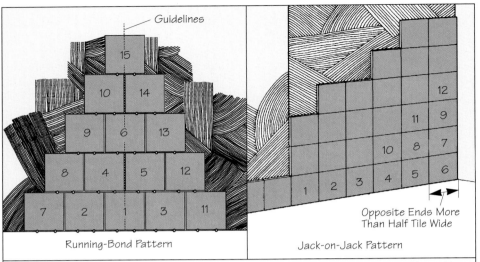

Guidelines

15	
10	14
9	6	13
8	4	5	12
7	2	1	3	11

Running-Bond Pattern

Jack-on-Jack Pattern

Opposite Ends More Than Half Tile Wide

Planning the Job. Tile a wall from the bottom up, either by setting tile in a pyramid on either side of a vertical center guideline or by stepping up the wall from the guideline toward the corner. Two popular patterns, running bond and jack-on-jack, are shown. Note tiling sequences.

applying grout. You will also need a chalkline, a line or water level, and a tape measure.

Planning the Job. There are two basic ways to lay tile on a wall: build tiles up from the center of the wall in a pyramid shape; or start by laying the entire bottom row, and then work from one corner, stepping the tiles up the wall. Before starting, decide whether you want to stack the tiles with straight, unbroken vertical grout lines, called a jack-on-jack pattern, or if you'd rather stagger the vertical grout lines in a running-bond pattern. (Even though the drawings show the patterns built up using a particular setting method, you can use whichever method you find easier to set your desired pattern.)

Marking Guidelines

1. Determine the Center of the Wall. Measure the length of the wall, and then divide the length in half and mark this midpoint measurement on the wall. Next, lay out a course of tiles with the desired grout spacing (tiles with lugs on the edges are self-spacing, so butt these tiles together), and mark the centers of the grout spaces on the wall. Check whether the last tile on either side of the midpoint is at least a half tile wide. If it's less, mark half the width of a tile to the right or left of the midpoint, and use this as the position of the vertical guideline.

2. Mark the Vertical Guideline. Use a level to mark the vertical guideline at the proper point.

3. Find the High and Low Points. First, find out if the surface you are tiling from—the floor, tub, or countertop—is level. Mark a reference point on one end of the wall; then use a water level or line level to transfer the mark to the opposite end of the wall. Connect the marks by snapping

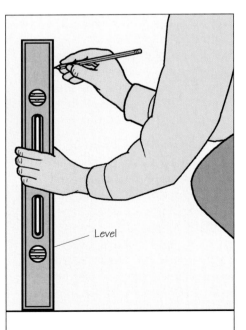

Center of Wall

Allowance for Grout Spaces

Opposite Ends More than Half Tile Wide

1. Locate the midpoint of the wall; then measure across the wall in tile widths, including grout space, to position the vertical guideline.

Level

2. After locating the position of the vertical guideline, use a level held straight up and down to mark guidelines on the wall.

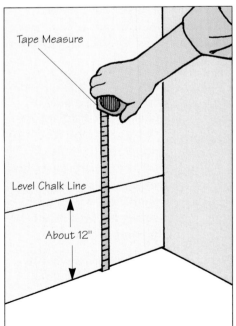

Tape Measure

Level Chalk Line

About 12"

3. Use a level to mark a horizontal reference line about 1 foot above the floor; then measure from the line to the floor to locate the highest and lowest points.

a chalk line, and measure from this level line to the floor. Find the lowest and highest points, and mark them on the wall.

4. Establish the Horizontal Guideline. Place a field tile (or a trim tile if you are using base trim) against the wall, and mark one grout space above the tile. (A typical grout space is $^3/_{16}$ inch wide.) Exactly where you mark the wall depends on the difference between the high and low points. If the difference is less than $^1/_4$ inch, mark the highest point; you can make up the difference by vary-

ing the size of the grout joints. If the difference is greater than $^1/_4$ inch, mark the wall at the lowest point. Then use a line level or water level to transfer this mark to all of the walls you will tile. Connect the marks by snapping chalk lines. These will be your horizontal guidelines.

5. Lay Out the Courses. If you used the floor's lowest point to establish the horizontal guideline, you will need to cut the bottom course of tiles so that they align with the horizontal guideline. You also may need to cut the top course along the

ceiling. Check by marking off the total height of a tile, plus a grout joint, in increments down the wall to the horizontal guideline. The increment above the guideline is the height to which the top course of field tiles must be trimmed to fit along the ceiling. If it's less than a half tile, avoid an unattractive narrow top course by setting two top courses of cut tiles. See "Cutting Tile," page 79.

An alternative to all this cutting would be to end the tile partway up the wall. In this case, measure the height of a tile plus a grout joint; then mark off this height in increments from the horizontal guideline up the wall to the desired height, and snap a level chalkline. If you are tiling a shower surround, the tiles should extend at least one full course above the shower head.

6. Mark Accessory Positions. If you are mounting the kind of soap dish that sits flush to the wall, or other similar ceramic accessory, find the position where the piece is to be located and then mark its outline on the wall. Most accessory pieces will have flanges that fit over surrounding tiles.

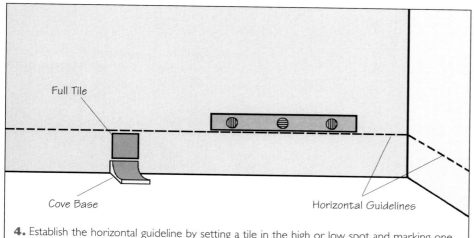

Full Tile

Cove Base

Horizontal Guidelines

4. Establish the horizontal guideline by setting a tile in the high or low spot and marking one grout space above it; at this point, snap a level chalk line on the wall.

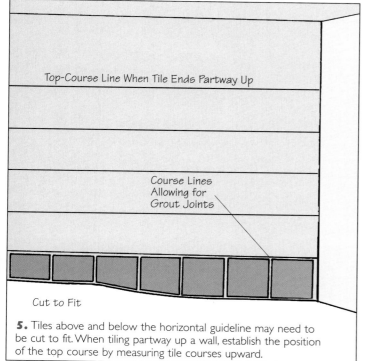

Top-Course Line When Tile Ends Partway Up

Course Lines Allowing for Grout Joints

Cut to Fit

5. Tiles above and below the horizontal guideline may need to be cut to fit. When tiling partway up a wall, establish the position of the top course by measuring tile courses upward.

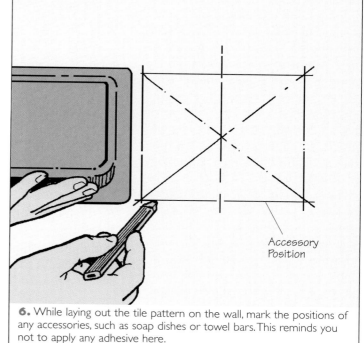

Accessory Position

6. While laying out the tile pattern on the wall, mark the positions of any accessories, such as soap dishes or towel bars. This reminds you not to apply any adhesive here.

Installing Tile

1. Apply Tile Adhesive. Tile can be bonded to the wall with a mix-it-yourself cement-based adhesive or, with greater ease, a premixed mastic adhesive. The basic method of applying a mastic adhesive is to spread it with the long edge of a notched trowel across a wall. The depth of the tile adhesive should be consistent, and if you have the right trowel, the right amount of adhesive will squeeze through the notches as you run the trowel against the wall. Start at the guidelines and work out, leaving the lines visible. The adhesive dries slow enough to give you time to make adjustments, but don't cover such a large area that the adhesive begins to lose its tackiness before you get to it. When starting out, cover only a small area—about 4 feet by 4 feet—and make sure the surface is entirely and evenly covered. Then, as you become more skilled working with tile, you can cover larger areas. Do not spread tile adhesive over areas designated for soap dishes and other ceramic accessories.

2. Lay the First Two Tiles. Install the course of cove or other trim tiles at floor level by lining up the first tile along the vertical guideline and tipping it into position. Give the tile a slight twist to spread the adhesive beneath it more evenly. Settle the tile half a grouting space away from the horizontal and vertical lines. If the tile has lugs at its edges, set them even with the lines. Then set a second tile on the other side of the vertical line in the same manner. If this tile has lugs, butt them against the lugs of the installed tile. If it doesn't, you can position for the grouting space by eye if you have a very precise touch, or use temporary cross-shaped plastic spacers to keep the tiles one grout joint apart. If the tiles start to settle out of position, you will need to space them with nails driven partially into the substrate.

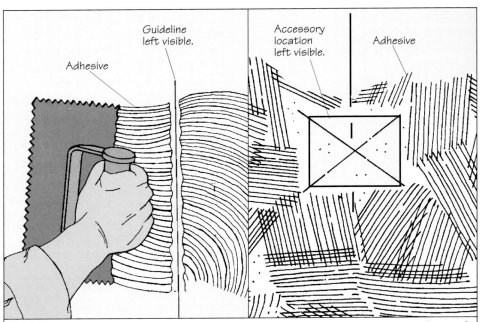

1. You will need a notched trowel to spread adhesive in a thin, ridged coat over a small area of wall. Work out from the guidelines, leaving them and any accessory locations visible.

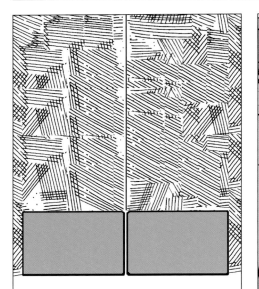

2. Tip the first tile into position at the intersection of the vertical and horizontal guidelines, and give the tile a slight twist to set it into the adhesive. Set the second tile the same way.

3. Using the tiles and the guidelines for reference, set the rest of the tiles in a pyramidal or diagonal stepping pattern. You can use lugs on tile edges or temporary plastic spacers to keep the tiles aligned.

3. Position Subsequent Tiles. Use the pyramid or diagonal method described earlier to position subsequent tiles. If the tiles are laid carefully along the guidelines, their straight edges will serve as in-place guides for the next tiles, and they in turn for subsequent ones. Measure for any cut tiles, and set them after all the full tiles are installed.

4. Mount Accessories. A soap dish or other ceramic hardware should be the last piece installed. Its substrate should be free of tile adhesive. Soap dishes must be adhered to the wall

Special Accessory Adhesive

4. A soap dish or similar ceramic accessory is installed with epoxy adhesive applied directly to the soap dish. After sticking the accessory on the wall, secure it with strips of masking tape while the adhesive dries.

with care, because they may be subject to unusual stress and should not give way suddenly. Use epoxy putties or special mastic-like adhesive designed to hold under stress.

Cutting Tile

Making Straight Cuts. Use a tile cutter to make straight cuts. The tile cutter holds the tile in place while you score the surface with a wheel at the end of a handle mounted on a fixed track. Run the cutting wheel back and forth, applying some pressure to cut the surface; then tip the handle sideways to break the tile along the score line. Always cut tiles with ridges on the back in the direction the ridges run. The cut edge will be rough, so smooth it by rubbing it over a piece of metal lath.

Making Curved Cuts. To fit tile around such edges as a shower head or a pipe, you must cut it bit by bit with tile nippers. This takes a strong grip and some patience because numerous nips through the very tough tile may be needed to carve out the shape. Most pipe areas and holes you must cut around will later be covered by an escutcheon, or flange, concealing the edges of the cut, so you needn't worry about a ragged edge as long as the cut is large enough. To fit around pipes, mate edges of whole tiles or cut one tile into two sections that will meet at the center of the pipe, nipping out a semicircle to fit around the pipe on mating edges. If you need a very precise circular cut in a tile, you can drill it with a carbide-tipped hole saw, cutting from the back of the tile.

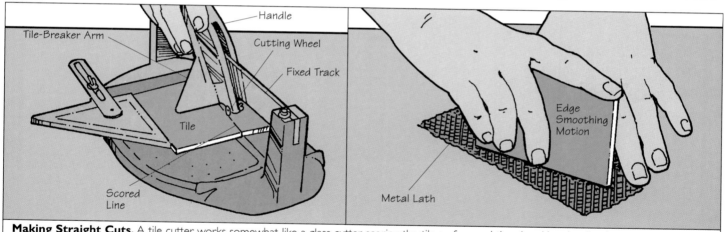

Handle
Tile-Breaker Arm
Cutting Wheel
Fixed Track
Tile
Scored Line
Edge Smoothing Motion
Metal Lath

Making Straight Cuts. A tile cutter works somewhat like a glass cutter, scoring the tile surface and then breaking the tile along that line. Smooth the cut edge by rubbing it on a piece of metal plaster lath.

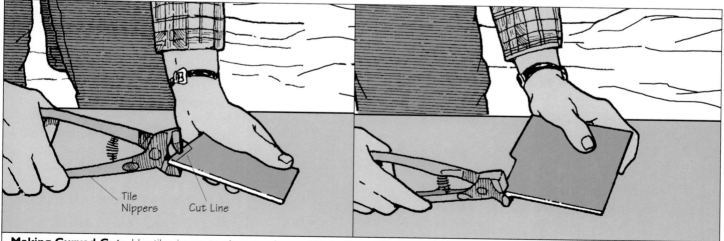

Tile Nippers
Cut Line

Making Curved Cuts. Use tile nippers to nip away pieces of tile to the cut line. The edge need not be perfectly smooth if it will be covered by an escutcheon, or flange.

Grouting

1. Prepare the Tile. Let the tile set at least 24 hours, and then use an old scratch awl to pick out the spacers, crumbs of adhesive, and any other debris from the grout joints. If you're working with unglazed tile, seal it and let the sealer cure fully before grouting. Otherwise, the grout will stain it.

2. Spread the Grout. Mix the grout, and apply it with a squeegee, spreading it diagonally across the joints between the tiles. Make sure the grout is packed firmly into every joint.

3. Shape the Joints. As soon as the grout becomes firm, use a wet sponge to wipe off any excess from the tile surface. Shape the grout joints with a softer-than-tile striking tool.

4. Clean the Tiles. Wipe the tiles and smooth the joints with a damp sponge. Allow a dry haze to form on the tile surface; then polish the tiles with a clean, damp cloth. In most cases, the grout will take several days to harden completely.

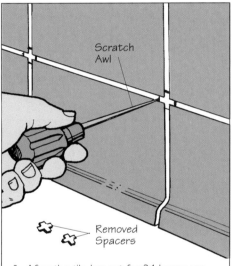

1. After the tile has set for 24 hours, use a scratch awl to remove plastic spacers and chunks of adhesive, and to clean the grout joints.

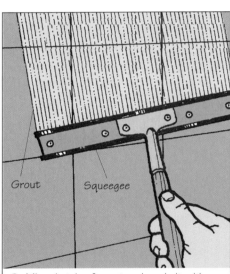

2. Mix a batch of grout and apply it with a squeegee, making several diagonal passes across the tiles to pack the grout into the joints.

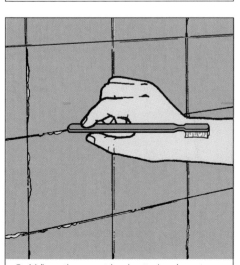

3. When the grout begins to harden, smooth and shape it with a soft shaping tool, such as the end of a toothbrush, which won't scratch tiles.

4. Wipe down the tiles with a damp sponge to remove grout residue from the tile surface, and give a final shaping to the grout joints.

WALLPAPERING BASICS

Wallpaper is a general term that applies to a number of wall coverings, from traditional paper to fabric-backed vinyl, paper-backed grass cloths, and other exotic variations. Wallpaper can add elegance and distinction to a plain room, and it requires less maintenance than paint. Papering a wall is not difficult, but it takes patience and care to match patterns and make tight seams.

If the area to be covered gets a lot of wear and tear, use a durable, washable covering, such as solid-vinyl paper. For moderate-wear areas, such as bedrooms and halls, use vinyl-coated papers. Low-traffic areas can take more delicate wallpapers, such as flocked wallpaper, which has slightly raised patterns of velvet-like synthetic fibers; paper-backed foils, which have a metallic surface for a dramatic effect; or grasscloths, which have a natural netting that lends a textured look to the walls.

Some wallpaper is available prepasted; some must be pasted at home, sheet by sheet as it goes up. However it is pasted, wallpaper must be applied to a clean, smooth surface; any blemish in the wall beneath will show through clearly and spoil the effect. It is best to strip walls of old wallpaper before applying new paper. If a wall is not sufficiently smooth, wallpaper liner—a thick, blank wall covering—should be pasted on the wall to provide a smooth foundation.

To paper a room you will need a bucket of water, a bucket for mixing paste, a wallpaper smoothing brush—long and narrow with moderately stiff but pliable bristles—a long table, a long straightedge, scissors, a seam roller, a level, and measuring tools.

Planning the Job. Wallpaper is sold in rolls of various widths typically containing 36 square feet of material.

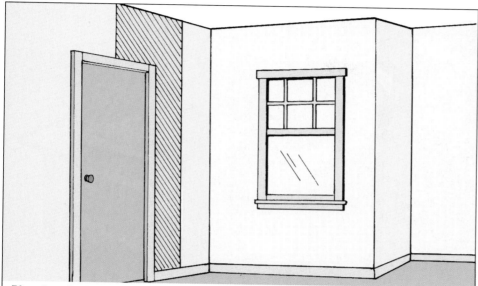

Planning the Job. If you are papering all the way around a room, plan to have the last sheet meet the first sheet in the least conspicuous corner of the room.

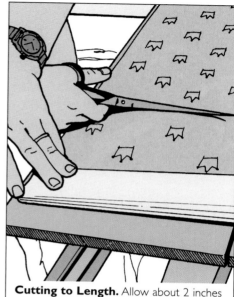

Cutting to Length. Allow about 2 inches of overlap at the top and bottom of each strip. Unroll the paper, mark it, and cut it.

However, once you're done matching patterns and trimming off excess, you'll end up hanging about 30 square feet per roll and throwing away about 6 square feet. So to figure out how many rolls you'll need, determine the number of square feet in the area to be covered, subtract openings, such as windows, doors, and fireplaces; and divide the total by 30 if you're using standard 36-square-foot rolls. Then round up the result to the nearest whole number.

If you are papering an entire room, chances are you won't be able to match the pattern where the papering job starts and ends. So plan the papering so that this meeting place is in the least conspicuous part of the room, such as over a door or in a corner.

Cutting Wallpaper

Cutting to Length. Wallpaper initially must be rough-cut to about 4 inches longer than the wall height. This lets you adjust a sheet up and down a little to meet the pattern properly. Use a sharp pair of scissors to cut the paper squarely across its width and long enough to allow about 2 inches of overlap at the top and bottom of the wall. You'll trim off this excess after the paper is on the wall.

Pasting Wallpaper

1. Prepare the Paste. Wallpaper paste is available both premixed in liquid form and dry for mixing with water at home. Paste that you mix yourself is more economical, and you can make only the amount you'll need. If you are mixing your own, paste manufacturers usually recommend that you mix about 30 minutes before you start.

1. If you mix your own paste, work the powder into the water until it has a smooth, somewhat viscous consistency.

2. Brush On the Paste. Lay a piece of the paper that has been cut to length on your pasting table with one edge flush with a long edge. Paste the paper with a paste brush from the middle to the table edge and about half its length. Shift the paper across the table so that the other edge lines up along the other edge of the table. Lining the paper up with the table edges prevents paste from getting on the table top.

Middle to Edge

2. With a wallpaper-pasting brush, spread the paste evenly from the middle of the sheet toward the edges and corners. Align the paper with the edge of the table.

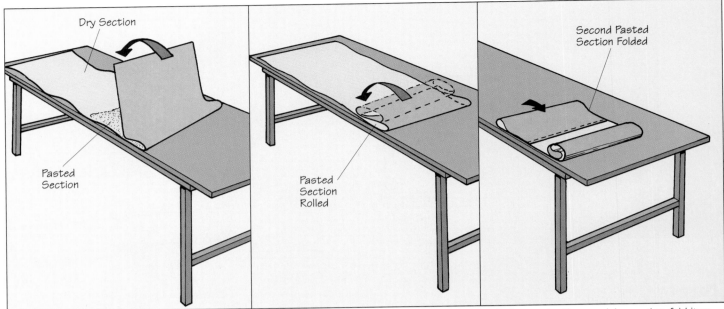

3. Fold the pasted section of a strip over on itself (paste to paste), and roll up the folded section, and after pasting the remaining section, fold it as you did the first half. Allow the paste to soften the paper for a few minutes.

3. Roll Up the Pasted Paper.

Fold the pasted section of the paper over on itself. Loosely roll up the section as you would a newspaper, and pull the remainder up on the table to paste. When the entire sheet is pasted, fold it as you did the previous section, and set the sheet aside a few minutes to allow the paste to soften the paper.

Hanging the First Sheet

1. Mark a Vertical Starting Line.

Start the job at a corner, beginning at the left side of the corner if you are right-handed, or at the right side if you are left-handed. From the corner, measure horizontally a distance equal to the width of your wallpaper minus 2 inches. Make a plumb line at this point from the ceiling to the floor.

2. Fold the Paper for Easy Installation.

Unroll the pasted paper as if you were addressing a king with a scroll announcement.

1. To aid you in hanging the paper straight up and down, mark a vertical line from the floor to the ceiling 2 inches less than the paper width away from the starting corner.

2. Hold the top edge of the paper between thumb and forefinger, with the middle folded over your middle fingers and the bottom edge held with your other fingers.

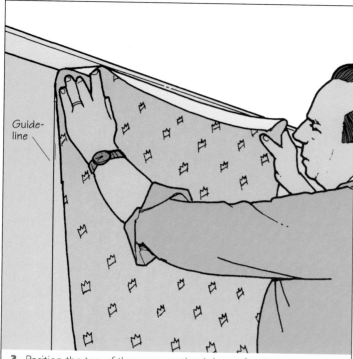

3. Position the top of the paper so that it laps a few inches onto the ceiling, and let the bottom drop down the wall. Align the edge of the paper with the vertical guideline, and press the paper into place.

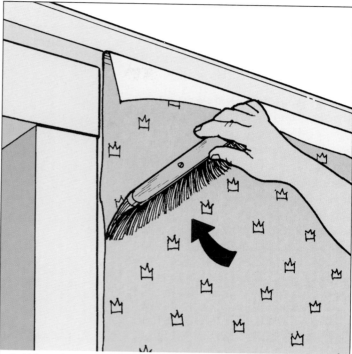

4. When the strip is in position, flatten it against the wall with a wallpaper brush, stroking from the center out.

Gently grasp the edges of the paper where the top and bottom meet, holding it as shown with the top corners between thumb and forefinger, and your other fingers supporting the fold and the bottom edge. This enables you to position the paper at the ceiling as you let the rest of the sheet fall into place.

3. Position the Sheet. Put the top of the paper against the ceiling, leaving a few inches of overlap, and shift it into position along the vertical starting line.

4. Smooth Wrinkles with a Brush. Once the sheet is in position, smooth it reasonably flat by hand, and then use a wallpaper brush to smooth out wrinkles. Brush from the middle of the sheet toward the edges and corners. Use the brush to tuck the paper into corners, along the ceil-

ing line, and above the baseboard. Then wipe the entire sheet with a damp sponge.

Trimming for an Exact Fit

1. Mark and Trim Excess. When the paper is hung and brushed out, use the back of a scissors blade to force the paper tightly into joints

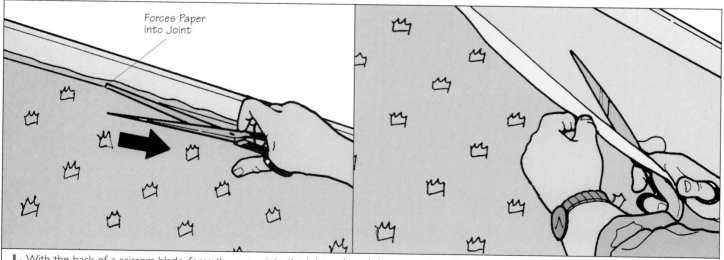

1. With the back of a scissors blade, force the paper into the joints where it laps onto the ceiling, into corners, and along the baseboard. Peel the excess paper away from the wall, cut along the crease, and then brush the paper back into place.

along the ceiling, floor, or corner. Peel the paper down enough to permit cutting. Cut along the crease with scissors, and stick the paper back against the wall, brushing it flat.

2. Cut Around Windows and Doors. Hang a full sheet over a window or door, positioning the sheet so that the pattern aligns; use scissors to rough-cut an opening 1 or 2 inches from the molding. Then carefully make 45-degree relief cuts back to the edge of the molding, and press and brush the paper into place. Then score and cut as above.

Hanging Tight Seams

1. Butt the Edges. Position a second sheet along the edge of the first so that the pattern lines up and the edges of the sheets are butted together tightly—not overlapped or pulled apart—with a very slight ridge at the junction. This ridge will subside as the paper dries out.

2. Roll the Seam. After the paste has started to dry and the seams have

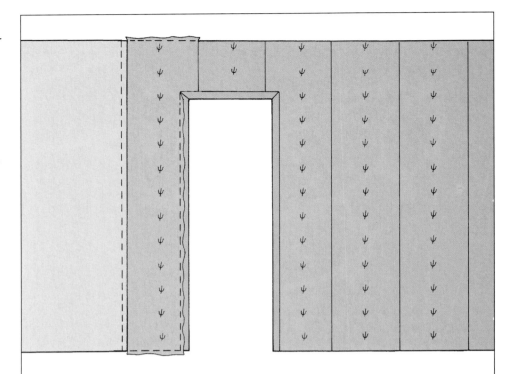

2. Hang the paper at the ceiling, drape it down over a window or door, and rough-cut the opening. Then make 45-degree relief cuts to allow you to press the paper to the wall.

sunk back to the wall, use a seam roller to flatten the seam and press the edges of the sheets firmly into the paste. Roll only one time up and down; repeated rollings may create a shiny track on the paper.

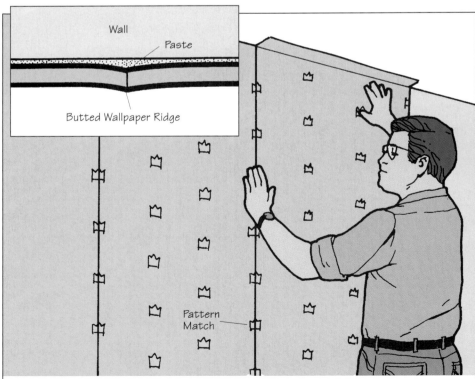

1. Hang the second sheet so that the pattern matches up; the strip should be butted tightly to the previous one, forming a slight ridge.

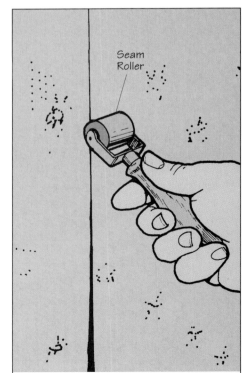

2. Use a small wallpaper roller to flatten the seam. Don't go over the seam repeatedly, or you will leave a track.

Turning Inside Corners

1. Fit a Strip into the Corner. If your wallpaper pattern repeats infrequently, you'll need to cut the paper to carry the pattern around a corner. Measure from the edge of the last full sheet to the corner at both the top and the bottom of the wall. Add ½ inch to the larger measurement; transfer this to a sheet, and cut it lengthwise. Then hang the sheet against the edge of the previous sheet, letting the other edge turn the corner by the extra ½ inch. Brush the sheet out and tuck it cleanly into the corner.

2. Mark a Vertical Guideline. Measure the width of the narrow strip of wallpaper left over from cutting the previous sheet. Subtract ½ inch, transfer this measurement to the unpapered portion of the wall corner, and use a level or plumb bob to make a vertical line at this point.

Use the vertical line as a guide for hanging the narrow strip.

3. Hang the Adjacent Sheet. Hang the narrow strip, positioning it against the guideline and brushing out as usual. Use the brush to tuck in the edge that meets the corner.

4. Trim the Second Sheet. If the second sheet overlaps the corner, score it with scissors, peel it back slightly, and cut along the scored line.

1. For inside corners, cut a strip ½ inch wider than necessary, and use the brush to push the paper into the corner.

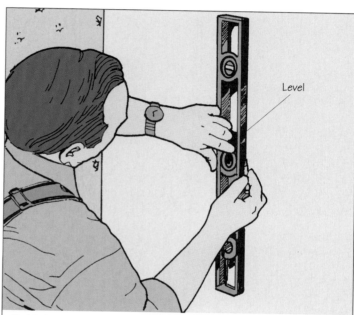

Level

2. Mark a vertical line a distance from the corner equal to the width of the remainder of the strip minus ½ inch.

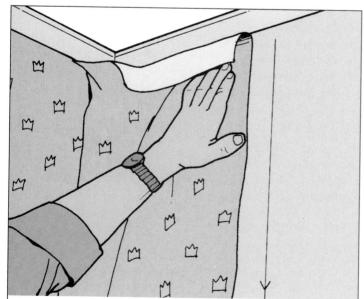

3. Use the vertical guideline to position the second strip. Brush the overlap into the corner.

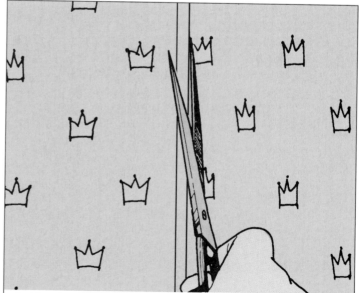

4. After the second strip is hung and brushed out, crease it in the corner and cut it to fit.

FLOORS

This book considers three kinds of floors: concrete floors, floors of various surfaces on subflooring laid over joists (the kind of floors on the upper stories of most houses), and masonry floors. This section includes instructions for pouring new concrete floors and repairing old ones, rehabilitating the structure of floors on joists, repairing the surface of hardwood floors, and installing a variety of new floor surfaces from brick to carpet.

Concrete Floors

Although a concrete floor is essentially just a slab of concrete, it hides some structural elements. A plastic barrier separates the slab from the ground, wire mesh reinforces the concrete, and drain pipes carry moisture to a sump. Concrete floors are poured in sections separated by key joints that allow these sections to expand without cracking. "Placing Concrete Floors," page 97, shows you how to build and set up forms for the sections of the floor, and also how to level the floor and give it a smooth finish. "Repairing Concrete," page 100, explains how to seal small cracks, and how to break out and replace large damaged areas. "Warming a Concrete Floor," page 102, shows how to frame an insulated wood floor over a concrete slab, an important project if you ever want to turn your basement into a comfortable living space.

Wood Floors

In wood-frame construction, floors are built with joists, which are covered with some kind of subflooring—sheets of plywood, or particle board, or planks. The finished floor is installed on this subflooring. For extra stability, the joists often are tied together with cross bridging, which keeps them from twisting. The first-floor joists bear on mudsills on top of the foundation. If a house is very narrow, the joists will span from one foundation wall to the other. Usually, however, joists are supported midway by a girder, which typically consists of several pieces of wood nailed together. The ends of the girder rest on the foundation walls, and the middle of the girder is supported by wood posts or steel Lally columns.

"Leveling Wood Floors," page 103, shows how to fix wood floors that have sagged but are otherwise structurally sound. Two common problems are addressed: straightening a sagging basement girder, and reinforcing sagging floor joists. Straightening a basement girder requires the use of a heavy-duty hydraulic jack to push the girder straight; then a new steel post is installed to keep the girder straight. To reinforce sagging joists, you simply cut new lumber to fit, and then nail it to the old joists, a process known as sistering joists.

If a joist breaks or fails for some other reason, the floor will be deformed. If it is a hardwood board floor, the boards above the failed joist may ride together and make a noise when stepped on. "Silencing Squeaking Floors," page 105, shows several methods for quieting wood floors, and "Silencing Squeaking Stairs," page 106, presents solutions for noisy stairs.

Baked-earth, terra cotta tiles are highly popular. As visible here, the porous surface of unglazed tiles stains easily. So before use, unglazed tiles should be sealed to prevent staining.

Floor bricks can be actual bricks extruded from shale to the thickness of tile, as shown here. Or they can be simulated bricks, which are simply glazed or unglazed ceramic tiles. Before selecting bricks for flooring, ensure that the manufacturer recommends them for high-traffic areas. For kitchen floors and other areas subject to spills, seal unglazed bricks after installation.

Finish Flooring

In an older house, hardwood floors may be in bad repair. "Replacing Damaged Strip Flooring," page 107, tells how to make hardwood floors whole again by cutting out damaged areas and filling them with new strips. "Refinishing Wood Floors," page 110, explains how to remove an old finish and apply a new one. You fill any cracks, sink any loose nails (silence any squeaky boards at the same time), and sand the surface with a rented floor sander—a noisy, dusty but rewarding job. The sanded floor is then sealed and finished to reveal its original beauty. To start fresh, "Installing Wood Strip Flooring," page 131, shows how to lay a new floor from scratch. And "Installing Wood Flooring in a Basement," page 134, shows the special flooring products and installation techniques proven to stand up to damp basement conditions.

Where you wish to recondition an old floor by installing an entirely new surface, you will need the instructions in "Preparing Floors for New Surfaces," page 112. This section explains how to prepare a sufficiently sound and smooth floor to accept adhesive for resilient sheet flooring, or for resilient, ceramic, or parquet tiles. To do this, sheets of plywood, called underlayment, are nailed over the old floor, and the seams between the sheets are filled to make a uniformly flat surface.

In addition to hardwood, there is a wide choice of floor coverings. One of the most versatile is resilient tile, appropriate almost anywhere in the house and practical because it is easy to clean. "Laying Resilient Tile," page 114, tells how to plan the job and make it easy. No matter what pattern you want to lay, a clean surface, straight work lines, and patience are all you need to lay a perfect floor. Resilient sheet flooring has the same practical advantages as resilient tile, but it requires different installation procedures; these are covered in "Installing Resilient Sheet Flooring," page 117. Parquet tiles—blocks of hardwood strips available in different designs—are installed in much the same way as resilient tiles. Using the directions in "Laying Wood Floor Tiles," page 119, and your own imagination, you can achieve the elegant effect of a handcrafted floor. For a solid, country look in a garden room or solarium, "Laying Brick Floors," page 121, shows you how to pave your floor.

Wall-to-wall carpet softens and warms a floor, and has the additional advantage of making rooms below it quieter. "Installing Wall-to-Wall Carpeting," page 123, explains the equipment and techniques necessary to do the job like a professional. If you have damaged carpeting, consult "Repairing Carpets," page 127.

Where you need tough, waterproof, easy-to-clean floor surfaces, such as in bathrooms and kitchens, "Laying Ceramic-Tile Floors," page 128, may provide the answer. Beyond its practical value, tile offers endless design possibilities.

Resilient sheet flooring is more challenging to install than resilient tiles because it usually comes in 6-foot- and 12-foot-wide rolls that require precise cuts around furnishings. Resilient flooring may be either cushioned or unbacked. Cushioned flooring is more comfortable to walk and stand on.

In addition to providing a sea of color, wall-to-wall carpeting dampens room noise and the noise transmitted to rooms beneath, while also inviting comfy walking in stocking feet. Solid colors show dust and stains more readily than patterns.

At first you might mistake this for resilient flooring. In fact, it's a combination of wood-ply tiles and planks, some with wood grain and others with a granite look, arranged to taste. The planks and tiles are glued to one another, not to the floor, and float on an underlayment of foam and a moisture barrier.

Especially created for do-it-yourselfers, these 12-inch tiles are applied after simply peeling off a backing material, no additional adhesive required. In laying all types of tile, conduct a dry-run layout, as explained in "Laying Resilient Tile," on page 114.

Resilient sheet flooring is also available with unique central statements. Of course, this compass is best suited for a small floor area.

With cherry wood in short supply, you might expect to gasp at the cost of this floor, which is in fact far less expensive 3x36-inch vinyl "planks" that simulate cherry wood. Simply install the planks over adhesive applied with a notched trowel, no nailing required.

This wood floor features 12-inch three-ply maple tiles with diamond accents selected from a range of color choices. For added durability, all tiles come with multicoats of heat-treated urethane. This pattern is called Diamond Stone.

In rooms with interrupting partitions and counters, it's especially important to conduct dry-run layouts. The goal is a satisfactory compromise between minimizing cutting and providing eye-pleasing full-tile rows at the most visible wall edges. In this case, the installers butted 12-inch tile edges to the white brick partition and also to the far back wall.

The floor at left consists of hardwood planks and inset ceramic tile. The tile provides spill resistance needed in kitchens, and the planks afford the warm, friendly surface more appropriate for the living room. Note how the tile turns the corner along the far wall, unifying the two living spaces.

Combined with an early 19th-century decor, wood floors in herringbone pattern suggest old-world craftsmanship. Yet the only especially time-consuming part of installation is the measuring and cutting of 45-degree miters for pieces that abut the perimeter.

One attribute of a tile floor near a southerly window is its ability to serve as a heat sink, absorbing the sun's rays and slowing reradiating heat to the room. When planning an elaborate pattern such as this, it's wise to sketch the room's floor plan on graph paper, experimenting with pattern options.

Hardwood flooring comes mostly in 2¼-inch to 3¼-inch widths in differing grade designations, according to standard species groupings. The flooring shown is of oak, which—like ash—comes in grades of clear, select, No. 1 common, and No. 2 common, depending on color, grain, and imperfections.

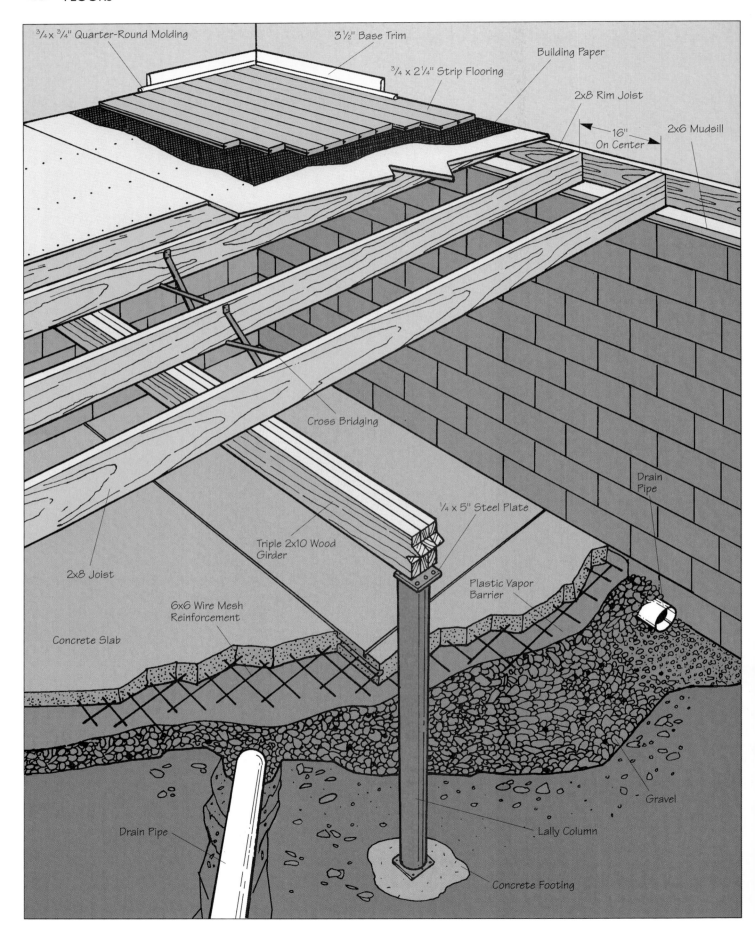

³/₄ x ³/₄" Quarter-Round Molding

3½" Base Trim

³/₄ x 2¼" Strip Flooring

Building Paper

2x8 Rim Joist

16" On Center

2x6 Mudsill

Cross Bridging

Drain Pipe

Triple 2x10 Wood Girder

¼ x 5" Steel Plate

2x8 Joist

6x6 Wire Mesh Reinforcement

Concrete Slab

Plastic Vapor Barrier

Gravel

Drain Pipe

Lally Column

Concrete Footing

PLACING CONCRETE FLOORS

A concrete floor instead of a dirt floor can make a basement more usable; at the same time, it can reduce dampness. Typically, a concrete slab 4 inches thick is placed on top of 4 inches of gravel. So if you're planning to turn a basement into living space, consider that a new concrete floor will eat up 8 inches of headroom. Building codes require that at least half of the basement have a minimum ceiling height of 90 inches. (Bathrooms, kitchens, and hallways in a basement may have 84-inch-high ceilings.) If a quick measurement of the existing ceiling height shows that you won't have the proper clearance, you will have to remove some dirt. If your basement tends to flood, you must slant the dirt surface toward one corner of the room so that water can drain into a dry well or sump pump. Also, you should dig trenches around the room perimeter, and diagonally across the room so that you can install perforated drain pipes.

You may be required to obtain a building permit, which includes an on-the-scene inspection of your grading job. So before undertaking this project, check with your local building department. Once your plans are approved, you can install forms, spread a layer of gravel, cover the gravel with plastic sheets, and install wire reinforcement and then place the concrete.

The truck bringing the ready-mix concrete may have to drive onto your property to within 10 feet of the basement window for the chute to reach. Prepare the ground around the area with 2x10 planks and plastic sheeting to catch any spills. If you can't provide access, consider using a concrete pump, which can deliver concrete through hoses from a truck several hundred yards away.

Pour and spread concrete rapidly. Fill the forms one floor section at a time before going on to the next. Then use a screed to level the concrete surface and a darby or bullfloat, as shown on page 99, to push down gravel aggregate and bring the sand and cement to the surface. Allow "bleed water" to evaporate before cutting control joints and troweling the surface to a smooth finish.

When all is completed, the concrete slab must cure slowly to reach its full strength. You can purchase a curing compound from a building supplier, or keep the floor damp for a week or longer.

Preparing the Grade

1. Level the Old Floor. Dig out the old dirt floor so that its surface is 8 inches below the new concrete floor surface. The dirt floor should slope 1 inch every 8 feet to the lowest corner, where the sump pump or dry well will be located. You can check the new floor level by snapping level chalk lines on the walls 8 inches above the dirt surface. Tie strings across the room to nails located every 4 feet along the chalk line; then measure down from the strings.

2. Install Drainage. Dig a hole for the sump pump $2\frac{1}{2}$ feet deep and 2 feet wide in the lowest corner of the room. If you are not using a sump pump, fill the hole with clean gravel. Then dig a trench 4 inches deep and 6 inches wide around the perimeter of the room, and dig a similar trench diagonally across the room. Pour a 2-inch layer of gravel into the trenches, and lay lengths of perforated plastic pipe on the gravel to form a conduit around and across the room. Lay the pipes with the perforations down; the pipe ends should drain into the hole or be attached to the sump pump.

1. Dig out the old floor 8 inches below the level wanted for the new one; use string guides to keep the depth even.

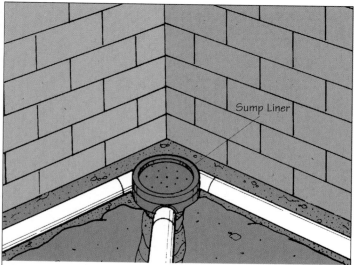

2. Dig a 30-inch-deep sump in the low corner; dig drainage trenches around and diagonally across the room, and install perforated drain pipes. Set a sump liner in the hole with the rim at finish-floor height.

Preparing to Pour

1. Set Up the Forms. Make key-jointed form boards. To do this, make 45-degree bevels on opposing edges of 8-foot 1x2s as shown in the drawing. Nail the 1x2s to 8-foot 2x4s as shown. Make up as many of these form boards as you need to span the length of the room and half of its width if the floor is to be poured in smaller sections. It's best to pour small sections if you have little experience and only one helper. With more helpers and some experience, you can pour a lot more concrete.

Then, in each key-jointed form board, drill three ¾-inch holes: one in the center and two 1 foot from the either end. These holes are for iron rebar dowels that will hold the slab sections together. Make three stakes for each form board from 2x4s. Nail the stakes to the flat side of the form boards as shown, with the tops of the stakes and forms flush. Along a line dividing the basement in half, drive the forms into the dirt floor until the tops of the forms are 8 inches above the floor. The beveled 1x2s should face the side of the room you intend to pour first. Check that the forms are level.

2. Install the Base Materials. Rake out and tamp a 4-inch layer of gravel over the entire dirt floor, taking care not to disturb the form boards. The gravel surface should be reasonably level. Lay down 6-mil polyethylene sheets over the gravel, extending the plastic up the walls to the chalk lines and overlapping the edges at least 6 inches. Unless you are using fiberglass-reinforced concrete, lay out reinforcing wire mesh on the plastic.

3. Insert the Form Dowels. Insert a steel dowel (an 18-inch length of ½-inch reinforcing bar) through each ¾-inch hole you drilled in the form boards so that half the dowel is on each side. Use wooden wedges in the back of the form to hold the dowels in place and pack gravel tightly behind the form boards. Then brush clean motor oil on the forms so that concrete will not bond to them.

2x4 Form

1x2 Key

1. Have a helper hold the key-jointed form. Drive the stakes down to the level indicated by the string.

6" Overlap

Steel Dowel

2. After the floor is filled with 4 inches of gravel covered with a plastic sheet, put down 6-inch wire mesh. Overlap sections of wire 6 inches and tie the pieces together with wire.

3. After wedging steel dowels firmly in the form, pile gravel behind the form to hold it as you place the concrete.

1. Dump concrete near the wall, and push the concrete against the wall to form a flat strip even with the chalk line. Beginning at one end of the room, place and rake out concrete between the forms and the concrete strip.

2. With the forms and concrete strip to guide you, pull a long, straight 2x4 in a backward zigzag motion to level the concrete. Rake away concrete that builds up in front of the 2x4.

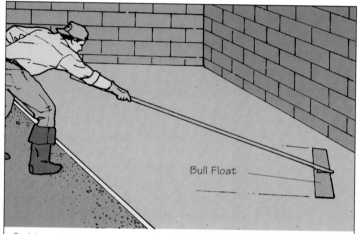

Bull Float

3. Use a darby or rent a bull float to smooth the surface; then wait until the surface water evaporates.

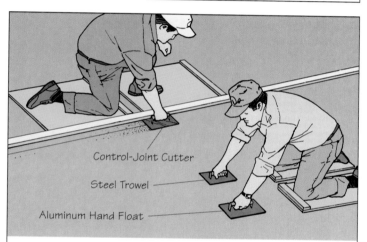

Control-Joint Cutter

Steel Trowel

Aluminum Hand Float

4. Use a 2x4 straightedge to guide the control-joint cutter, and then smooth the surface in wide arcs with a float; follow immediately with a trowel to smooth away the marks left by the float.

Spreading the Concrete

1. Fill the Forms with Concrete. Pour a 1-foot-wide strip of concrete next to the basement walls. Use a hand float to bring the concrete strip level with the chalk lines. Allow the concrete to set for an hour or two. Then deposit more concrete to cover 8 to 10 feet, and spread it with a rake or hoe. Also use the rake or hoe to pull the reinforcing wire halfway up through the wet concrete.

2. Level the Concrete. Level the concrete with a straight 2x4 screed rail. One person can pull the screed rail in a sawing motion along the top of the form on one side and along the top of the concrete strip next to the wall. A second person should rake away any concrete that builds up in front of the screed rail. Screed small sections before pouring more concrete.

3. Smooth the Surface. While the concrete is wet, smooth the leveled surface with a 3-foot-wide bull float attached to a long pole. The bull float is pushed and pulled across the slab surface; lift the handle as you pull and lower the handle as you push. "Bleed water" will appear on the top of the slab, making it shiny. When completely dry, the surface will be dull.

4. Finish the Slab. When the concrete can withstand the toss of a 1-inch stone so that it bounces, leaving only a slight indentation, cut 1-inch-deep control joints every 10 feet. Then smooth the surface between the joints with an aluminum hand float and a steel trowel, moving backwards. If the concrete is too hard, dampen it a bit. In five to six hours, wet the surface again and cover with polyethylene sheets for 24 hours. Then remove the gravel packing and the forms. The steel dowels remain in the edge of the slab. When you pour the companion slab, the dowels will lock the two slabs together.

REPAIRING CONCRETE

There are two kinds of damaged concrete floors: those that are merely cracked or pitted, with a structurally sound subbase, and those that have buckled or heaved because of poor drainage or an unstable subbase. The former can be patched easily; the latter should be broken up and completely replaced with a new concrete slab after the structural problems underneath have been repaired. For example, a subbase of compacted gravel with a drain pipe should be installed before the new slab of concrete is poured.

If the subbase is sound, a ½-inch layer of new concrete can be poured directly over a cracked or spalled slab. On a large floor, it is easier to pour the new surface in sections, using form boards to divide the room. Align the forms directly over the control joints of the old floor. They should be the thickness of the intended surface and may be applied with paneling adhesive. This will hold the forms in place, but will let them be removed after the concrete is poured. Cut new control joints over the old ones.

Very small holes in a sound floor can be patched simply with epoxy. Small holes and cracks should be scraped clean and patched with any of several cement patching compounds. More serious cracks and large holes need more extensive preparation, including breaking up the damaged area and removing the debris. You should always wear goggles and gloves for such work to protect your eyes and hands. When patching large holes, build up the patch in layers until you can trowel it flush with the existing slab.

Filling Large Holes

1. Break Out the Damage. To prepare the damaged area, break up the cracked concrete with a sledgehammer or an electric chipping

1. Break up damaged concrete back to the solid slab with a sledgehammer or electric chipping hammer. Clear out the debris with a wire brush. Wear goggles.

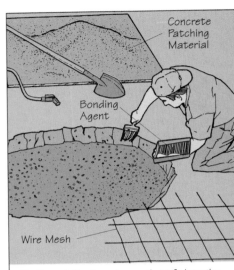

2. Cut reinforcing wire mesh to fit into the hole, remove the mesh, and paint the perimeter of the hole with bonding agent.

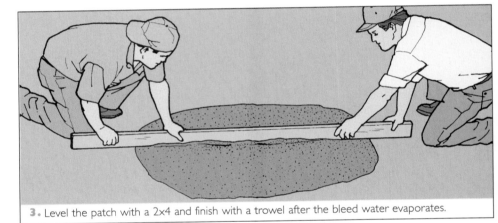

3. Level the patch with a 2x4 and finish with a trowel after the bleed water evaporates.

hammer until the pieces are small enough to remove easily. Angle the edges of the hole toward the center with a chisel and hammer. With a stiff wire brush, roughen the edges of the hole and remove any loose chips or particles. Excavate the subbase so that the bottom of the hole is 8 inches below the existing concrete surface, and then tamp the bottom of the hole with the head of the sledgehammer. Fill the hole with clean ¾-inch gravel up to the bottom of the concrete slab.

2. Prepare the Old Concrete. Cut a piece of reinforcing wire mesh to fit inside the hole about 2 inches below the concrete surface. Remove the mesh, then brush an epoxy bonding agent onto the exposed

concrete edges. Before the epoxy dries, mix a batch of concrete, and then fill the hole halfway with concrete, replace the wire mesh, then fill the hole to the top. Add a few more shovelsful of concrete to counter any settling or shrinking.

3. Level the Concrete. With an assistant, level the patch with a 2x4, sweeping it back and forth to smooth the new concrete. Fill any depressions that develop with more concrete, and screed them smooth with the 2x4. When the bleed water evaporates and the surface looks dull, use a trowel to smooth the final finish. If the patch is too large for you to reach the center, lay boards across it to kneel on, moving them back with you as you go along. The patch should cure for three to seven days. Then sprinkle it with water and cover it with a sheet of polyethylene to prevent the moisture from evaporating. Check it every day and add more water if the surface becomes dry.

Filling Cracks

1. Clear the Crack. Some cracks in concrete are small enough to be patched only. If a crack is a hairline or slightly larger, patch it with epoxy cement. If a crack is ¼ inch or wider, widen it with a hammer and cold chisel, and cut under the sides as shown so that the patching material can anchor itself under the beveled edges. Chisel down into the concrete about 2 inches, and sweep out debris and dust.

2. Flush the Crack with Water. Flush out the opening with pressurized water; then brush on a mixture of portland cement and water to help the patching material bond to the old concrete.

3. Apply Patching Material. While the cement bonding agent is still wet, mix the patching material and pack it into the crack with the edge of the trowel. Force the patching material into all the crevices and undercutting you have cleared out. Don't spare the patching material, pack in as much as you can. When the crack is filled, level and smooth it with a trowel.

Sealing a Floor. To prevent stains in a concrete floor, seal it with a mixture of boiled linseed oil thinned with mineral spirits. Apply the sealer with a brush or a roller. If you want to clean a stained slab, you should consult your home-center dealer for the right chemicals to use on your particular problem; there are as many solutions as there are stains.

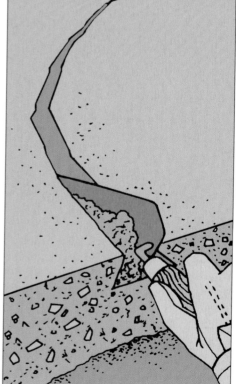

Sealing a Floor. Apply a coat of boiled linseed oil and mineral spirits to a concrete slab to protect it from stains and frost.

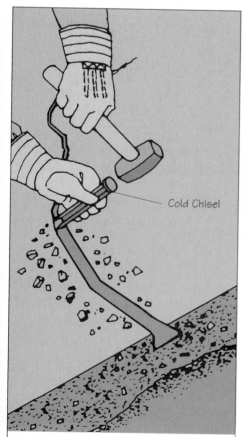

1. Enlarge a crack with a cold chisel, cutting under the edges to widen it at the bottom so that the patch won't pop out.

Cold Chisel

2. Water clears out small pieces of debris and prepares the concrete for the cement bonding agent.

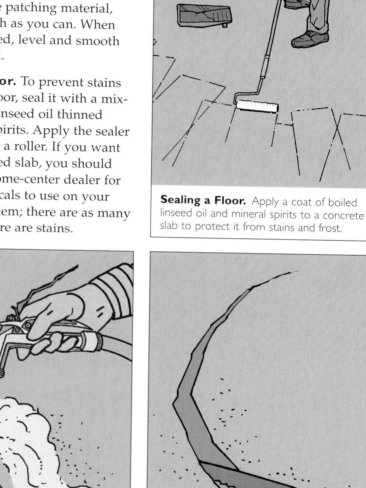

3. Pack the patching material under the beveled edges of the crack with the edge of a trowel to fill every crevice.

WARMING A CONCRETE FLOOR

Many concrete floors, whether they're in a basement or on the first floor of a slab-on-grade house, tend to be uncomfortably cold in winter and damp with condensation in summer. If you've noticed these problems in your house, consider installing an insulated subfloor over the concrete. An insulated subfloor isolates the finished floor from the slab, resulting in a warmer floor and helping to prevent moisture from damaging the finished flooring.

The insulated subfloor consists of plywood nailed to sleepers (2x4s laid flat). Rigid insulation fits between the sleepers. Subflooring plywood comes in two edge configurations: square edge and tongue-and-groove edge. Although either configuration can be used for a basement subfloor, tongue-and-groove plywood eliminates the need for blocks placed beneath unsupported edges of the plywood. Remember, there must be at least 90 inches of headroom (84 inches in kitchens, hallways, and bathrooms) after the insulated subfloor has been installed.

You can install the flooring of your choice over the insulated subfloor. An exception is solid-wood flooring; see "Installing Wood Flooring in a Basement," page 134, for information on installing a wood-flooring product recommended for basement installations.

1. Put Down a Vapor Barrier. After sweeping the floor slab, cover it with clear plastic sheets, known as 6-mil polyethylene. Overlap each seam by a minimum of 6 inches, and let the sheets lap up the wall about 2 inches. Lift up the edges of the polyethylene, and use a caulking gun to put down dabs of construction adhesive to hold it in place. Adhere the plastic sheets to the walls with a bead of adhesive.

1. Roll polyethylene sheets over the floor, overlapping the seams by at least 6 inches. Press the sheets into dabs of construction adhesive on the slab.

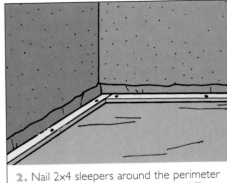

2. Nail 2x4 sleepers around the perimeter of the room, butting joints as needed. The 2x4s must be straight and flat. Use masonry nails spaced every few feet to secure them to the slab.

3. Space 2x4 sleepers 24 inches on center. Align them to provide solid bearing for the plywood, then nail them to the floor.

4. Cut rigid foam to fit between the sleepers and drop it in place.

2. Install the Perimeter Sleepers. Use 2¼-inch-long masonry nails to nail sleepers around the perimeter of the room. If the lumber is dry and straight, you can install a nail or two every several feet. Use shingle shims to fill any gaps occurring under the sleepers, where they bridge dips in the concrete surface. Mark the perimeter sleepers for additional sleepers 2 feet on center. This spacing is suitable for ¾-inch plywood.

3. Install the Interior Sleepers. Align the interior sleepers square to the marks on the perimeter sleepers. Use one nail at the end of each board and one about every 4 feet. If one sleeper does not extend completely across the room, butt two sleepers end-to-end.

4. Insert the Foam. Medium-density extruded polystyrene foam

5. Use 6d nails to attach plywood to the sleepers. Place the nails at 6-inch intervals around the perimeter of each panel, and 12 inches over intermediate supports.

is best for concrete floor slabs. Use a thickness that matches the thickness of the sleepers. Cut each piece to fit snugly between the sleepers.

5. Attach the Subfloor. Use ¾-inch-plywood subflooring (either straightedge or tongue-and-groove). Install the plywood so that it spans across rather than parallel to the sleepers. Stagger the plywood so that the two pieces butt together at the middle of a sheet of plywood in the previous course.

LEVELING WOOD FLOORS

The structure that holds up a house must bear tremendous weight, adjust to seasonal changes of weather, and withstand the constant traffic of those who live there. In older homes, where the original wooden posts, girders, joists, and bridging have been in place for years, gravity will have taken its toll in the form of sagging floors. More often than not, a sagging floor is a nuisance, but not a portent of disaster. For example, a small dip in a floor is probably a minor problem; however, a deep sag may be an indication of more serious structural damage, such as a rotten girder or a termite-eaten post. In some cases, old posts may have sunk because of inadequate footings.

Most sags occurring on the first floor can be repaired quite easily from the basement or crawl space. Repairs to second-story floors are more difficult because of cosmetic considerations; the ceiling on the first floor must be removed and replaced, for instance, and a post cannot be left in the middle of the floor as a permanent solution. You should consult a professional before undertaking any work above the basement level.

This section deals with two common problems in old houses: sagging joists and a sagging basement girder, or carrying beam. One way to remedy sagging joists, called sistering joists, is to install new joists alongside the old. Straightening a girder that is sagging but otherwise sound—not rotted, cracked, or termite-infested—requires jacking up the girder to remove the sag and adding a new adjustable steel post. For this job, you will need a 12- or 20-ton hydraulic

jack, a ¼-inch thick steel pressure plate, and a 6x6 jacking post. You will install the new post on a footing dug in the basement or crawl space.

Sometimes, straightening a sagging floor can cause more problems than it eliminates. You may find that the doors no longer swing freely across the floor. Or you may discover that removing the sag has caused walls to crack or a tile floor to loosen. In short, consider the big picture; if the sag is minor, you may be wiser to live with it rather than to repair it.

Reinforcing Sagging Joists

1. Inspect the Joists. Check the sagging joists for rot or termite damage by jabbing a pointed tool, such as a screwdriver, into the wood. Soft spots indicate deterioration. Also look for structural damage, such as cracks. If the joists are sound, you can straighten the floor by sistering new joists onto the old. Measure the existing joists, and buy lumber that matches as closely as possible the width of the existing joists.

2. Cut the New Joists. Cut the joists to length. When retrofitting joists, often the biggest challenge is getting them to stand on edge between the mudsill and the subfloor. You can ease the work by notching the ends of the new joists about ¼ inch narrower than the existing joists. Another trick is to remove, or chamfer, opposite edges of the joists, as shown, so that you can roll the joist into place.

3. Install the New Joist. Rest the new joist on the mudsills and girder. If you cannot maneuver the joist into position on edge, set it in place flat, and then roll it into position against the old joist. Drive wooden shims under the ends to force them up firmly against the subfloor, and then drive 10d nails in rows of three every 16 inches to sister the new joist to the old. Repeat the process for all sagging joists.

1. Jab a pointed tool into the sagging joists to make sure they are solid. Look for cracks and splits.

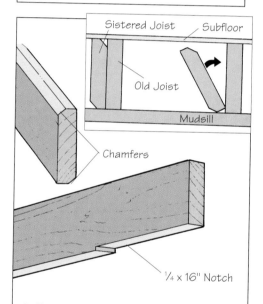
2. Fitting new joists between the mudsills and subfloor is easier if you notch the ends of the new joists, or chamfer opposite edges.

Sistered Joist
Subfloor
Old Joist
Mudsill
Chamfers
¼ x 16" Notch

Shim
3. Set the joist on the mudsills, and roll it on edge against the old joist. Shim each end to force it against the floor; then sister the new joist to the old with three 10d nails every 16 inches.

Straightening a Girder

1. String a Reference Line. At each end of the sagging girder, start an 8d nail 1 inch from the bottom edge. Tie a string from these nails along the girder. Make sure the string doesn't touch the girder. Use this string to guide you in straightening the girder.

2. Place a Footing. If the girder sags over a post, you will have to replace the old post with an adjustable steel support post. If there is no footing beneath the post, you will have to place one there before installing the new post. This is also true if the girder sags because there simply is no post at all. In this case, you must add a new footing and a post.

On the floor where the new post will be located, mark a footing the size your building code requires. Use a rented hammer drill to break through a concrete floor, and remove all chunks of slab. Dig a hole in the subsoil the depth the building code requires. Dampen the hole, and fill it with concrete. Release air bubbles by repeatedly thrusting a shovel into the wet concrete. With a straight piece of lumber, level the concrete surface. Cure the concrete for two weeks by keeping the surface wet and covered with plastic sheeting.

3. Jack Up the Girder. Position a hydraulic jack close to the footing, set a 1/4-inch steel plate on the jack, and use a 6x6 post on the jack to raise the sagging girder. Make sure the jacking post is plumb. Raise the girder until it is straight by checking its position against the reference string. Then pump the jack one more time to put a slight crown in the girder. Remove any existing post.

4. Install the New Post. Set the adjustable steel support post on the footing. Unscrew the post's plate to fit snugly under the girder, then insert a long screwdriver into the pivot holes and continue turning the screw until it is very tight. Use a level and a sledgehammer to knock the post into plumb. Then release the jack completely.

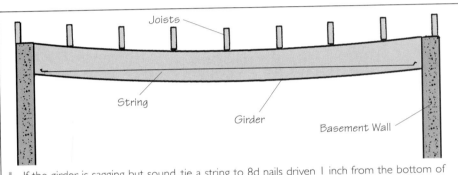

Joists
String
Girder
Basement Wall

1. If the girder is sagging but sound, tie a string to 8d nails driven 1 inch from the bottom of the girder at each end.

String

2. After marking the post position on the floor, break through the slab and dig a hole for a footing; level the concrete footing flush with the floor.

String
6x6 Post
Hydraulic Jack   2x8 Pad

3. Near the footing, set up a 20-ton jack and raise the girder until it is slightly crowned. Remove any existing post.

Adjustable Post

4. Set the adjustable steel support post on the footing, unscrew the plate to fit snugly under the girder, plumb the post, and release the jack.

SILENCING SQUEAKING FLOORS

There aren't many homes that don't have a squeak or two in the floors. Although they are aggravating, squeaks don't indicate anything seriously wrong with the floor or its structure. Frequent causes of squeaks are two boards that have warped and now rock when they are stepped on, or cheaply manufactured floor strips with tongues and grooves that don't fit tightly. You might be able to fix a squeak simply by sweeping talcum powder into the joint between the squeaking boards.

Sometimes the squeak is produced by a subfloor that has separated from the joists because of settling, or because the joists have dried out and shrunk away from the subfloor. Weak or rotten joists also can pull away from the flooring, as can those with faulty bridging between them. Occasionally, inadequate nailing of the subfloor to the joists causes squeaks. If these problems are causing a squeaky floor, you may have to shim the floor, add blocking, or reattach the floor boards.

Locate the squeak by having someone walk over the noisy area of the floor while you listen and watch from below. Look for springy boards, movement between joists, and bridging that gives when a weight is brought to bear. Just to be on the safe side, inspect the area around the squeak for structural damage needing more extensive repair, such as the replacement of girders, posts, or bridging.

Shimming a Squeaky Floor. You can use wood shims to silence squeaks caused by movement between a joist and the subfloor. Locate the squeak, and gently tap shims into the space between the joist and the subfloor to prevent movement. Do not drive the shims too forcefully, or they will widen the gap and cause more squeaks elsewhere. Instead,

wedge the shims in just firmly enough to fill the space and eliminate the movement that was causing the squeak.

Cleating the Subfloor. If the squeak is caused by several floor boards running perpendicular or diagonal to the floor joists, you can eliminate movement with a 1x4 or 1x6 cleat. Start some 8d nails in the cleat, locate the squeaky boards, and place the cleat against the joist supporting the loose boards. With a 2x4 block, push the cleat tightly against the floor, and nail the cleat to the joist. When the cleat is solidly attached, remove the 2x4 block.

Reinforcing the Floor. If the squeaking is from an area spanning several joists, the problem may be that the joists are shifting. You can stiffen them by installing steel bridging. Some types of steel bridging don't even require nails; you simply drive the pronged ends into the joists. First, hammer the straight-pronged end into one joist near the top. Then drive the curled prongs on the other end into the opposite joist at the bottom. Install the companion bridging in a crisscross fashion, and proceed to the other joists. The result will be a series of joists more firmly braced and less liable to give beneath the weight of the floor.

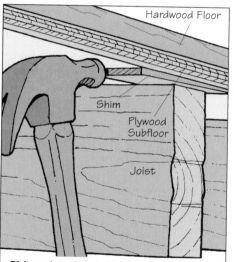

Shimming the Subfloor. If floor joists are not tight against the subfloor in the area that is squeaking, shimming may solve the problem. Wedge shims between the joist and subfloor and tap them into place.

Cleating the Subfloor. Where several boards in the subfloor above a joist are moving, nail a cleat to the joist to support the springy boards. While nailing, press the cleat under the floor with a 2x4 block.

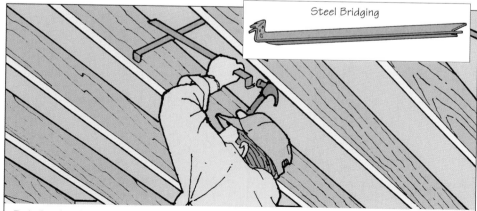

Reinforcing Joists. Squeaking over a large area may indicate that the joists beneath the floor are shifting slightly and giving inadequate support to the subfloor. Steel bridging, attached between joists as shown, holds the joists from moving side to side and stabilizes the subfloor.

Screwing from Below. When individual boards are loose or bulging, you might be able to pull them tightly against the subfloor with screws inserted from below. Use roundhead wood screws of a length that will reach no farther than ¼ inch below the surface of the finish floor. First, choose a drill bit whose diameter equals the diameter of the screw you are using, including the threads. Use the bit to drill a pilot hole through the subfloor but not through the finish floorboard. Put a washer on the screw and slip it into the hole. As you tighten the screw, it will bite into the finish floorboard and pull it down.

Surface Nailing. If you can't gain access to the subfloor, you can drive 6d blunt flooring nails through the finish floor to anchor loose boards. Drive the nails at an angle into the subfloor, or drive 8d nails straight into a joist. Drill a pilot hole narrower than the nail shank to reduce the chance of splitting the wood. Set the nailheads below the floor surface, and fill the holes with wood putty the same color as the floor.

Squeak-Controlling Products. A number of products are manufactured specifically to fix a squeaking floor. These products are available at home centers and hardware stores, and are simple to install. One type is a metal bracket screwed between a joist and the subfloor. As you turn the screws, the bracket tightens itself against the subfloor to eliminate gaps and stop squeaks.

SILENCING SQUEAKING STAIRS

The most common cause of squeaky stairs is a loose tread rubbing against other parts of the stairway. If the tread is separated from the riser (the vertical board of each step), squeaking will result. To eliminate the squeak, first determine how the tread and riser are assembled, and then close the gap where the two separate. Techniques for closing the gap include nailing the tread down, gluing together the tread and riser, inserting wedges in the gap, and reinforcing the tread and riser with wooden blocks. Occasionally, a tread may be rubbing on the carriage (the diagonal, terraced structure supporting the risers and treads).

To locate the exact spot causing the squeak, have someone step on each tread and rock back and forth. Watch closely both the middle of the tread and the ends to determine where the greatest movement occurs. Most squeaks can be eliminated from either above or below. Stairs that are open or accessible from below are easier to fix because you don't have to be concerned with breaking through and subsequently needing to refinish existing walls or ceilings.

Tightening or Replacing Loose Wedges. In many staircases, the treads and risers are held in place with wedges underneath. Sometimes, you can eliminate a squeak simply by locating it and then using a hammer to tap the appropriate wedges farther

Tightening or Replacing Loose Wedges. Sometimes, you can tap old wedges tight again. Other times, you need to break them out with a chisel and replace them.

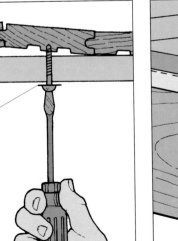

Screwing from Below. Drill a pilot hole that does not penetrate the finish-floor surface; then use a wood screw and washer to pull the loose board down onto the subfloor.

Washer

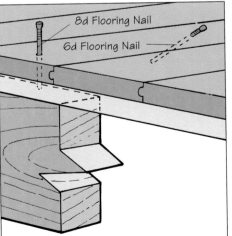

8d Flooring Nail

6d Flooring Nail

Surface Nailing. Nail down from the top with 6d blunt flooring nails when you can't get access to the floor from below. Try to locate joists and drive 8d nails into them.

Squeak-Controlling Products. One type of squeak-control product fits between a joist and the subfloor. Tightening the screws forces the bracket upward, where it presses against the subfloor to take up any slack and eliminate squeaks.

Nailing and Gluing a Squeaky Tread.
Have a helper stand on the glued tread
while you drive the nails.

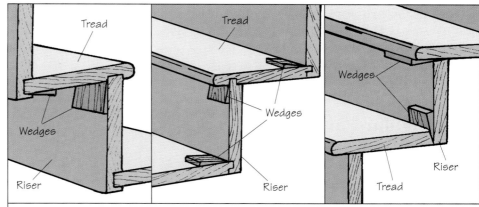

Wedging a Loose Tread. The three examples above show the placement of wedges for different kinds of joints. Cut off wedges in place and conceal with quarter-round molding.

in. Other times, though, you can't move the wedges because they are glued in. In that case, split out the old wedge with a chisel, and clean out the dried glue. Cut a new wedge to fit, coat the notch with glue, and hammer the new wedge firmly into place, but not so hard that it lifts the tread.

Nailing and Gluing a Squeaky Tread. Have someone stand on the loose tread while you drill $3/32$-inch pilot holes at opposing angles through the tread and into the riser at the point of the squeak. If the squeak is near the end of the tread, drill the holes into the carriage. Have the helper step off the tread, and apply a bead of white wood glue between the tread and riser. Then fasten the tread to the riser with two 8d finishing nails set below the tread surface. If nails will not hold the tread, drill a $3/8$-inch countersink hole partially into the tread, and an $11/64$-inch pilot hole into the tread and riser. Fasten the tread to the riser with a $2\frac{1}{2}$-inch #8 wood screw, and plug the hole with a piece of dowel.

Wedging a Loose Tread. If there is quarter-round molding at the back of the tread, remove it. Determine the kind of tread joints by inserting a knife between the tread and riser. Whittle sharply pointed wedges an inch or two long, and drive them into the gap between the tread and riser

at the points shown. Insert them just enough to silence the squeak. To conceal the wedges, cut off the ends with a utility knife and replace or add quarter-round molding in the joint.

Installing Wood Blocks. Working under the stairs, coat two sides of a 2x2 wood block with yellow glue, and press the block into the squeaking area between the tread and riser. Drill pilot holes and drive two $1\frac{1}{4}$-inch drywall screws into the riser, and one up into the tread. Add as many blocks as are necessary to stop the squeak.

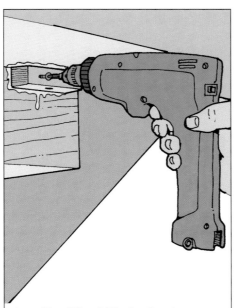

Installing Wood Blocks. Put glue on adjacent sides of a 2x2 wood block, press the block into the joint between the tread and riser, and fasten the block with drywall screws.

REPLACING DAMAGED STRIP FLOORING

The causes of damaged wood strip flooring are usually obvious. Furniture and heavy appliances can mar, crack, and tear wood fibers. Burns and stains are also common. If the cause is not immediately obvious, check out the entire floor, not just the damaged area. Also inspect the substructure for sagging girders, settling posts, or moisture and rotting due to plumbing leaks or insects.

When buying replacement strips, take a sample of the old floor to your lumber dealer to make as close a match as possible. Be prepared to discover that nothing matches your floor completely and that you may, therefore, have to refinish the floor when the new boards are in place. A floor made of prefinished wood is not difficult to match, although every floor changes with wear and tear over time and takes on its own unique characteristics.

The tools you'll need for replacing wood strips are a hammer, a 1-inch chisel, a framing square, a pry bar, a circular saw, 8d nails, and wood putty.

There are two methods of replacing strip flooring. The easier way is to remove a rectangular area encompassing the damaged strips, but the straight line where the old strips end and the new strips begin will be apparent. The second method is to remove individual strips in a staggered pattern. This is a little more difficult, but the patch is less noticeable.

Rectangular-Pattern Replacement

1. Cut Out the Damaged Strips. With a square and a pencil, measure a rectangle encompassing the strips to be removed, but mark the line ¾ inch from all joints between strips to prevent cutting through nails. Adjust the blade of the circular saw so that it just cuts through the strips but not through the subfloor. Lower the blade to the wood, and work from the center of a line outward. With a hammer and chisel, finish the cut, keeping the beveled side of the chisel facing the damaged area. Then beginning at the midpoint of a cut side, lift the strip out with a pry bar. You should usea small block of wood for leverage, and be careful not to mar good wood strips in the area.

2. Cut Away the Remaining ¾ Inch. Use the hammer and chisel to cut the ¾ inch remaining behind the saw cuts. Then, starting at one end, separate the strip from the other flooring by tapping the chisel gently into the edge joint. Work carefully and slowly so as not to ruin the adjacent strips. When the ¾ inch is removed, set any exposed nailheads in the strips bordering the cut area.

3. Install the New Wood Strips. Measure, cut, and install the new strips one at a time. Cut one end square, butt it against the old strip, mark the other end even with the strip beneath, and cut the new piece of flooring. Be sure to keep the saw on the waste side of the mark so that the cut won't shorten the board. Use a hammer and a small block of flooring to tap the new strip into place, locking the groove over the tongue in the old strip. Drill pilot holes through the

1. Cut around the area with a saw set to cut through the finish flooring but not the subfloor; finish the corners of the cut with a chisel.

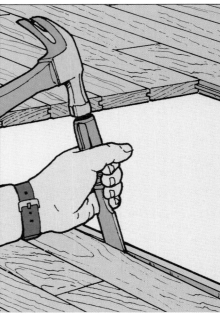

2. Use a chisel to cut away the ¾ inch of the wood strips remaining along two sides of the cut, and set any exposed nails.

Flooring Scrap

3. Tap new strips in place with a scrap of flooring; then nail at a 45-degree angle through the tongue.

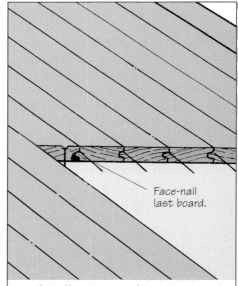

Face-nail last board.

4. Cut off the tongue of the last strip, and face-nail it in place as shown. Seal the ends of the patch with wood putty.

tongue at a 45-degree angle, and nail the new flooring strip with 8d finishing nails. Cut and install the remaining strips until you have reached the last one.

4. Install the Final Strip. To lay the final strip, first remove the lower lip of the groove with a chisel, and sand the rough edge. Insert the

tongue of the final strip into the existing flooring groove; and tap the strip down into place, using a hammer and a block of wood. In the face of the strip about ¾ inch from its groove edge, drill pilot holes every 12 inches; then face-nail the board with 8d finishing nails. Set the nails, and fill the holes with wood putty.

Staggered-Pattern Replacement

1. Chisel the Ends of Bad Strips. Mark the area you wish to remove; but instead of drawing a straight line across the strips, stagger the marks so that you cut each strip a different length. Use a hammer and 1-inch chisel to score the mark at each end of a damaged strip, holding the chisel with the beveled side facing the damaged area. Then hold the chisel on an angle a few inches back from the score, and chip out some of the wood. Deepen the score, chip out more of the wood, and repeat until you have cut the strip completely. The edge of the section not to be removed should be sharp and clean.

2. Pry out Bad Strips. Strike the center of the damaged strip with the hammer and chisel, holding the chisel parallel with the wood grain. Move the chisel along the strip, and keep striking until the wood splits. Split the strip again using the same technique, and insert a pry bar into the incision to pry out the middle portion. Then pry loose the section on the groove side of the strip and the portion on the tongue side.

Begin the removal of each strip in the center of the section and work out to the ends. Remove the remaining damaged strips by cutting the ends and splitting them out, and set any exposed nails in the section you won't remove.

3. Tap the New Strips into Place. Cut replacement strips to size. Using a scrap of flooring as a hammering block, tap a strip into place so that the groove side goes over the tongue of the old strip. Then drill pilot holes at an angle through the tongue of the new flooring, drive in 8d finishing nails, and set them.

4. Install the Final Strip. When installing the final strip, remove the lower lip of the groove, insert the tongue into the existing flooring, and tap the strip down. Drill pilot holes through the top of the wood strip, and fasten it with 8d finishing nails. Set the nails, and fill the holes with matching wood putty.

1. Mark off the damaged area, score crosscuts with a chisel, and then chisel toward these marks at an angle as shown.

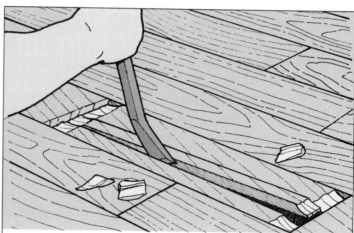

2. Break the damaged strips with lengthwise chisel cuts; pry out the middle piece, followed by the grooved side and then the tongue side.

3. Slip in a new strip, cut to fit, and tap it into place against the tongue edge of the old flooring.

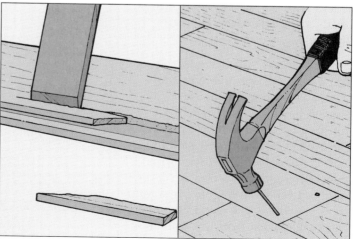

4. Remove the lower lip of the last strip, tap the strip into place, and then attach it using 8d finishing nails driven through the face.

Refinishing Wood Floors

When wood floors become so marred and scuffed that new coats of wax do little to improve them, it may be time for a major refinishing. Instead of hiring a professional floor service, you can save quite a bit of money by refinishing the floor yourself. This includes sanding off the old finish, applying a sealer, and then applying a topcoat. You can sand about 200 to 250 square feet of flooring in a day. If you use a waterborne acrylic sealer and waterborne urethane floor finish, you could seal and topcoat the floor in the same day. The use of waterborne sealers and finishes is recommended because these products dry quickly and don't smell so bad. However, you must wear rubber gloves and a respirator with an organic charcoal filter for protection from hazardous fumes.

Also, you will need to rent professional equipment from a reliable dealer. You'll need two kinds of sanders—a drum sander and an edger—and a floor buffer with nylon pads. Rent the sanders first and hold off on the buffer until you have sealed the floor. Be sure the equipment works before leaving the store, and have the dealer show you how to load the drum sander, change the edger's sanding discs, and fit the buffer with the nylon pad. Ask if you need special wrenches for loading the drum.

For each room, you will need 10 or 12 sheets of fine, medium, and coarse sandpaper for the drum sander, the same number of discs for the edger, and one nylon pad for the buffer. Each time you sand or buff the floor, you must vacuum the entire room, and wipe the floor with a clean, damp rag. If any stains have penetrated the wood, you may be able to bleach them out using a commercial floor bleach. Wear gloves and goggles to apply the bleach to discolored areas. When the area is bleached to the matching tone of the floor, wash the bleached area with warm water and allow it to dry completely.

If you wish to tint, pickle, or stain your floor, do so before sealing it, and be sure to let the stain dry at least 24 hours. Pickling stains may require as much as one week to cure; check with manufacturers for product compatibilities and recommended curing times. Then you can apply the waterborne acrylic sealer, which locks in the floor color, and creates a smooth base for the waterborne urethane topcoat. When the seal coat dries (after about four hours), buff the floor smooth with a nylon pad.

Two coats of waterborne urethane floor finish over the seal coat provide an extremely hard, protective glaze when dry. Allow the floor to cure for one week before subjecting it to daily wear and tear. Keep the floor clean, and it will provide years of beautiful service with no waxing necessary.

Preparing the Room

Before beginning to refinish the floor, strip the room of furniture and pictures. Dust will coat anything left in the room that is not covered. Take down drapes or pin them up from the floor, and wrap them in plastic bags. Cover or remove any heat registers, seal off doorways into other rooms, and open the windows for ventilation. Sanding will create extremely flammable dust, so turn off any pilot lights in the area.

Removing Shoe Molding. When the room has been stripped of furniture and wall hangings, remove the shoe molding at the base. Begin at the doorway, and carefully pry the molding away from the base trim. Use two chisels, one to separate the molding from the base and the other to pry the strips up from the floor. As you proceed, place wood shims behind and under the molding to prevent it from snapping back into place. As you move along, move the shims with you. Number the sections as you remove them so that you will

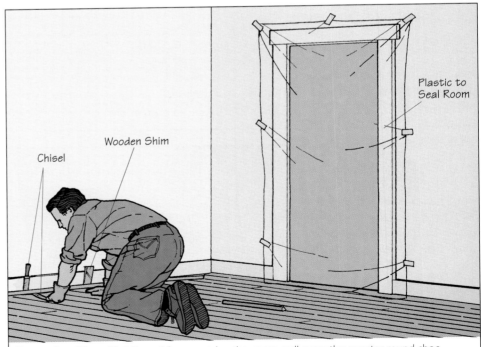

Removing Shoe Molding. After emptying the room, pull away the quarter-round shoe molding at the bottom of the base trim. Use a chisel to pry the molding away from the base and another chisel to pull the shoe molding off the floor. Use wooden shims to keep the shoe molding from snapping back in place. Remove all nails, and then seal off the room so that sanding dust won't escape.

Chisel

Wooden Shim

Plastic to Seal Room

know in what order to replace them when the job is over. Pull out any finishing nails that remain in the baseboard or floor. Set any flooring nails at least $\frac{1}{16}$ inch below the surface.

Sanding the Floor

1. Put in Sandpaper. Make sure the sander is unplugged before loading the sandpaper. Slip a sheet of 20-grit coarse sandpaper into the loading slot of the drum. Turn the drum one complete revolution and slip the other end of the sandpaper into the slot. Secure the paper by tightening the nuts on both ends of the drum. The sander should come with wrenches for this purpose.

2. Use the Drum Sander. Tilt the machine back so that the drum is off the floor, and turn on the sander. When the motor reaches top speed, lower the machine gently, and let it pull you forward slowly and steadily. Work with the grain. Never let the drum stand in one spot while it is running because it will gouge the wood. When you reach the wall, tilt the sander up, walk it back to where you began, and move it to the side 3 or 4 inches so that the second pass will overlap the first. Your goal is to strip the old finish from the floor. When the machine becomes less aggressive, change to a new sheet of coarse sandpaper. On parquet or herringbone patterns, you should sand at 45 degrees to the wood grain.

3. Use the Edger. When you finish drum sanding the floor with coarse paper, load the edger with a coarse disc, and sand close to the walls, working from left to right in a semicircular pattern to remove the old finish.

4. Scrape Hard-to-Reach Areas. In tight areas where neither the sander nor the edger can reach, such as around radiators and in corners, remove the old finish with a sharp paint scraper. Pull the scraper toward you with both hands, bearing down on it with firm, steady pressure. Scrape with the grain as much as

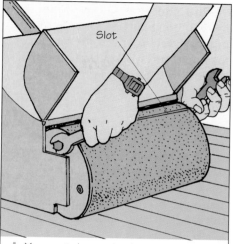

1. You must change the drum sander's sandpaper as it wears down and as you need finer grits to finish the floor.

2. When the sander is running, slowly lower the drum to the floor, and let the action of the drum pull the sander along. Sand with the grain of the wood.

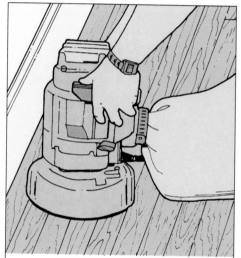

3. Use the edger to sand along walls and other areas you can't reach with the drum sander. Work with the grain, moving left to right in a semicircular motion.

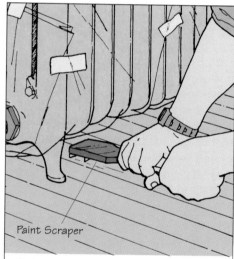

4. In areas where the edger can't reach, such as corners and around pipes, remove the old finish with a well-sharpened paint scraper.

possible, and be careful not to splinter the wood. When the blade becomes dull, sharpen it with a file. When you have removed the finish in these areas, sand them by hand with coarse-grit paper.

5. Fill Cracks with Putty. Use a putty knife to force wood putty into any cracks and nailholes. Scrape off the excess putty to make a smooth surface. Then sand the floor with medium grit followed by fine grit in both the drum sander and the edger, and sand hard-to-reach areas by hand with medium and fine grit.

5. After sanding with coarse grit, use a putty knife to force wood putty into cracks or holes. Scrape the surface smooth, and sand the floor with medium and fine grits.

For parquet and herringbone patterns, do the medium-grit sanding at 45 degrees in the cross direction from the coarse-grit sanding; the fine-grit sanding can go straight across the floor.

Sealing and Finishing

1. Seal the Floor. After vacuuming thoroughly, wipe the floor with a clean, damp cloth. Allow the floor to dry; then, wearing rubber gloves and the respirator, use a natural-bristle brush to seal the floor along the walls and in corners. Brush with the wood grain.

Next, seal the rest of the floor with a tubular synthetic pad applicator. Begin against the wall opposite the door so that you won't seal yourself into a corner. Pour out a line of the sealer, and, working with the wood grain, pull the finish along the floor. Coverages vary, but a good rule of thumb is that one gallon of acrylic sealer will cover about 500 square feet of floor. When you have completed the floor, ventilate the room, and allow the sealer to set for at least three hours.

2. Buff the Seal Coat. Mount the nylon buffing pad on the buffer's pad pusher. Start buffing at the far end of the room, and work toward the door. Work with the grain, moving sideways in overlapping passes. You'll have to do the corners, edges, and hard-to-reach areas by hand. Buffing knocks down any raised wood grain, and smoothes the sealer to a level surface. The process creates a coating of white powder on the floor; so when you finish buffing, you must vacuum and wipe off the floor with a clean, damp rag.

3. Apply the Topcoats. Strap on the respirator, pull on the rubber gloves, and brush on the urethane floor finish along walls, in corners, and in other hard-to-reach areas. Then switch to a tubular pad applicator, pour out a line of finish along the far wall, and pull the finish over the floor. Typically, one gallon of waterborne urethane will cover 800 square feet of flooring. After three or four hours, buff the surface with a nylon pad as shown. Vacuum and wipe with a clean, damp cloth. Apply a second coat, and let it dry 24 hours before moving furniture back into the room.

PREPARING FLOORS FOR NEW SURFACES

If your remodeling plans call for new resilient flooring, whether tiles or sheet goods, you may need to install underlayment to eliminate irregularities in the existing subfloor. You'll also need underlayment if you plan to install ceramic tile over an existing wood floor because flexing between individual joints can loosen tiles and crack grout. New underlayment isn't needed below wood finished floors.

Resilient flooring applied to an uneven floor will begin to show the irregularities of that floor, a problem called "telegraphing." Over a plywood subfloor, the underlayment may be ¼-inch plywood; over a board subfloor, use ¹¹/₃₂-inch or thicker plywood. Always be sure the plywood is rated for use as underlayment, which means the faces are smooth, and there are no voids in the center plies. If the floor will be subject to lots of moisture, use underlayment rated for exterior use.

1. After brushing the waterborne acrylic sealer into hard-to-reach areas, pour some sealer on the floor and spread it with a tubular pad applicator. Work with the grain, and move toward the door.

Respirator

Rubber Gloves

2. After the seal coat is dry, use a buffer with a nylon pad to smooth the surface. Vacuum and wipe away the white, powdery residue.

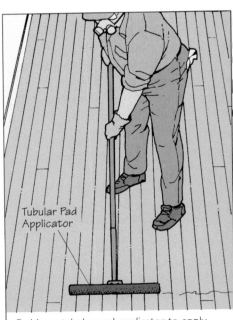

Tubular Pad Applicator

3. Use a tubular pad applicator to apply two coats of polyurethane, and buff between coats. Let the first coat dry three or four hours, the second, 24 hours.

Store plywood underlayment where it will be protected from physical damage and moisture. Store the panels flat, and keep them off the floor. Several days before the installation, bring the underlayment into the room, and stand it against the walls, with an air space between each panel, so that it can adjust to the room's temperature and humidity conditions. Try not to install underlayment in exceedingly moist or humid weather, or at times when the atmosphere is unusually dry, because such weather extremes will cause the plywood underlayment to swell or shrink.

Installing Underlayment on a Plywood Subfloor. Remove the baseboard molding using a pry bar, and pull out the nails through the back of the molding using a nail puller or pliers. Immediately before installing the new flooring, lay down the underlayment with the smoother side up, and with staggered joints that don't coincide with joints in the subflooring. If the edge of an underlayment panel falls directly over a seam in the subfloor, cut the underlayment so that its edge is at least 2 inches from the subfloor joint. Leave a $\frac{1}{16}$-inch space between panels; later, you will fill these spaces, and any other gaps, cracks, and holes with a filling product the flooring manufacturer recommends. Fasten the underlayment with ring-shank nails, which have cone-shaped threads that grip the wood. The nails should be long enough to penetrate the subfloor but not the floor framing.

Installing Underlayment on a Board Subfloor. Use underlayment panels that are at least $\frac{11}{32}$ inch thick, and lay them across the direction of the boards in the subfloor. If the end of a panel falls directly over a seam in the subfloor, cut the panel so that it falls in the middle of the board. Use ring-shank nails every 6 inches along the edges, keeping the nails $\frac{3}{8}$ inch from the edges, and every 8 inches in the center. Nails should be long enough to penetrate the sub-

floor boards but not the floor framing below. Leave $\frac{1}{32}$-inch gaps between sheets of underlayment for minor expansion and contraction.

Nailing Ring Shanks. Ring-shank nails are difficult to drive. When you hit them slightly off center, they bend and fold up or break because of the shank's reduced diameter size between rings. Also, the hammer tends to slip off the small nail head. One way to minimize these problems is to hold the hammer loosely rather than tightly. Another tip is to sand the

hammer head with fine sandpaper. When the hammer begins slipping off the nails, sand the head again.

Don't hammer hard on the assumption that forceful strokes will pull the underlayment tightly against the subfloor. Instead, start nailing at one edge of the underlayment and work your way across the panel, smoothing it out so that there is no void between it and the subfloor. Hammer with easy strokes, and apply pressure to the underlayment with your free hand, kneeling close to the spot you

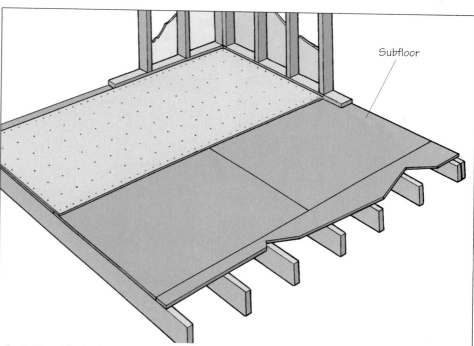

Installing Underlayment on a Plywood Subfloor. Over a plywood subfloor, use plywood underlayment at least $\frac{1}{4}$ inch thick. Arrange the panels with staggered seams that do not fall directly over seams in the subflooring. Fasten the underlayment with ring-shank nails every 3 inches along edges, and every 6 inches in the centers. Do not nail into the floor framing.

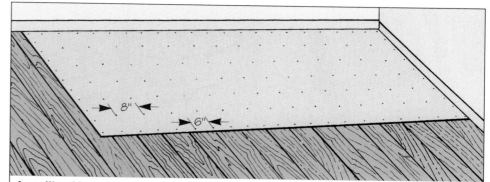

Installing Underlayment on a Board Subfloor. Over a board subfloor, use plywood underlayment at least $\frac{11}{32}$ inch thick. Arrange the panels with staggered seams that occur over the middle of subfloor boards. Fasten underlayment with ring-shank nails every 6 inches along edges, and every 8 inches in the centers. Do not nail into the floor framing.

are nailing, or have a helper exert pressure. Your last blow should drive the nailhead flush with the surface. Do not dimple the underlayment with the hammerhead. Dimples can telegraph through to the flooring above, appearing as slight depressions.

Removing a Bent Nail. If you try to remove a bent nail by grabbing the nailhead with the claw of the hammer, you will probably snap the nailhead off the shank. Instead, tap the claw of a cat's paw or pry bar into the shank with a hammer; the soft metal in the nail can be forced into the claw rather easily. Always wear safety goggles when you strike a metal tool

with a hammer. Lean back on the cat's paw, using leverage to pull out the bent nail.

Finishing the Surface. The purpose of underlayment is to provide a perfectly smooth surface on which to place new finish flooring. (One exception would be tile, which doesn't require a smooth setting bed.) After you have put down the underlayment, fill all gaps, holes, and cracks with a filler the flooring manufacturer recommends. If you have dimpled the surface with the hammer, fill the dimples. Smooth all patches with a putty knife, and sand them smooth once they have dried.

LAYING RESILIENT TILE

Homeowners with a creative bent often enjoy installing resilient tile because it is easy and fun to do. For a successful job, however, you've got to plan ahead, make proper preparations, design your pattern and color combinations, measure accurately, and work on a day when you won't be interrupted. Also, you must have a proper underlayment for the tile, and follow the instructions that come with the product you bought.

The best setting beds for resilient tile are sturdy, smooth, dry, and clean. A plywood floor makes a suitable base only if all seams, gaps, and holes have been filled. Wood-plank flooring over a durable subfloor will suffice if the floorboards are at least 4 inches wide, and they are also smooth and sound. If there are any damaged boards, replace them. Nail any loose boards down tight, sand them smooth, and fill cracks and splits with a filler the flooring manufacturer recommends. Before laying the tile, cover the wood floor with 15-pound building paper. If the entire floor is in poor condition, or if it is only a single layer of wood subfloor, install an underlayment.

Concrete can serve as a base for resilient tile only if the slab is smooth and dry. If it is not perfectly dry throughout the year, it will harm the tiles. Be sure the slab is never subject to moisture penetration; check it during the rainy and humid seasons of the year. If you think it is safe, follow the manufacturer's directions to fill the cracks and dimples with a latex underlayment compound.

You should keep the tile and all the materials at room temperature for 24 hours before and after installation.

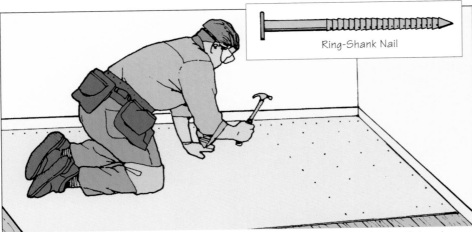

Ring-Shank Nail

Nailing Ring-Shanks. Nailing down underlayment is tricky because ring-shank nails bend or break easily. Working from one end of a panel to the other, hammer with easy strokes, pressing down on the panel with your free hand. Keep a piece of sandpaper on hand to polish the hammer head when it begins to slip off the nails.

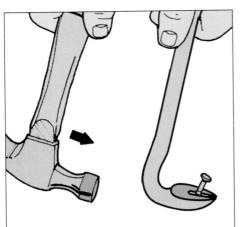

Removing a Bent Nail. The easiest way to remove nails, a common occurrence in putting down underlayment, is to tap a cat's paw into the shank of the nail. Pull back on the tool to extract the nail.

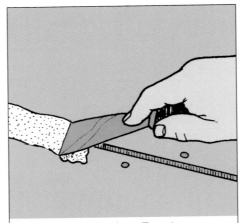

Finishing the Surface. To make a smooth surface suitable for resilient flooring, fill all dents, cracks, nailholes, and gaps between sheets of underlayment; then smooth off and sand the patches.

Calculating the Number of Tiles Required

Resilient tiles come as 9-inch squares or 12-inch squares. To calculate how many 12-inch squares you'll need, just multiply the length of the room times the width in feet. For example, a 16x16-foot room is 256 square feet and will need 256 12-inch tiles. To calculate how many 9-inch tiles you need, multiply the square footage by 1.78. A 256-square-foot room will need 456 9-inch tiles.

Plotting a Design. Unless you plan tiles that are all the same color, or plan simply to alternate colors, you'll need to plot out your design on graph paper, letting each square represent one tile. Then you can count squares to determine how many of each tile color you will need.

Preparing to Lay the Tile

1. Mark Wall Center Points. Tack small nails at the center points of two opposite walls, and stretch a chalk line between the nails. Do the same on the other walls. Do not snap the lines yet. Use a framing square to determine that they intersect at a true 90-degree angle.

If the pattern is to be laid on a diagonal, snap the chalk lines; then measure the shorter chalk line from the intersection to the wall. Measure out that distance on either side of the nail, do the same on the opposite wall, and drive nails into the four new points. Stretch chalk lines between these nails so that they intersect at 90 degrees.

2. Do a Dry Run. Beginning at the intersection of the lines and working back toward the walls, lay dry tiles along the strings, as shown. Duplicate the color combination you drew on the graph paper. If you discover the last tiles are less than half a tile width from the wall, move the chalk string to make a wider border at the wall.

If the last tile is more than one-half a tile width from the wall, leave the chalk string where you have it. Then snap the chalk lines on the floor.

For a diagonal pattern, lay dry tiles point-to-point along the chalk lines, and rows of tiles along the intersecting diagonal chalk strings. Check the size of the border tiles; adjust the chalk strings, and then snap them.

3. Set the Tiles. Spread adhesive along one chalk line with a notched trowel angled 45 degrees to the floor. Begin at the intersection and work toward the wall, leaving part of the chalk line exposed for guidance. Set

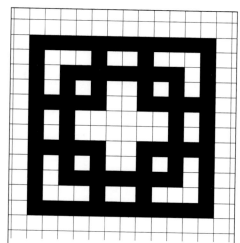

Plotting a Design. If you are using different colors, plot out the design you want on ¼-inch graph paper, using one square for each tile.

1. Measure the walls to find their midpoints, and stretch strings or chalk lines between them; add diagonals as described for diagonal designs. For diagonal patterns, lines "X" and "Y," shown in the inset, are the same length.

2. Lay out tiles along two of the guidelines, and check the fit at the walls; adjust the lines to avoid having thin border tiles.

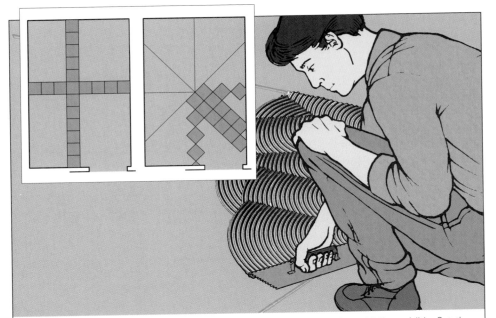

3. Apply adhesive with a notched trowel in one quadrant, leaving the guidelines visible. Set the first tile at the intersection of the guidelines, dropping—not sliding—it into place.

a row of tiles along the line, letting each tile butt the preceding one. Drop tiles into place; do not slide them. Set a row perpendicular to the first, and fill in the tiles between them.

For a diagonal pattern, begin at the intersection of diagonal lines, and lay a row along one diagonal. Use this as a base line on which to build your pattern. After finishing a section, roll it with a J-roller or a rolling pin.

Cutting Tiles

Trimming a Border. Align a dry tile over the last set tile from the wall. Then place a third tile over these two and push it to within ⅛ inch of the wall. Using this top tile as a guide, score a line with a utility knife on the tile immediately under it. Snap the tile on the scored line, and fit in to the border the piece that the top tile did not cover. For a diagonal pattern, score the border tiles from corner to corner with a straightedge and a knife. Snap them to make triangular halves to complete the saw-tooth border pattern.

Cutting around a Corner. Align a tile over the last set tile on the left side of the corner. Place a third tile over these two and push it to within ⅛ inch of the wall. Mark the edge with a pencil. Then, without turning the marked tile, align it on the last set tile to the right of the corner. Mark it in a similar fashion. Cut the marked tile with a knife, and remove the corner section. Fit the remaining part around the corner.

Making Irregular Cuts. To cut an irregular shape, use the procedure for borders and corners, but move the top tile along the irregular shape to locate its surfaces on the tile to be cut. At curved surfaces, bend a piece of solder wire and transfer the curve to the tile being marked.

Trimming a Border. Set two tiles atop the one closest to the wall, slide the top tile against the wall, and mark the one beneath. Score the marked tile with a utility knife and break it along the line.

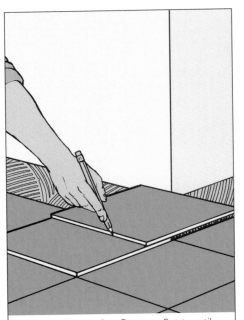

Cutting around a Corner. Set two tiles atop the tile closest to one side of the corner to be cut out, and mark that dimension; then shift the two tiles to the other side of the corner to mark the other dimension.

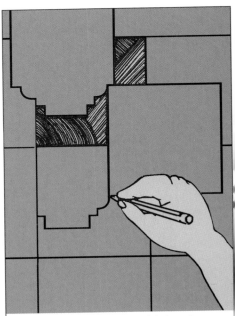

Making Irregular Cuts. Mark an irregular cut with the tile-over-loose-tile method, moving the guide tile along the irregular surface and marking at each point; connect the marks to outline the cut.

INSTALLING RESILIENT SHEET FLOORING

Manufacturers have developed many new types of resilient sheet flooring. These products are vinyl, not linoleum, and they're available in a huge assortment of colors, patterns, and textures. Typically, sheet flooring comes in 6-foot- and 12-foot-wide rolls, and may be cushioned or unbacked. Cushioned sheet flooring presents a more comfortable walking surface than unbacked flooring. After deciding on the type of sheet flooring you want, order it to arrive at least three days before you intend to lay it so that the flooring can adjust to the temperature conditions in your home.

There are several ways to install resilient sheet flooring; one popular technique, called a perimeter-adhered or tension floor, is to glue down the edges and seams only.

Although resilient sheet vinyl flooring can be installed over several types of old flooring, the existing floor must be in good condition. You can lay resilient flooring over old linoleum as long as the old flooring is completely smooth and tightly adhered to the subfloor. Concrete must be dry, level, and clean. A wood floor is suitable if the boards are not rotten or warped, and only if they are firmly nailed down. If these conditions cannot be met, then it's best to install plywood underlayment.

Prepare the room by removing the furnishings, including the covers on the floor registers, and the baseboard molding. But when you remove shoe moldings and baseboards, number the pieces so that you can replace them in the same order.

Lay out the room's shape and dimensions as accurately as possible on a piece of graph paper. Using the scale $\frac{1}{4}$ inch equals one foot, draw an overhead view of the room, including closets, alcoves, fireplaces, and doorways. If your floor is very irregular, you may want to make a full-size paper template to guide you when cutting the sheets. The largest flooring sheets available are 12 feet wide. If the room will require more than one sheet of flooring, determine where the seam will go as to design, pattern, and traffic flow. It's best not to put a seam where traffic is heaviest.

Installing Flooring without a Seam

Unroll the flooring in a large open space to make a rough cut. Transfer the floor plan onto it with a water-soluble felt-tipped pen, and cut the flooring so that it's about 3 inches oversize all around. You will cut the excess away after the flooring is in place.

Take the flooring to the room, and lay the longest edge against the longest wall first. Position the entire piece, making sure it curls up 3 inches on every wall. Then trim the sheet to make it fit the room, following the cutting instructions in "Installing Flooring with a Seam." Leave a $\frac{1}{8}$-inch gap at the walls to allow for expansion. Once it's trimmed to fit, you can staple the flooring around the perimeter or roll it back and trowel a 6-inch-wide band of adhesive around the floor perimeter.

Installing Flooring with a Seam

Take your floor plan to your dealer, and have him make the rough cuts. If you do it yourself, use a linoleum knife and heavy scissors to cut the most intricate piece first, making it 3 inches oversize on all sides, including the seam. If you are using adhesive, spread it on the floor with a notched trowel, but do not adhere the seam. Position the flooring. Then cut the second sheet so that it will overlap the first piece at least 2 inches. Spread the adhesive for the second sheet, but do not glue the seam area.

Usually, matching the pattern along the seam is a simple matter of overlapping the second sheet on the first so that the patterns align, and then cutting both sheets at once. To make a large, centered pattern, you sometimes must reverse the second sheet.

Relief Cut

Installing Flooring with a Seam. To make a perfect seam, overlap the two pieces of flooring, matching their pattern as shown. Trim the ends of the seam so that the flooring butts into the wall; then cut through the overlap to make the seam.

Position and align the second piece carefully. Make a semi-circular relief cut where the seam overlaps the wall so that the seam will lay flat where it meets the wall. Guiding a utility knife with a straightedge, cut through both sheets at the line for the seam. Lift up both halves and apply adhesive. Clean the seam and use the seam sealer recommended for your flooring.

Trimming

1. Trim the Outside Corner. Trim for an outside corner by cutting straight down the curled-up flooring. Begin at the top edge and cut to where the wall and floor meet.

2. Trim the Inside Corner. Trim for an inside corner by cutting the excess flooring away with increasingly lower diagonal cuts on each side of the corner. Gradually, these cuts will produce a wide enough split for the flooring to lie flat in the corner.

3. Trim Along the Wall. Remove the curled-up flooring at the walls by pressing it down with a 2-foot-long piece of 2x4. Press the flooring into the right angle where the wall and floor meet until a crease develops at the joint. Then position a metal straightedge into this crease and cut along the wall with a utility knife. Leave a 1/8-inch gap between the wall and the edge of the flooring so that the material can expand without buckling.

4. Cut the Flooring at the Door Jamb. The best way to have the flooring meet a door jamb is to cut the curled-up flooring to match the angles and corners of the door jamb. Make cuts straight down to the floor, and cut off the strips along the crease that appears when you force them tightly against the jamb and the floor.

Finishing the Job. Using a solvent the flooring manufacturer recommends, clean adhesive from the flooring. Then use a J-roller to press the flooring firmly into the adhesive. Replace the baseboard molding, and cover any exposed edges in doorways with metal threshold strips.

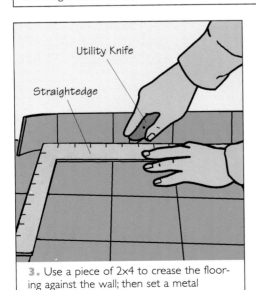

1. Start at the top of the flooring where it overlaps the corner, and cut straight down to the floor.

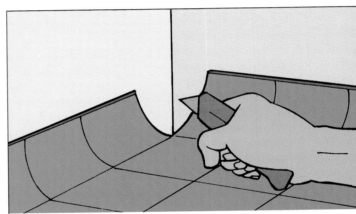

2. At an inside corner, cut the flooring in V-shaped sections until the flooring can lie flat.

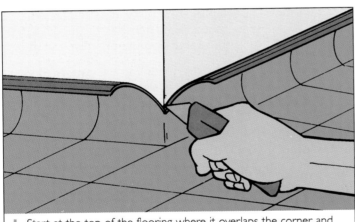

Utility Knife

Straightedge

3. Use a piece of 2x4 to crease the flooring against the wall; then set a metal straightedge along the crease, and cut the flooring 1/8 inch away from the wall.

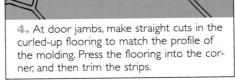

4. At door jambs, make straight cuts in the curled-up flooring to match the profile of the molding. Press the flooring into the corner, and then trim the strips.

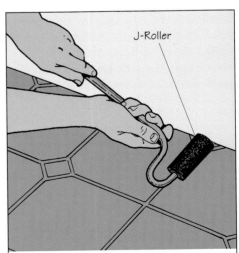

J-Roller

Finishing the Job. Use a J-roller to press the edges of the flooring into the adhesive. Wipe away any adhesive with a solvent the manufacturer recommends.

LAYING WOOD FLOOR TILES

Wood tiles, also called parquet tiles, are arranged and laid in much the same way as resilient floor tiles, except that wood tiles have tongue-and-groove edges that must be fitted together. Also, wood tiles must be sawed, not snapped, when smaller pieces are needed for borders. Like resilient floor tiles, wood tiles are set in adhesive; however, it's a good idea to leave a $\frac{3}{8}$-inch gap between wood flooring and the wall to allow for expansion. If you plan to put wood flooring over a concrete basement floor, see "Installing a Wood Floor in a Basement," page 134.

The surface over which you will lay the wood tiles should be smooth, dry, clean, and level. Parquet can be set on old wood floors if they are smooth and even. Remove old floor finish by sanding it using a rented drum sander. Nail down any loose boards, and set all nails. If any boards are badly damaged or rotten, you should put an underlayment down before laying new parquet flooring. Parquet should not be installed over old resilient flooring. Either remove it or cover it with plywood underlayment.

Estimating the Amount You Need. Wood tiles come in a great variety of sizes and designs, but the most popular tile designs come in 12-inch and 9-inch squares. To calculate the amount you need, figure out the area of the floor in square feet. This number will equal the quantity of 12-inch tiles required; or else multiply the square footage by 1.78 to figure out the required number of 9-inch tiles. It's a good idea to order five percent extra for miscuts and other mishaps.

Preparing to Lay the Tiles

1. Establish Working Lines. After removing the baseboard molding, mark the working lines by measuring the center points of the walls. Drive nails at the center points, and stretch chalk lines that divide the room into quarters; but do not snap the chalk lines yet. With a framing square, determine that the lines intersect at a true 90-degree angle. Adjust the lines if necessary.

2. Do a Practice Run. Practice laying out tiles along the chalk lines. Begin laying the tiles at the intersection, and work toward the walls. Get used to the tongue-and-groove construction of the tiles. Alternate the grain from wood tile to wood tile, placing the tongues into the grooves to create the basket-weave pattern of the parquet floor. If you find that you need a small piece at the border, move the strings before snapping the working lines.

1. Find the midpoints of the walls, stretch chalk lines, and check the intersection for square.

2. Set tiles in place along the working lines. Alternate the grain of the tiles, fitting the tongue into the groove. If necessary, reposition the chalk lines to avoid having to use a thin strip next to the wall.

Laying and Setting the Tiles

1. Set the First Tiles. With a notched trowel angled at 45 degrees to the floor, apply adhesive along the chalk lines. Begin at the intersection and work toward the wall, and don't cover the lines. Spread enough adhesive to set about three tiles in both directions. Lay the first tile into a corner of the intersection. Align the edges of the tile, not the tongues, with the lines. Place the second tile against the first one, engaging the tongue and groove; then place the third tile to form a right angle. Avoid sliding the tiles any more than is necesssary. After setting six tiles as shown, strike them with a rubber mallet to bed them.

2. Cut the Border Tiles. To make a border, align a tile over the last full one, and place a third tile over those two, holding it ⅜ inch away from the wall. Use a wood spacer to keep an even gap. This gap is needed for the cork expansion strip that comes with the tiles. Mark the middle tile, using the top one as a guide; then saw along the mark. The exposed portion of the middle tile will be the piece to place in the border.

3. Fit the Tiles Under the Door Trim. Using a tile for a guide, mark how much of the door jamb must be removed to allow the tile to fit under it. Then trim the bottom of the jamb with a saw.

Finishing the Job. Allow the adhesive to dry overnight; then insert the cork expansion strip between the tiles and walls. Next, replace the baseboard and shoe molding; be sure to drive nails into the baseboard, not down into the tiles. If an inward swinging door will not clear the raised floor, remove the door and trim the bottom. If the tiles are not prefinished, finish them following the instructions in "Refinishing Wood Floors," page 110.

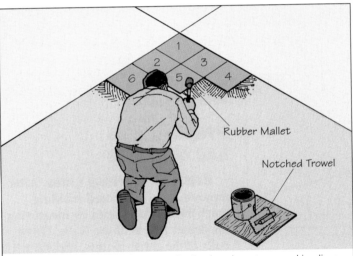

1. Use a notched trowel to spread adhesive along two working lines; then set the tiles in the order indicated by the numbers. Bed the tiles with a rubber mallet.

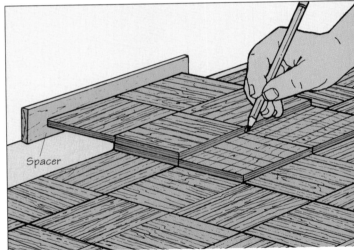

2. Place a loose tile directly over the last full tile, then set another tile over those two, butted against a spacer. Mark the tile as shown, and cut it with a saw.

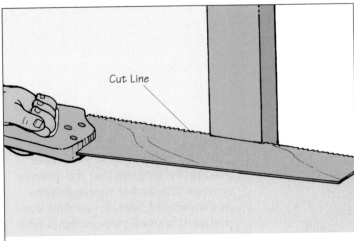

3. Use a tile to mark the cut on door jambs. Then cut below the line with a hand saw.

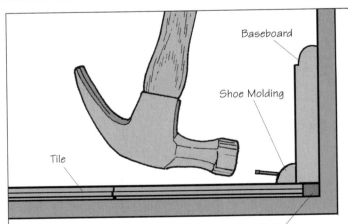

Finishing the Job. Cover the cork expansion strip with base moldings. First nail up the baseboard; then add the shoe molding, nailing it into the baseboard, not the tile.

LAYING BRICK FLOORS

Brick is a surprisingly inexpensive flooring option. It's particularly well-suited for greenhouse or solarium additions because it stores the warmth of the sun. Bricks come in a huge assortment of sizes, colors, and grades; but for floors, brick pavers are recommended because of their compressive strength and resistance to abrasion.

With few exceptions, you'll want to consider brick only for new construction. That's because paver bricks are at least 1½ inches thick, and you probably won't want to cut down existing doors by that much. Usually, brick floors are laid over a concrete slab. If you plan to lay bricks on a wood-frame floor, consult an engineer to find out if you need to reinforce the floor structure to support bricks.

Bricks may be laid either with mortar or without. Mortarless construction is recommended over a wood-frame floor. In a mortarless system, the bricks are laid over two sheets of building paper. The bricks are set tightly together, and sand is swept into the joints. If you're installing the bricks over a concrete slab, you can set the bricks in a mortar bed. This allows you to use mortar joints for a more traditional appearance. When laying bricks on concrete, the slab must be clean and dry; but irregularities can be eliminated with mortar.

Establishing the Starting Line

Begin your brick installation after the room has been painted. Remove any baseboard molding; and if you are doing a mortarless installation, put down two layers of 15-pound building paper over the entire floor.

Usually, the long side of the brick is parallel to the shorter wall in a rectangular room. Determine whether the shorter walls in your room are straight. Place identically sized bricks into each corner. Strike a chalk line along the outside edges of the bricks. If the wall is crooked, you will notice variations in the distance between the chalk line and the wall. Find the shortest distance between the chalk line and the wall, place a brick at this point, and strike a second chalk line parallel to the first. This will be your starting line. Variations that are less than the thickness of the baseboard molding won't matter; but if the wall is way off, you will have to cut narrow bricks to fill gaps.

Laying Mortarless Brick

1. Lay Straight Brick Courses. Before starting to lay the bricks, strike more chalk lines every few feet across the shorter dimension of the room, parallel to the starting line. As you install the bricks, use these reference lines to help you keep the courses straight.

Place a brick in the corner, and then set a half brick beside the corner brick. Alternating a full brick with a half brick will result in a classic running-bond pattern. You will need a mallet and wide masonry chisel called a brickset to cut bricks. Wear goggles or safety glasses. Give the brick a gentle blow on each side to score it; then whack it hard to break it. The brickset's bevel should face away from the piece you plan to use. Place the cut end of the brick against the wall so the baseboard can hide any irregularity in the cut.

Lay bricks along both walls, and work across the floor, butting each brick tightly to the adjoining bricks.

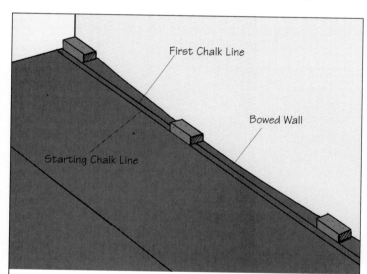

Establish the Starting Line. Snap a chalk line between the outer edges of two bricks set in the corners. Find the shortest distance from the line to the wall; set a brick at this point, and strike a second chalk line, parallel to the first. This second chalk line is the starting line.

First Chalk Line

Bowed Wall

Starting Chalk Line

Brickset

1. After striking the starting and reference lines on two layers of building paper, set one brick in the corner and a half-brick in front of it to establish the running-bond pattern. Continue laying courses along two adjacent walls, measuring the distance to the reference lines to keep straight courses.

2. Cut the bricks to fit along the other two walls. To cut a course of narrow bricks, use the same technique as when cutting half bricks.

3. Use a stiff-bristle broom to sweep a few shovelsful of fine mason's sand into the brick joints. Repeat the process after two or three days.

Laying Mortared Bricks

1. Do a Dry Run. Along the two longer walls in the room, nail 1-by boards on edge. The top edge of the boards should be at the finished height of the brick floor, which is usually ⅜ inch greater than the thickness of the bricks. Along these boards, set one row of bricks, with the short ends butting against the boards. Don't use mortar. If the wall is straight, place the first brick against it; if not, align the brick with the starting layout line. Continue setting bricks one in front of the other, spaced ¼ inch apart, until you reach the opposite wall. Adjust the spacing so that you won't need to cut narrow bricks for the last course. Try not to space courses farther than ⅜ inch apart. When you are satisfied with the spacing, mark the front edge of each brick on the layout board, and drive small nails at these marks. Then repeat the process along the other layout board, and attach a string to the nails indicating the first course.

2. Establish the Center Line. For rooms more than 8 feet wide, you should tie a string to establish the center of the course. Set bricks lengthwise against the shorter walls (the ones without layout boards), spaced ⅜ inch apart. Adjust the spacing so that the end brick is no less than a half length. Once you're satisfied with

You can walk on the bricks as they are laid. Make each course of bricks as straight as possible by maintaining an even distance to the reference lines. You may adjust the joints between bricks now and then, but remember that the best floor will have very tight joints.

2. Cut and Install Border Bricks. Unless you are very lucky, you will have to cut bricks to fit against the other two walls. If you need to cut a course of narrow bricks, use the same technique as for cutting short bricks. The bricks don't need to fit tightly to the walls; the baseboard molding will cover small gaps between the bricks and the wall.

3. Fill the Joints with Sand. When you have finished the borders, spread fine mason's sand over the entire surface, and sweep it with a stiff-bristle broom diagonally into the joints between the bricks. Most rooms require only two or three shovelsful. After two or three days, sweep in more sand. After one month, apply several coats of masonry sealer to lock the sand in place and protect the bricks from stains.

Starting Layout Line

Leading Edge

1x3 Layout Board

1. In dry-run positioning, space bricks uniformly and no more than ⅜ inch apart. Mark the leading edges with small nails.

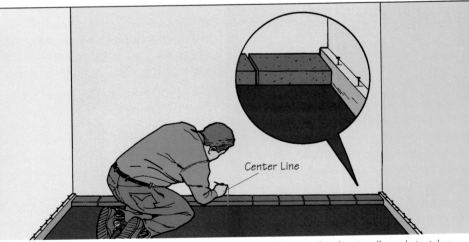

Center Line

2. For rooms wider than about 8 feet, mark the center joint on the short walls, and stretch a string at this point to help you align the brick pattern.

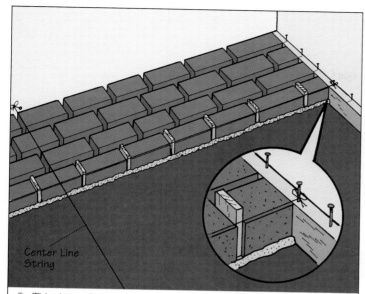

3. This shows four courses set in mortar. Keep top edges aligned with the layout string. Use ⅜-inch wood spacers to ensure uniform joints and cut the last brick to fit.

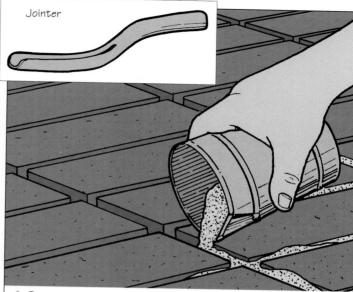

Jointer

4. Pour soupy mortar from a coffee can into joints between the bricks. When the mortar has dried sufficiently, shape it with a jointing tool.

the spacing, mark the location of the center brick, then do the same on the opposite wall. Drive small nails at these marks, and attach a string.

3. Set the Bricks in Mortar. Mix a bag of mortar to a whipped-cream-like consistency, and trowel a patch onto the slab, stretching from the center string to one of the layout boards. The first brick you set will be in the center; the next will be a full brick at the end of the course. Bed each brick into the mortar by tapping it with the trowel handle. Finish laying bricks in half the course; then set bricks on the other side of the center brick, working toward the wall. Use wood spacers to maintain the proper joint width between bricks; pieces of ⅜-inch plywood work well. Cut the last brick to fit. Keep the bricks aligned and level with the layout string. Once you've finished a course, move the string to the next set of nails; align the center brick for the next course so that you create the running-bond pattern, then place the rest of the bricks in that course, working toward the walls. Cut the last bricks to fit.

4. Mortar the Joints. After 24 hours, mix small batches of soupy mortar (three parts sand and one part cement), and pour it from a

coffee can with a bent rim into the joints. Be careful not to spill the mortar onto the brick surface; if you do, wipe it up immediately with a wet sponge. When the mortar is hard enough to hold an impression, carve each joint with a convex tool such as a jointer or a dowel. After several hours, wipe up mortar crumbs with a burlap sack. When the floor is completely dry, finish it with a water-based acrylic sealer.

INSTALLING WALL-TO-WALL CARPETING

Conventional wall-to-wall carpeting is installed on a pad and secured with tackless strips around the perimeter of the room to create tension. Cushion-backed carpeting is easier to lay down because it does not use tackless strips. It is laid in latex or fastened with double-faced tape. Although cushion-backed carpeting is less expensive than conventional carpeting, it will not last as long.

Before ordering your carpeting, prepare a scale drawing on graph paper, and let each square equal 1 foot. Mark all doors, alcoves, obstacles, and other unique features of the room you

intend to carpet. The more accurate you make the scale drawing, the easier it will be for your carpet dealer to recommend the type and amount you need.

If you can't carpet your entire room with one piece, you will have to allow for a seam. Seams are weak spots in the carpet, so they should not be placed where traffic flow is heaviest. If possible, seams should be laid away from the primary visual focus in the room. Seams are less visible when they run parallel to light rays and should, therefore, run toward the room's primary source of light, which is usually the wall with windows.

Prepare the subfloor before laying carpeting by nailing down loose boards, fixing squeaks, and replacing any rotten or particularly damaged boards. If you intend to lay carpet on concrete, it must be dry and not subject to sweating. If the slab gets damp, cover it with a sealer.

Remove the shoe molding from the baseboards. Most rooms with wall-to-wall carpeting don't have any shoe molding at all; but save it in case you decide later that the carpet will look better with it.

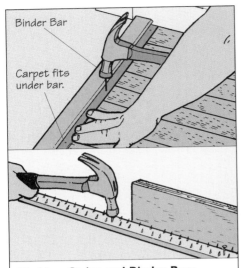

Tackless Strips and Binder Bars.
Fasten metal binder bars where carpet edge will be exposed. Attach tackless strips near the walls.

1. Staple the pad in front of the tackless strips; allow the pad to overlap the strips, and butt seams together tightly.

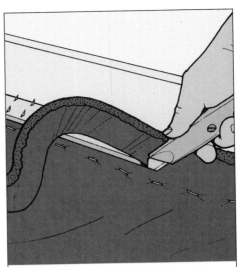

2. Trim the pad against the tackless strips with a utility knife; angle the cut inward slightly to prevent the pad from climbing onto the strips.

You will need to rent two tools for stretching the carpet: a knee-kicker and a power stretcher, both available at your carpet dealer. You may want to rent a carpet cutter, too.

Tackless Strips and Binder Bars.
Despite their name, tackless strips are strips of wood that are pierced through with numerous tacks. Their name comes from the fact that they eliminate the need for individual carpet tacks. Install tackless strips around the perimeter of the room with the tacks slanting toward the walls. Cut the strips with a hand saw, and nail them down a distance from the wall equal to two thirds the thickness of the carpet. When you have determined this distance, use a cardboard or wooden spacer so that you can place all the strips evenly. Attach metal binder bars in doorways and other places where the carpeting ends without a wall. The binder bar in the doorway should be directly under the door when it is closed.

Laying the Padding

1. Cover the Floor with Padding.
Cut the padding so that it covers the entire floor. Butt pieces evenly at any seams. If the padding has a waf-

fle pattern, that side goes up. Staple the padding down at 6-inch intervals around the perimeter of the room, and any other places where you think it might slip. On non-wooden floors, use the adhesive your carpet dealer suggests.

2. Trim Excess Padding. After fastening the padding securely all around the room, trim off the overlap with a sharp utility knife just along the inside of the tackless strips. Leave a 1/8- to 1/4-inch gap between the tackless strip and the pad. If the padding is urethane or rubber, tilt the knife

slightly away from the wall to create a beveled edge that will prevent the pad from climbing.

Making Rough Cuts. Roll out the carpet in a large, clean, dry, and flat area. Measure very carefully and allow at least a 3-inch overlap for the perimeter of the room and for any seams. You should cut loop-pile carpeting from the front. Snap the chalk line and cut it with a utility knife. But you should cut cut-pile carpeting from the back. First, notch the ends of the cut; then fold the carpet over and make chalk lines on the back between

Chalk Line

Cut-Pile Carpet

Making Rough Cuts. How you cut carpet will depend on the type. Cut-pile is cut from the back; loop-pile, from the front. Use a utility knife, or rent special carpet cutters.

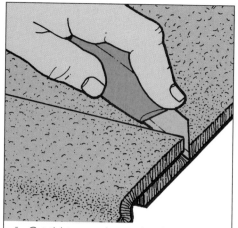

1. Cut tight seams by overlapping the fitted piece on the piece to be cut; use the top piece as the cutting guide.

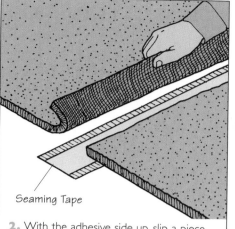

Seaming Tape

2. With the adhesive side up, slip a piece of seaming tape, cut to length, directly under the carpet seam.

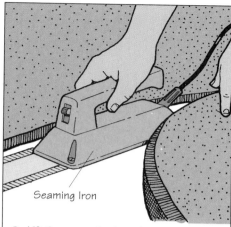

Seaming Iron

3. Lift the carpet back, and run a hot seaming iron over the tape; press the carpet onto the heated adhesive.

the notches. Cut along the line with a utility or carpet knife, taking care to cut only the backing.

Seaming the Carpet

1. Overlap and Cut the Carpet. To cut a seam, place one piece of carpeting over the other so that the overlap is about 1 inch. Use the top piece as a guide to cut the bottom piece.

2. Apply the Seaming Tape. Make sure the two pieces butt tightly. Then situate a length of hot-melt seaming tape directly under the seam. Make sure the adhesive side is up and the printed center is aligned with the edge of the carpet. Warm up a seaming iron to 250 degrees F.

3. Bond the Carpet to the Tape. Hold back one edge of the carpet, and slip the seaming iron under the edge of the other piece. Hold the iron on the tape for about 30 seconds. Then slide it slowly along the tape while you press both halves of the carpet down onto the heated adhesive. Go slowly and be sure the two edges are butting. If not, pull them together and place a heavy object on them until they have time to bond to the tape. Let the seam set.

Installing the Carpet

1. Hook the Carpet. Cut all corners so that the carpet lies flat; cut away the excess from inside corners, and cut around grates and other

obstacles. First hook the carpet at one corner (point A in top Drawing 3 on next page) by placing the knee-kicker about 1 inch from the tackless strip at a slight angle to the wall. Bump the kicker with your knee so that it moves the carpet and hooks it onto the tackless strip.

2. Stretch the Carpet. Use a power stretcher to pull the carpet taut from the hooked corner to the corner at the other end of the wall. Pull the carpet with minimal force so that it doesn't tear.

3. Stretch, Hook, and Affix the Carpet. Using your hands and a hammer, press the edge of the carpet onto the tackless strip along AB,

1. Set the end of the knee-kicker 1 inch from the tackless strip, and jam the carpet up over the strip.

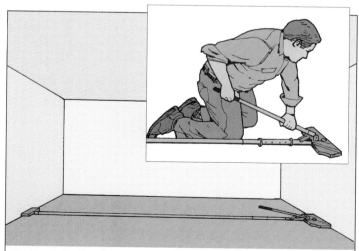

2. Crank the handle on the power stretcher to extend the bar and stretch the carpet. Apply only enough force to move the carpet; otherwise, it will tear.

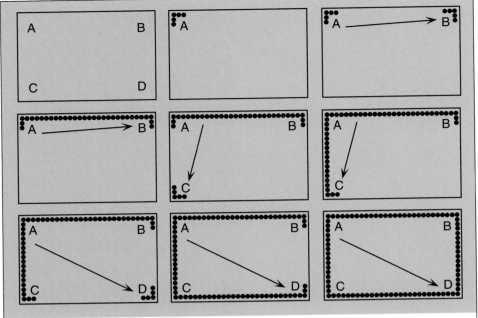

3. Carpeting should be installed in the sequence shown above. The circles indicate points of attachment, and the arrows indicate the direction of stretching.

2. Tuck in the Carpet Edge.
Use a putty knife to push the edge of the carpet into the gully between the tackless strip and the wall. If the carpet edge bunches up and creates an unsightly bulge, trim it a bit to make it shorter.

3. Clamp the Carpet to the Binder Bars. The final step is to clamp the carpet to the binder bars at the doorways and wherever else you have installed them. Trim the carpet with a utility knife so that it will fit under the binder bar. Tuck the carpet under the metal lip. Then, with a block of wood and a hammer, gently tap the lip down over the carpet edge so that it holds firmly.

shown in the drawing. Then follow the sequence shown in the drawing to hook, stretch, and affix the carpet. Stretch the carpet from A toward C, where it is hooked with the kicker, and press edge AC onto the strip. Next, stretch from A to D, hook at D, and affix along CD, using a kicker, your hands, and a hammer. Leave the stretcher in place, and use the kicker to hook BD onto the tackless strip.

Check the carpet to make sure it is evenly stretched. If the seams or the pattern are distorted, unhook the carpet and stretch it again.

Finishing the Job

1. Trim the Carpet at the Wall.
Trim the carpeting between the wall and the tackless strip. Use a rented wall trimmer to make the job easy. If you can't get one, a utility knife will do. First adjust the trimmer to the thickness of the carpet. Slice downward into the carpeting at a 45-degree angle, leveling it out when you reach the floor, and leaving just enough edging to tuck down into the gap between the strip and the wall. Make cuts in corners and around obstacles with a utility knife.

1. Cut the carpet at the wall with a rented wall trimmer, or use a utility knife if a trimmer is not available. Leave enough carpet to be tucked against the wall.

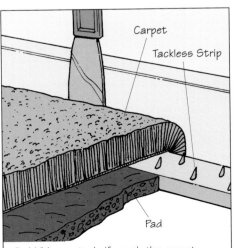

2. With a putty knife, push the carpet down between the tackless strip and the wall.

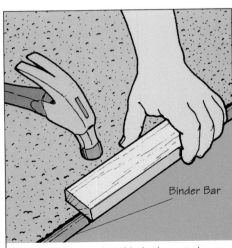

3. Slip the carpet into binder bars at doorways, and close bars with gentle taps on a wood block.

REPAIRING CARPETS

There are two secrets to making carpet repairs: One is to work slowly and patiently, and the other is to have scraps of extra carpet on hand from previous installations. If you have no scraps, take patches for holes from unseen areas like the back of a closet or under furniture you never move.

You can often repair small areas by setting in new tufts with a tuft setter. Tuft-setters are available from carpet dealers.

To patch a ripped carpet, fold back the torn section and apply latex seam adhesive to the backing. Tuck the torn part back into the carpet; then use a large bottle and a smooth rolling action to press it. If adhesive oozes up, clean it with water and detergent. When the adhesive has dried, replace any loose or missing pile as explained below.

If the rip goes through the backing, release the tension, using a knee-kicker in the corner nearest the rip. Lift the corner off the tacks and roll it back. With thread to match the color of the pile, mend the rip with 1-inch-long stitches spaced ¼ inch apart. Depending on the direction of the rip, run the stitches either parallel to rows of pile or perpendicular to them. Check frequently to make sure you

are not stitching the pile down on the face of the carpet. Then work in a thin, wavy strip of adhesive and cover the wet backing with a paper towel. Roll the carpet back to the wall and rehook it on the tacks.

Always match the pattern of any carpeting, and keep patches and tufts of pile oriented in the same direction as the rest of the carpet.

Patching a Small Area. Cut the damaged pile down to the backing with a cuticle scissors, and pick out pile stubs with tweezers. Then apply a little latex cement to the backing. Set replacement tufts, cut from the edge of a piece of scrap carpet, into the cement. For loop pile, poke one end of a long piece of yarn into the backing and make successive loops, adjusting the length accordingly.

Patching a Large Area

1. Reduce Carpet Tension. Reduce the tension slightly with a knee-kicker, and tack down strips of carpet on all four sides of the damaged area.

2. Remove the Damaged Section. Use a screwdriver and framing square to gently separate carpet-pile tufts, exposing carpet backing along a square-cornered outline. Then, as shown, use a utility knife and framing square to cut through the carpet backing. Remove the damaged section. If

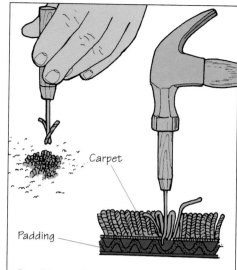

Patching a Small Area. Remove pile down to the backing in the damaged area; for the repair, use a tuft setter and tufts cut from scraps of the same carpet.

the undercushion is also damaged, cut and remove it too. Repeating the same techniques, mark and cut a replacement patch the exact size of the removed section. (If the carpet has a pattern, first match the replacement section's pattern to it.)

3. Install the Replacement Patch. Apply seam cement to backing, as shown, after having slipped double-faced carpet tape partway under the existing carpet. Press the replacement patch carefully into place. To hide the seam, use the screwdriver to gently interweave pile tufts of the two pieces of carpeting.

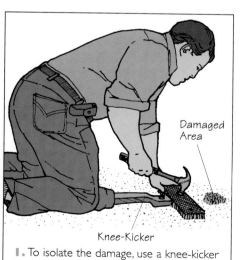

1. To isolate the damage, use a knee-kicker to slacken tension as you tack upside-down strips of scrap carpet on all four sides.

2. After parting pile tufts with a screwdriver, use a utility knife to cut through carpet backing. Remove the damaged section.

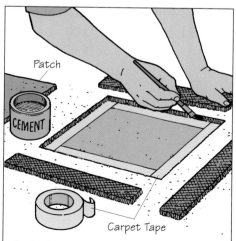

3. Apply seam cement, after having slipped double-faced carpet tape partway under existing carpeting. Press the patch into place.

LAYING CERAMIC-TILE FLOORS

Ceramic tiles provide a durable, easy-to-maintain surface that is particularly well-suited for kitchens and baths, but will complement practically any room setting and all furnishings. To help your tile dealer suggest which tiles are best for you, and how many you'll need, make a scale drawing of your room on graph paper. Be sure to order about 10 percent extra tiles for mistakes, trimming, and cracked or chipped pieces. You'll also want to have a few on hand for repairs.

In deciding on color and design, remember that floors with busy patterns or several colors tend to look smaller. Small tiles give the illusion that the floor is larger; large tiles make the floor look smaller. Similarly, dark colors make the floor look smaller, and light colors make the floor seem larger.

There are several different types of adhesives, but manufacturers recommend specific kinds for their tiles. For most applications, you can use a "thin-set" rather than a heavy mortar base. Thin-set adhesives come with cement, organic, and epoxy bases. Cement bases are excellent for applying tiles to concrete or masonry subfloors. Organic bases, called mastics, are easy to apply, but many are not waterproof and won't hold up in wet areas such as bathrooms. Epoxy is the strongest base, having high bonding power, but it hardens quickly and is therefore trickier to work with. Both organic and epoxy adhesives can irritate the skin, eyes, and lungs, so you should wear gloves, goggles, and a respirator.

Installing the Tiles

Ceramic tiles should be installed only over sound subfloors. Concrete is the best subfloor, but it must be dry, clean, and free of holes. Some adhesives require that a sealer be laid on concrete before they can be spread. A plywood base is suitable if the panels are exterior grade and securely fastened to the joists, and also if the structure itself is strong and stiff enough to support the weight of the floor without flexing. Sound, single-layer linoleum and vinyl floors will take ceramic tiles; but multiple layers, or even a single layer of cushioned resilient flooring, is too soft and springy and should be removed.

1. Lay Out Test Rows. First, decide on the width of your grout joints. This will depend on the size of the tiles, the look you want to achieve, and the application. (Wider grout lines are harder to keep clean.) Some tiles come with nubs that space them apart, and you can make the job easier by letting these nubs determine grout spacing. Or, you can purchase plastic spacers. These come in various sizes and are left in place as you lay the tile.

Let's say, for example, that you are using 12-inch-square tiles with a $\frac{1}{4}$-inch grout line. Starting $\frac{1}{4}$ inch from adjacent walls, lay out a row of properly spaced tiles. Unless you are extremely lucky, the space at the end of the row will be equal to less than a full tile. Whatever the leftover distance, subtract one grout line and divide the remainder in half. Let's say the leftover space is $8\frac{1}{2}$ inches. In the example, you would start each row with a $4\frac{1}{8}$-inch-wide piece of tile. Of course, you don't want to work with slivers of tiles. So if the leftover space is small, you may want to cut tiles on only one side, or you might even be able to use full tiles by adjusting the grout-line width. Repeat this process for the adjacent wall.

2. Snap Starting Lines. Lay out starting lines to define the inside edges of the first row of tiles as shown. (This distance from the wall equals one grout joint plus the width of the cut starter tile.) Make sure the lines intersect at a 90-degree angle. If

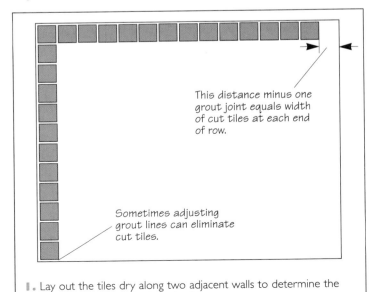

This distance minus one grout joint equals width of cut tiles at each end of row.

Sometimes adjusting grout lines can eliminate cut tiles.

1. Lay out the tiles dry along two adjacent walls to determine the size of the cut tiles on both ends of the row.

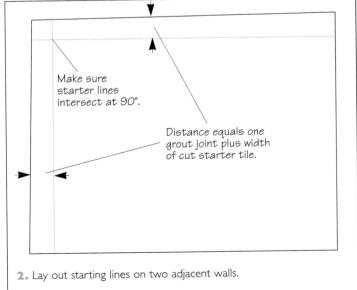

Make sure starter lines intersect at 90°.

Distance equals one grout joint plus width of cut starter tile.

2. Lay out starting lines on two adjacent walls.

3. Use a snap cutter to cut the partial tiles for each end of the rows. Lift and drag the handle to score the tile. Then hit the handle sharply downward to snap the tile.

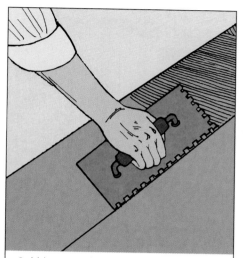

4. Using a notched trowel that meets the adhesive manufacturer's specifications, spread the adhesive evenly, leaving work lines visible.

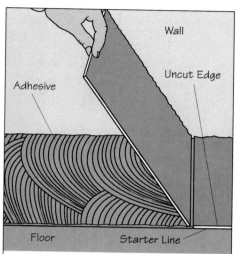

5. Place the starter rows of cut tiles in the adhesive with the cut edge toward the wall.

the angle is 90 degrees and the lines get farther away from the walls as you leave the intersection, your walls are out of square. If the problem is slight, you can let the size of the grout joints increase along the walls. If the problem is severe, you'll have to cus-tom-cut the tiles. If the distance from the wall decreases as you leave the intersection, put the intersection at the opposing corner so the distance will increase.

3. Cut the Partial Tiles. Cut all the border tiles now, using a snap cutter. With a felt-tip pen, mark the tile, and position it in the cutter with the pen line directly under the scor-ing wheel. Hold the tile with one hand; and with the other, lift the handle and pull it toward you to score the tile. Next, position the handle over the lower third of the tile, pressing the handle down slight-ly with your thumb; with the heel of your other hand, strike the handle sharply to snap the tile. Test fit these tiles with their uncut sides against the starter lines and their cut sides toward the walls.

4. Spread Adhesive. Use a notched trowel to spread the adhesive be-tween the walls and the starter lines. The size of the notches will determine how thickly the adhesive is laid

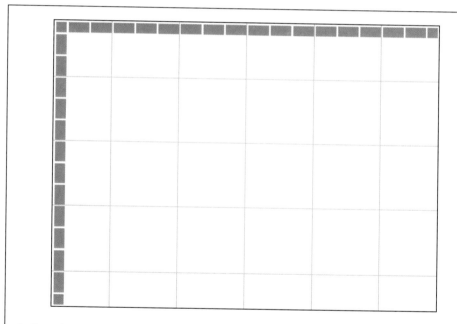

6. Snap the guidelines every three rows or so to ensure that the tiles are running in a straight line.

down. Use a trowel with notch sizes recommended on the label of the adhesive can. Note carefully the time you have to work with the adhesive before it dries. Always spread the adhesive just up to the chalk lines, with enough left exposed to guide you in laying the tiles.

5. Lay Tiles along Starter Lines. Lay the first two adjacent rows of tiles in the adhesive with their uncut edges against the starter lines. When laying

tiles, place each one where it should go, and wiggle it with a gentle twist-ing motion to get it into place. Insert a plastic spacer (if you are using plastic spacers), and lay the next tile. If you discover that the tiles are running out of line with each other, wiggle them into position rather than lifting them off the adhesive.

6. Lay Out Guidelines. Tiles are rarely perfectly uniform, especially handmade tiles. So it is a good idea to

7. When laying individual tiles, seat them firmly into the adhesive by tapping on a bedding block covered with old carpet.

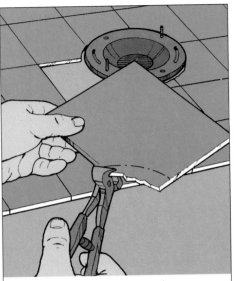

8. Use nippers to make curved cuts for fitting tiles around such objects as toilet flanges.

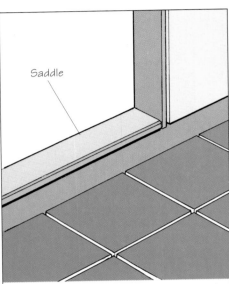

9. If you are finishing a doorway with a saddle, put it in place with adhesive before cutting tiles to fill the border.

snap grid guidelines along the floor so you can check and adjust alignment every three or four rows. Use the grout lines you established in the first two adjacent rows as a guide.

7. **Bed the Tiles.** After laying several rows of adjoining tiles, bed them so that they are level with each other. An easy way to do this is to make a bedding block. Use a block of wood large enough to cover several tiles at once, and cover it with a padding of felt or thin carpet. Then bed the tiles by laying the block over several rows and tapping it firmly with a hammer. Slide the bedding block along the tiles, and continue tapping it firmly to achieve a smooth, even surface. Every so often, use a framing square to check positioning and a level to check the bedding. Make adjustments as necessary.

8. **Make Curved Cuts.** To cut a tile to fit around a curving obstruction, such as a toilet flange, use nippers. If the obstruction has a complex shape, make a cardboard template, trace the shape onto the tile, and cut it with nippers.

9. **Lay a Saddle.** Cut off the bottom of the door if necessary. Apply adhesive to the floor and the bottom of the saddle. Leave a thin gap on each

side between the saddle and the door jamb, and a normal grout joint between the saddle and the tile floor. After installing the saddle, fill in the border tiles.

Grouting

1. **Apply Tile Grout.** Using a rubber-faced float or a squeegee, spread the grout over the face of the tiles and force it down into the joints between them. Then scrape off the excess with a squeegee or float. Work diagonally across the tiles; and as you remove the excess, check to make sure the joints are

filled and there are no air pockets.

2. **Clean Tiles with a Damp Sponge.** When the grout becomes firm, wipe the tiles with a sponge soaked in clean water. Rinse the sponge frequently, changing the water when it gets dirty.

3. **Tool the Joints.** Smooth and shape the grout joints with a convex striking tool, a tapered piece of wood, or the end of a toothbrush. Then clean off the tiles and smooth the joints with a damp sponge.

Wait about 30 minutes for a thin haze to appear on the tile surface, and

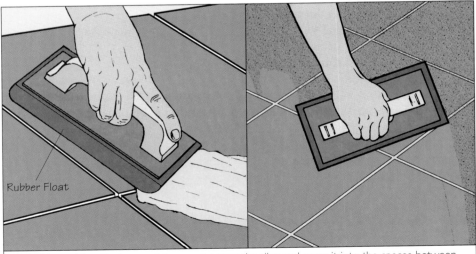

Rubber Float

1. With a rubber float, spread the grout across the tiles and press it into the spaces between tiles.

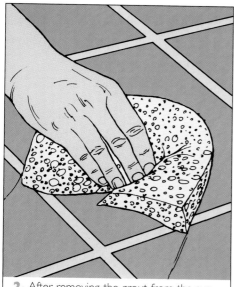

2. After removing the grout from the surface with the float, clean the floor with a sponge, rinsing it frequently.

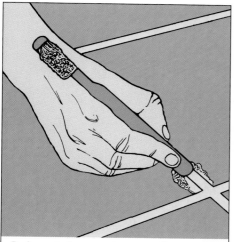

3. Smooth the grout between tiles with any rounded tool, leaving a slight depression. The handle of a toothbrush works well.

wipe it off with a clean, damp cloth. Put plywood over the floor to keep from stepping on new grout. Some grout can take two weeks to cure; check the length of time the manufacturer suggests. When cured, the grout should be sealed.

Sealing Unglazed Tile. Before grouting unglazed tile you should seal it. Use a damp cloth to wipe away any dried adhesive on the tile surface. With a screwdriver or other pointed tool, scrape out any adhesive that may have squeezed up between tiles. Let the tiles set for the length of time the manufacturer of your adhe-

sive recommends. After the tiles have set completely, apply a sealer the tile manufacturer recommends. The easiest way to apply the sealer is with a foam roller.

Caulking. You should caulk the gap between the tile and the wall, as well as any joints larger than your established grout joint, especially around the walls in a bathroom or any areas that will be subject to prolonged wetness.

Sealing Unglazed Tile. Unglazed tile should be sealed with the sealant the tile manufacturer recommends. Apply this sealant with a foam roller.

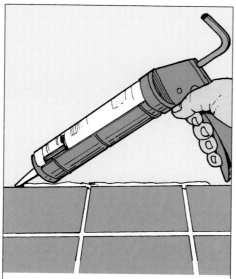

Caulking. Use silicone caulking compound in a caulking gun to fill gaps between the floor and walls, and especially between a tub and the floor.

INSTALLING WOOD STRIP FLOORING

Installing a wood strip or plank floor is a job requiring thorough knowledge of the process and certain expertise in handling wood. If you are undertaking this project for the first time, study the procedure in detail, so you know what you're getting into before you start.

Most common types of wood flooring are graded according to color, grain, and imperfections such as streaks and knots. Ash, oak and pine boards are designated in order of decreasing quality as follows: clear, select, No. 1 common, and No. 2 common. Birch, beech, maple, and pecan are designated from best to worst as first grade, second grade, and third grade. When ordering 2¼-inch-wide flooring (the most popular size), multiply the number of square feet in the room by 1.383 to determine the amount of board feet you will need, including waste. For strips or planks of other sizes, ask your dealer how to compute the quantity.

The subfloor must be adequately prepared to receive the new flooring. A wood floor will make a good subfloor if there are no seriously damaged areas. Drive down all nails flush, and replace badly damaged boards or panels. With a resilient-tile floor, be sure the tiles are all fixed tightly; replace or re-cement any loose ones. If a wood or tile floor is badly damaged, lay a new subfloor.

Concrete makes a good subfloor if it is dry and level, but if it is at or below ground level, see "Installing Wood Flooring in a Basement," page 134, for the recommended flooring products and installation techniques.

To prepare the room, remove the shoe moldings and base trim (numbering the pieces so that you can replace them in the same sequence), radiator grates, and floor vents. Also lay a piece of new flooring near the door to see what may need to be shaved off to permit an unobstructed swing. Allow for the height of the threshold if there will be one.

1. Put Down Building Paper.

Mark the joist positions on the walls. Lay a covering of 15-pound building paper over the subfloor. Butt the seams tightly, and cut the edges flush with the walls. Staple the edges of the sheets to the floor, making sure the staples are set flush. Then snap the chalk lines marking the positions of the joists.

2. Snap the Starting Line.

Because you'll be installing the flooring across the joists, make sure the walls running perpendicular to the joists are parallel. Measure the distance between the walls at several locations, and if the measurements are within ½ inch of each other, snap a starting line along one of the walls. If you are using 2¼-inch-wide flooring, position the line so that it is 2¾ inches from the wall. (The extra ½ inch allows for an expansion gap between the flooring and the wall.)

If the walls aren't parallel, you'll have to snap a starting line that is half as skewed as the walls. For example, if the walls are out of parallel by 2 inches, snap the starting line 2¾ inches from the wall at one end, and 3¾ inches from the wall at the other. Again, these dimensions assume you are installing 2¼-inch-wide flooring. Always leave at least ½ inch between the flooring and the wall. Any gap between the first course and the wall can be filled with strips trimmed to fit or covered by the base trim and shoe molding.

3. Install a Starter Course.

With tongues facing out, lay out the starter course (the first row of strips) the full length of the wall. The bottom edge of the strips must align with the starting line, with the tongues extending beyond the line. Drill holes along the back edges of the strips and over the joists, slightly smaller than the nails.

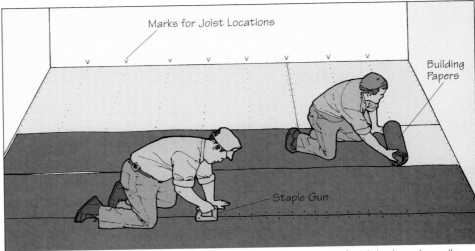

1. After marking the joist locations on the wall, cut building paper to fit tightly along the walls; staple down the sheets with seams butted together.

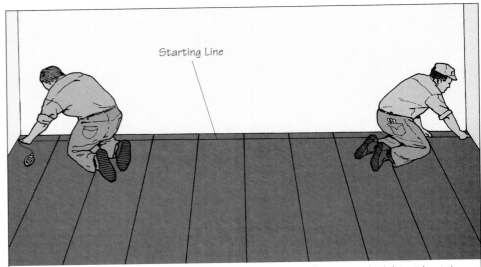

2. After snapping lines to show joist locations, snap a starting line across the joists at least the width of the flooring strips plus ½ inch from the wall.

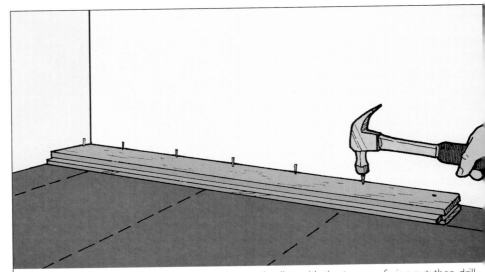

3. Position the first course of strips along the starting line with the tongues facing out; then drill the back edge, and face-nail the strips to the joists with 8d finishing nails. Set the nails.

Then face-nail with 8d finishing nails, setting them below the surface.

4. Nail through a Tongue. The first few rows of flooring strips will be too close to the wall for you to use a power nailer. Holding a drill at a 45-degree angle, bore holes through the tongue of the first course of strips into the joists. Drive in spiral-shank nails most of the way; then use a nail set to drive them the rest of the way and set them.

5. Lay a Field. Lay out several courses of strips in the way you intend to install them. Plan six or seven rows ahead in an attractive layout. Stagger the end joints so that each joint is more than 6 inches from the joints in the adjoining rows. Leave $1/2$ inch between the end of each course and the wall. If you can't find pieces the right length, cut them to fit at the end of each row. Try to fit your pattern so that no end piece is shorter than 8 inches. When you have laid out a field of rows, begin to fit and nail.

6. Fit and Nail the Flooring. Use a scrap of flooring as a tapping block to bring the piece you are installing tight to the flooring that is already nailed down. Then fasten the strips to the joists and every 8 inches between. Although you must nail the first few rows by hand, the rest of the floor will go faster if you use a floor nailer, which you'll find at a tool-rental shop. Beginning about 2 inches from the wall, slip the floor nailer onto the tongue of the strip. Hold the board in position by placing your heel over it. With a rubber-headed mallet, strike the plunger hard enough to drive a nail through the tongue and into the floor. Drive a nail into each joist and into the sub-floor halfway between joists.

7. Cut around Obstacles. When you come to an obstacle such as a radiator or a corner, butt the end of the strip against the obstacle and mark it. Then butt the strip against the wall, and mark the obstacle along the edge of the strip. Join the marks using a try square. Clamp the strip to a workbench, and cut out the waste with a saber saw. If the cut is complex, make a cardboard

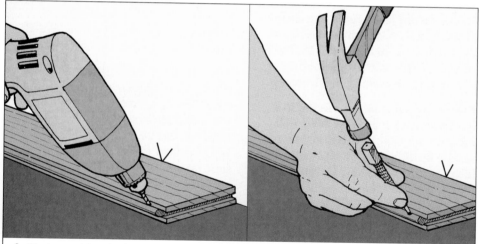

4. Most wood flooring is quite hard, so drill pilot holes at an angle over the places marked for joists. Hammer spiral-shank nails most of the way home; then finish with a nail set.

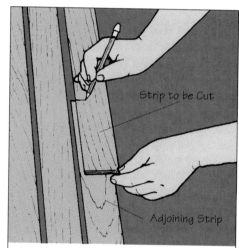

Strip to be Cut

Adjoining Strip

5. Butt strips to be cut against the wall, and mark where the adjoining strip ends.

Scrap Tapping Block

Floor Nailer

6. Fit strips together tightly by using a scrap piece of flooring as a tapping block. After hand-nailing the first few courses, use a rented floor nailer to fasten the strips to the joists and halfway between them. Strike the plunger sharply with a rubber mallet.

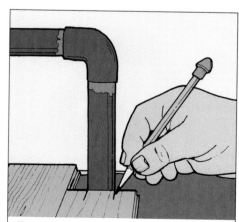

7. Butt the flooring up to the obstacle, and mark the strip end; then butt the strip against the wall, and mark the strip edge. Connect the marks using a try square.

8. Usually, the last course of boards must be ripped narrower and face-nailed. To get this last course tight against the rest of the floor, use a pry bar to lever it into position.

template to transfer the cut onto the board.

8. Install the Final Course. For gaps of more than ½ inch between the final strip and the wall, remove the tongue sides of as many strips as you need, cut them to width, and wedge them into place with a pry bar. Hold them tightly with the pry bar by placing your foot on the bar while its hooked end pulls the filler up tightly against the last strip. (Place a scrap of wood behind the bar to avoid marring the wall.) Face-nail these last strips, and then replace the base trim and shoe moldings.

Special Situations

Reversing Direction. If you intend to lay wood strip flooring in hallways or closets that open off the room, you may have to butt two strips groove edge to groove edge, at the transition point. You can join the groove edge by placing a slip tongue, available from flooring dealers, into the grooves of the last course of strips nailed down. Turn the next course of strips around so that the groove edge adjoins the slip tongue. Then nail the reversed strips into place, driving the nails through the tongues, and proceed as usual.

Framing Borders. Obstacles such as fireplace corners should have a professionally finished look. You can do this with a miter box to cut strips at 45-degree angles to make the corners of the frame. You'll have to remove the tongues from any strips that will run perpendicular to the flooring or that must butt against hearthstones.

Finishing Doorways. To finish a doorway where the new floor will meet a floor that is lower, install a saddle or threshold by face-nailing it into the subfloor. Some thresholds, called reducer strips, are made so that one side will fit over the tongue of the adjoining flooring strip. Also, the saddle can be butted to meet strips that run perpendicular to the doorway.

INSTALLING WOOD FLOORING IN A BASEMENT

A wood floor adds beauty and warmth to any room; but in a basement, dampness can cause traditional solid-wood flooring to swell, buckle, and even rot. Laminated wood flooring, on the other hand, is a viable alternative to solid wood flooring in a basement. Because laminated flooring is made from layers of wood plies, it is more stable than solid wood. It can also be installed where ordinary wood flooring might have problems, say below grade and over concrete. Because of this stability, the flooring can be installed as a floating floor system over a ⅛-inch-thick layer of high-density foam underlayment. The tongue-and-groove joints are glued; no nails are used in the installation.

Prefinished laminated wood flooring comes with a factory-applied, finished topcoat. This will save you the work and expense of finishing the flooring, but be aware that the hardwood veneer of the flooring is quite thin, so you won't be able to sand and refinish the flooring when the finish wears down. The flooring is ½ inch thick and comes either in strips 2 to 4 inches wide or in planks more than 4 inches wide. When they

Reversing Direction. Where you must change the direction of the tongue-and-groove pattern, butt flooring strips groove to groove with a slip tongue between.

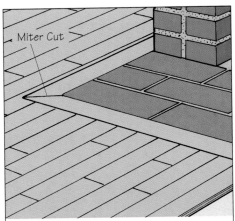

Framing Borders. Treat flooring as you would trim to border such areas as a hearth. Miter the strips, and rip off the tongue where necessary to fit.

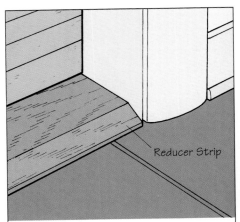

Finishing Doorways. A reducer strip is nailed over the edge of the flooring at a doorway to make a smooth transition from the flooring to a lower surface in another room.

are installed, the planks are often made of a number of narrow strips assembled to resemble strip flooring.

Although this section describes the installation of laminated wood flooring in a basement, this material may be laid over any smooth, dry, level subfloor.

Installing a Floating Floor

1. Put Down a Vapor Barrier. After sweeping the floor slab, cover it with clear plastic sheets, known as 6-mil polyethylene. Overlap each seam by a minimum of 6 inches, and let the sheets lap up the wall about 3 inches. Lift up the edges of the polyethylene, and use a caulking gun to put down dabs of construction adhesive to hold it in place. Adhere the plastic sheets to the walls with a bead of adhesive.

2. Put Down the Foam. Roll out the foam underlayment and cut it to fit the room. Butt the joints, and seal them with duct tape.

3. Lay the Planks. Leave a ½-inch expansion gap around the perimeter of the room. Start the installation on the longest wall of the basement, with the tongue facing away from the wall.

4. Join the Planks. Try to work in room-length runs. Join the planks by running a bead of carpenter's glue in the bottom edge of the groove as you install each succeeding section.

5. Finish the Job. Tap the sections together tightly with a hammer and a scrap piece of flooring as a hammering block. Mark, cut, and install planks in irregular areas just as you would a normal wood floor.

1. Roll polyethylene over the floor, overlapping the seams by at least 6 inches. Press the polyethelene into dabs of construction adhesive on the slab.

2. Roll out foam underlayment, and trim it to fit the room. Butt any seams rather than overlapping them.

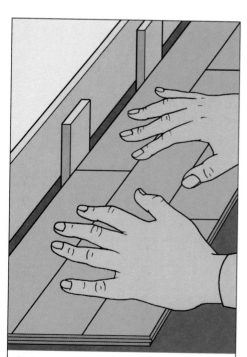

3. Leave an expansion gap of ½ inch around the room's perimeter, and begin laying the planking with the groove side against the wall.

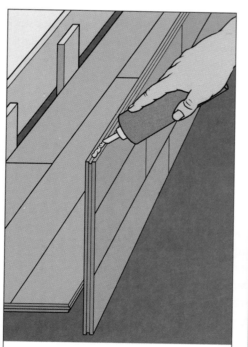

4. Squeeze carpenter's glue into the bottom of each groove, and then join the panels, tongue to groove.

5. With a hammer and block of scrap flooring, tap the joint tight along the entire run of planks.

CEILINGS

In frame construction, ceilings consist of a surface material, usually drywall or plaster over lath, attached to ceiling joists. If you're renovating a room, don't overlook the ceiling. Sometimes, a new coat of paint alone can rejuvenate an existing ceiling; other times, you must fix small areas of damage, resurface the ceiling, or even install a completely new ceiling. You can also add molding or beams. Ceilings with an attic or roof above allow you to install a skylight, but they also offer easy access for repairs. If there's a finished floor over the ceiling, you'll need to do your ceiling work from below, and that makes the work messier and more complicated.

Structure

Although a detailed description of how to lay out and frame a ceiling is beyond the scope of this book, two projects involve altering the existing ceiling framing. "Finishing Attic Ceilings," page 159, discusses how to frame a flat ceiling and how to use the existing rafters to create a sloped cathedral ceiling. It also includes suggestions for handling the joints between sloped ceilings and walls. The most complex ceiling project, "Installing Skylights," page 161, discusses how to make an opening in the roof and frame a light well. Skylight installations are a lot of work, but the effect of natural light overhead in a room makes the effort well worthwhile.

As a house settles over time, ceilings can sag or crack. This is a common problem in older homes with lath-and-plaster ceilings, and one solution is to remove the old ceiling and install a new one. Although removing the old surface is a lot of work, it gives you the opportunity to level the old joists using furring strips and shims. This procedure is discussed in "Hanging a Drywall Ceiling," page 148.

Surface

Whether you have new construction, an old ceiling in bad shape, or one that has never been finished, like an unfinished basement or attic, "Hanging a Drywall Ceiling," page 148-149, provides tips and techniques that simplify the tough, awkward job of lifting, holding, and installing drywall panels overhead. Once the seams are taped and finished, a drywall surface can be either

For pitched ceilings, the challenge is often to provide enough headroom, while still providing good ceiling insulation in order to retain room heat in winter and repel roof heat in summer.

The ceiling-to-roof depth shown would allow adequate insulation in most climates, as well as a ventilating airspace between insulation and roof.

When shopping for skylights, consider weather seals, quality of glazing, means of opening, and options for shades that can insulate by day and night.

painted or wallpapered. If your ceiling has extensive damage, especially an old plaster ceiling, you can use the information in "Resurfacing a Ceiling with Drywall," page 149, to impart a new look to an old ceiling without a lot of tedious patching. Instead, this section tells how to fasten a new drywall surface directly over the old ceiling surface and then tape and finish it as you would a wall.

If a ceiling has only minor damage, such as water stains or a few small cracks or holes, "Repairing Ceiling Damage," page 152, gives you instructions for repainting, patching, and finishing both plaster and drywall. On the other hand, if you are finishing a ceiling, you should consider whether soundproofing is necessary. One way

to soundproof a ceiling is to quiet the floor above with insulation board and hardboard covered with carpet. This will take care of impact noise only. To reduce airborne sound, you'll need to install resilient channels, insulation board, and a new drywall ceiling. Both procedures are discussed in "Soundproofing Ceilings," page 153.

Sometimes, you may want an attractive ceiling surface to cover up pipes and wires, but you also want access to these items for maintenance and repairs. "Installing a Suspended Ceiling," page 155, explains the process for hanging a metal gridwork from the ceiling joists and laying in panels (sometimes called ceiling tiles) that can be removed easily when you need to inspect the ceiling.

Finish

Ceilings offer lots of design opportunities, many of which can change the character of a room without altering its structure. If you have removed a bearing wall and have added a beam, you can disguise it by adding other beams, as described in "Making and Installing False Beams," beginning on page 164. By following the instructions outlined in "Installing Ceiling Molding," page 166, you'll learn how to lay out, cut and install crown or cove molding with tight joints. You'll also learn how to solve special molding problems. For example, some elaborate crown moldings are better avoided. And it's possible to create nailing surfaces when walls parallel to ceiling joists leave no structural wood to nail to.

Beaded wood paneling serves well for ceilings when cut to 4-foot squares and framed in molding. Note the contrasting wider cornice molding.

Older homes with ceilings over 8 feet allow large, elaborate false beams that are easier to construct than might appear. A good design concept is key.

Here a collar-tie beam is clad in wide planks, which also conceal indirect lighting. The gable dormer at left would have required tedious mitering of interior corners; instead the builders opted for a simple strip molding that visually ties the shapes together. With so much woodwork on the ceiling, the wallpapered end gable provides welcome contrast.

Although fans are usually associated with cooling, a ceiling fan in a cathedral ceiling can be equally important for distributing room heat in colder seasons. Because heat rises naturally, ceiling fans can help keep warm air nearer floor level.

Skylights beyond reach can be wired to allow switch control of ventilation and blinds. For such large expanses of skylighting, it's often helpful if shade trees screen out summer sun.

A molding-clad structural beam can become a pleasing design element when crossed with a false beam. Here a clear wood finish adds a cheery touch.

For new homes, Early-American timber-frame construction enjoys wide popularity. Saws and chisels create the joints, and wooden pegs secure them. Most homeowners prefer to showcase, rather than hide, the hefty structural members.

Recalling the days when timber-frame construction was the norm, false beams remain a handsome design element. When installing the false beam surface, stagger joints to avoid a continuous broken line around the "beam."

Below, acoustical ceiling tiles are bordered by a floral strip of wallcovering mounted over drywall. The cornice consists of polyurethane crown molding with rosettes. The tiles reduce room noise, as well as noise transmitted to the room above. They can be set into adhesive applied over drywall or plaster, or they can be installed over wood furring or metal tracks.

When planning locations of skylights, consider how they will relate to structural wall elements. In this case, it was essential to align the skylights with the three-paneled doorway.

Suspended acoustical ceilings are popular for basements. In addition to dampening sound and covering floor joists, the panels easily lift out of the way for access to plumbing and wiring. They also simplify installation of recessed lighting that may be required because of reduced headroom.

In this children's room, with a cow jumping over the moon, each acoustical panel was painted individually. If you wish to paint acoustical panels, do so on a tabletop and let them dry flat before installation. Otherwise, water in the paint could cause the wet tiles to sag.

For the intersection of wall and ceiling, crown moldings are available in countless ornamental patterns. The dark stain for this molding matches that of the built-up beam and helps showcase the ceiling and its light fixture.

White paint was stripped from this ceiling to reveal the original wood. For a similar cathedral effect, it may be necessary to create a false ceiling with false rafters. That's because it's important to provide adequate insulation to retain heat in winter and repel roof heat in summer. It's also important to provide a free-circulating airspace above the insulation to carry off water vapor.

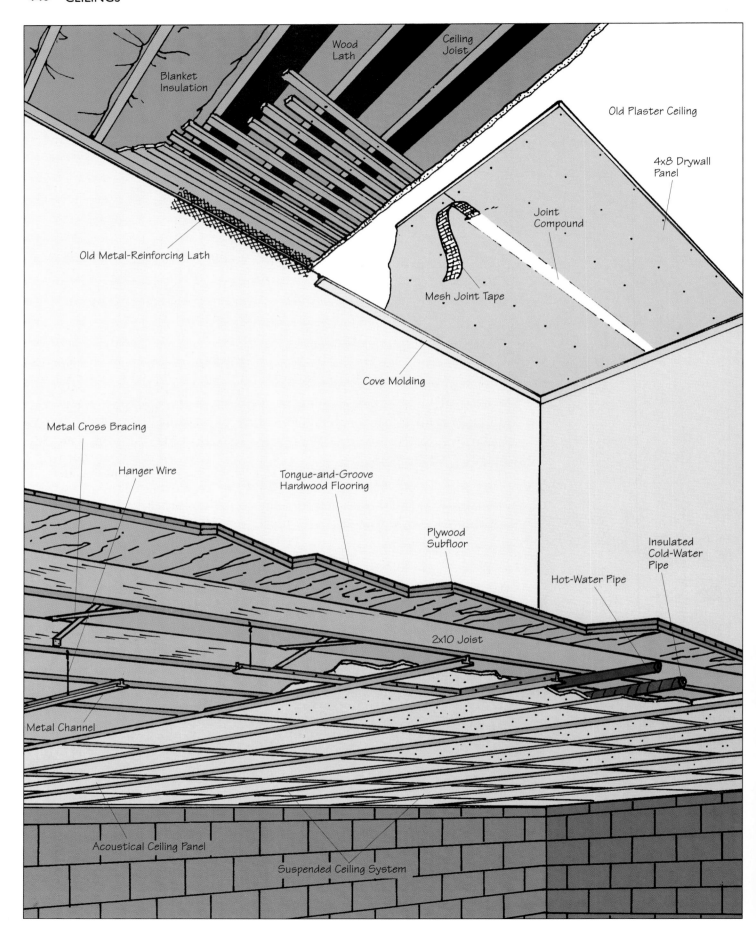

Wood Lath

Ceiling Joist

Blanket Insulation

Old Plaster Ceiling

4x8 Drywall Panel

Joint Compound

Old Metal-Reinforcing Lath

Mesh Joint Tape

Cove Molding

Metal Cross Bracing

Hanger Wire

Tongue-and-Groove Hardwood Flooring

Plywood Subfloor

Insulated Cold-Water Pipe

Hot-Water Pipe

2x10 Joist

Metal Channel

Acoustical Ceiling Panel

Suspended Ceiling System

HANGING A DRYWALL CEILING

Whether you're installing drywall in a newly framed room or resurfacing an old one, the ceiling is the place to begin. Drywall is a good choice for the ceiling surface because it's economical and attractive, and it won't sag. It is also the best choice if you need to soundproof the ceiling (see "Soundproofing Ceilings," page 153, for more information). However, putting drywall on a ceiling is a demanding job because you must work overhead. This section describes tools and techniques that will save you time and effort when hanging drywall on a ceiling. (To skin over an existing ceiling surface with drywall, see "Resurfacing a Ceiling with Drywall," page 149.)

Checking the Joists. Use a string to see if any joists are very high or low in relation to each other. Minor variations can be expected; but if one joist is more than about $3/4$ inch out of level, you should use 1x2s and tapered shims to "fur down" the high joist or fur down the joists on either side of one that's lower. The goal is to take out the serious humps and dents.

Providing Nailing Surfaces. Check along the walls parallel to the joists. Sometimes, a joist will sit right on top of a wall's top plate, leaving you no nailing surface for the ceiling drywall. If the joist doesn't stick out at least $3/4$ inch past the top plate, use 10d nails to attach 2x4s along the bottom of the joist; then build out the 2x4s, if necessary, with spacer blocks, as shown.

Planning the Job. Sheets of drywall are rectangular; they are fastened to the ceiling joists with the long edge perpendicular to the direction of the joists. The long edges of drywall panels are tapered so that joints may be finished flush with the drywall, using drywall compound. The short edges are not tapered, and joints along these edges—called butt joints—must be built up and feathered into a hardly noticeable hump. You should plan the job to maximize the amount of tapered joints and minimize butt joints. It is usually worth the extra trouble to put up the far heavier 10- or even 12-foot sheets to avoid butt joints. If you can't avoid them, it's a good idea to double the width of the joist where the butt joint will fall by sistering a 2x4 onto the joist. This provides a wider nailing surface

than a lone joist, making hanging easier. To make butt joints less apparent, stagger them so that no two are right next to each other. When you cut a sheet of drywall lengthwise, butt the cut edge against the wall.

Installing Temporary Bracing. Although you can install ceiling drywall by yourself, it's much easier for two people to handle the large, heavy panels. Because most of the work is done overhead, you and your helper should have solid step ladders. Better yet, you should consider renting a drywall jack, which lets you raise even 12-foot pieces with ease and put them exactly where you want them.

If you choose not to rent a drywall jack, make a T-brace, or deadman, to support the drywall as you're fastening it to the ceiling. To make the brace, cut two 2x4s: one $3/4$ inch longer than the ceiling height, and the other about 36 inches long. Using 8d nails, fasten the short piece perpendicular across the end of the long piece. Let the long edge of the short piece protrude about $1/4$ inch past the end of the long piece. When installing the new ceiling, wedge the brace between the drywall and the floor.

Checking the Ceiling. Hold a string under the joists at midspan to see if any are very high or low. Shim with 1x2 and shim stock, if necessary.

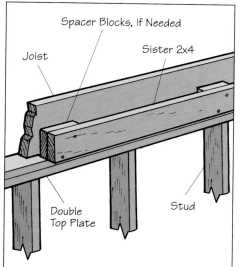

Providing Nailing Surfaces. If a joist sits too far back on the wall's top plate, provide a nailing surface by sistering a length of 2x4 onto the joist using 10d nails.

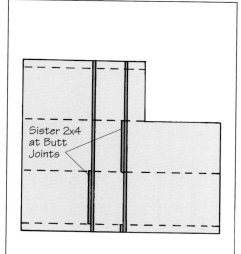

Planning the Job. Sketch a layout before cutting any drywall sheets. Plan where butt joints will fall, and sister 2x4s there onto the joists. Put cut edges against walls.

Installing Temporary Bracing. Use a T-brace to hold the sheet tight to the ceiling, and attach 2x4 cleats along the wall to hold the end of the drywall sheet temporarily in place. A rental drywall jack raises and positions even heavy 12-foot sheets against the ceiling.

screws just right: slightly dimpled, but not breaking the paper facing of the drywall.

Installing a Drywall Ceiling

1. Mark the Joist Locations.
On the top plate, mark the locations of the joists so that you will be able to mark them on the drywall when it is in place. If you tacked 2x4 cleats to the wall, mark them with the joist locations.

2. Measure for the Drywall.
Starting 2 feet from one corner of the ceiling, measure across the joists to find where the end of the first drywall sheet will fall. If it doesn't fall halfway across a joist, use a straightedge and a utility knife to trim the drywall sheet so that it will. (Or you can sister a 2x4 onto the joist to create a wider nailing surface; in this case, you should trim the sheet even with the sistered edge of the joist.) It's good practice to cut sheets about $\frac{1}{4}$ inch shorter than necessary to allow room to maneuver and to compensate for any irregularities in the cut edge.

Another way to hold drywall in place temporarily is to tack 2x4 cleats to the wall, positioned an inch or so down from the joists, to allow space to slip in the drywall sheets, as shown above. First snap chalk lines where you want the bases of the cleats. Then mount several short cleats with spaces between so that you can see when the drywall is tight against the top plate.

For fastening drywall to the framing, you can use either drywall nails, which have ringed shanks for holding power, or drywall screws. Screws hold better and won't pop over time; but unless you have a screw gun specially made for driving drywall screws, you'll find yourself setting many of the screws too deep. A screw gun automatically sets the

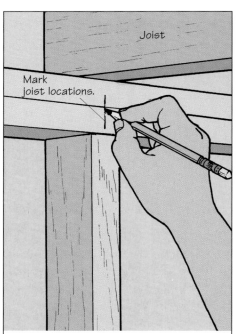

1. To make it easier to find the joists once they are covered, mark their locations on the studs or top plate.

2. Measure across the joists to see where the end of the sheet will fall. If it doesn't fall in the middle of a joist, trim the sheet so that it will, or add a sister 2x4 for nailing surface.

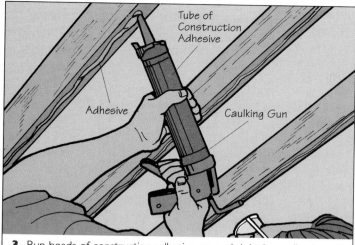

3. Run beads of construction adhesive on each joist immediately before installing the sheet.

4. Position the sheet carefully and brace it securely. Mark joist positions before driving 1⅝-inch drywall screws into the joists every 16 inches.

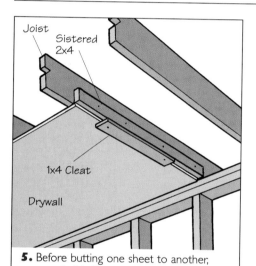

5. Before butting one sheet to another, screw a 1x4 halfway across the end of the drywall. This cleat temporarily supports the end of the next sheet.

3. Apply Adhesive. Use a caulk gun to dispense a bead of construction adhesive along each joist. This will mean you can use fewer screws or nails.

4. Hang the Drywall. Position the ladders directly under the area where the sheet will hang. With a helper, lift the drywall into place on the ceiling and have the helper prop up the sheet with the T-brace. Make sure the seams are tight, and then fasten the sheet to the joists with 1⅜-inch drywall nails or 1⅝-inch drywall screws placed at 16-inch intervals.

5. Use a Cleat for Butt Joints. After fastening the first sheet, use 2-inch drywall screws to attach a 36-inch-long 1x4 cleat at the end of the sheet. Use the cleat to support the butt end of the next sheet as you install it. Slip the sheet between the 1x4 cleat and the joists, and support the other end with the T-brace. Make sure the butt joint is tight; fasten the sheet, and then remove the cleat and finish screwing or nailing. Once the ceiling is covered, tape and finish the drywall as described in "Taping and Finishing Drywall," pages 44-47.

RESURFACING A CEILING WITH DRYWALL

Old plaster ceilings that show cracks can sometimes be patched. (For more information, see "Repairing Drywall and Plaster," page 58.) Often, however, cracks mean that the plaster has started to come loose from the lath. (Gravity causes this to happen sooner with a ceiling than a wall.) Test this by pushing against the ceiling. If it is loose in one place only, you can attempt to repair it; but chances are it eventually will come loose elsewhere, so you want a solution for the whole ceiling. You can remove the plaster before putting up new drywall, but that is a big job. It creates massive amounts of garbage and dust that permeate your whole house.

The best solution is to "skin over" the old plaster with drywall.

Sometimes, a drywall ceiling needs to be covered over. Perhaps there is water damage, or maybe the ceiling has a textured finish, such as a "cottage cheese" finish, that you don't like. Although removing drywall is easier than removing plaster, it's usually unnecessary. If the drywall is not crumbling from water damage, you can skin over it with new drywall, following the steps for "Installing Drywall over a Plaster Ceiling," on page 150. First, though, correct the source of the water damage.

In some ways, skinning over a ceiling is simple. Unlike with walls, there are usually no moldings to contend with. You can use lighter ⅜-inch drywall, making the job a bit easier. And if you install new molding where wall and ceiling meet, you will save yourself a good deal of taping work. However, working on a ceiling is awkward and strenuous. Have a good helper and two sturdy ladders, and use T-braces and 2x4 cleats along the top of the wall to brace the drywall panels temporarily as you install them (see "Hanging a Drywall Ceiling," page 147, for more information). And make some sort of safe scaffolding to walk on; a couple of 8-foot 2x12s set on strong wood horses works fine.

Typically, ⅜-inch drywall is used for skinning over old ceilings, simply because it is light and easy to work with; however, this thickness is available only in 8-foot sheets. Thicker sheets (½-inch and ⅝-inch) are available in 10-foot or 12-foot lengths. You might consider using these if they will span the whole ceiling because you won't need to tape and finish butt joints (where the untapered, short ends of the panels meet).

Dealing with Crown Molding.

Many older homes have an attractive crown molding where the walls meet the ceiling. Do not make the common mistake of simply butting the drywall to the molding and hoping that you can fill the joint in with compound; such a solution always looks unprofessional. Sometimes, the crown is divided into several pieces, and you can remove just one of them. (When you put that piece back, you may have to install a filler strip of molding to build out the gap made by the drywall thickness.) On the other hand, it's often difficult to remove the molding because coats of paint have sealed it to the plaster. The easiest solution is to install the drywall fairly close to the crown, and then add a new piece of molding to cover the gap, as shown.

Installing Drywall over a Plaster Ceiling

1. Prepare the Ceiling. Take care of anything that will cause the new drywall to be wavy. Knock out sections of old plaster that are hanging down and can't be pushed up. If any holes in the ceiling are larger than about 10 inches across, cut a piece of drywall the same thickness as the plaster to fill the opening, and screw the patch to the lath with 1¼-inch drywall screws.

2. Mark the Joist Locations. Probe for ceiling joists, using a hammer and an 8d nail. You can tell the difference between lath and joists because joists are solid; lath tends to bounce. Especially in older houses, do not assume that the joists will be located at regular 16-inch intervals. Find them all and mark them on the wall about 1 inch below the ceiling.

As you're probing for joists, check how deeply you must drive the 8d nail before it hits solid wood. Add 1 inch to this depth to determine the length of drywall screws to use. Usually, 2-inch screws will provide plenty of holding power.

3. Mark the Joist Layout. With your helper at one end of the joists and you at the other, stretch a chalk

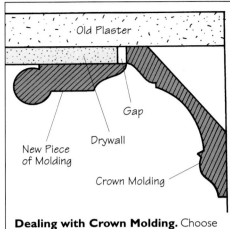

Dealing with Crown Molding. Choose an attractive molding to cover the gap between new drywall and crown molding.

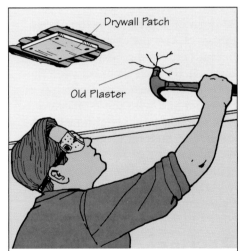

1. Knock down sagging plaster and fill in large holes with a drywall patch the same thickness as the plaster. Screw the drywall to the lath; the patch doesn't have to fit tightly.

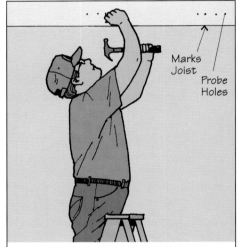

2. Use a hammer and an 8d nail to probe for the joists. Mark their locations clearly on the wall. Lath tends to feel bouncy. Joists will feel solid.

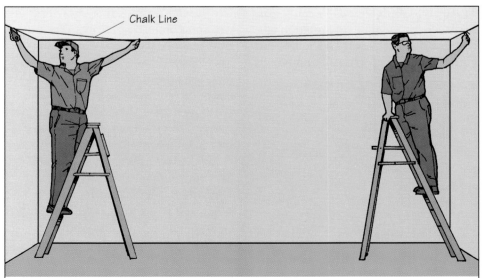

3. Stretch a chalk line across the ceiling at the joist locations, and snap the line to mark the joist layout.

4. Apply about ½ tube of construction adhesive to the back side of the drywall sheet immediately before installing it.

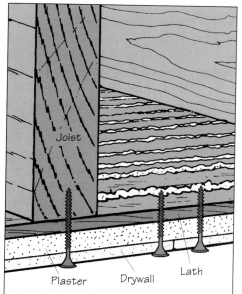

5. Using drywall screws long enough to penetrate the joists at least 1 inch, fasten the new drywall to joists where possible; for butt ends, attach the drywall to the lath.

ing, you can attach the butt ends of the drywall to the lath only, using 1⅝-inch drywall screws. After the last piece is attached, tape and finish the ceiling as described in "Taping and Finishing Drywall," page 44.

Shaping a Cove

Some older homes with plaster walls and ceilings have a curved transition between the walls and ceiling called a cove. With some extra work and a good deal of patience, you can reproduce a cove. If you plan only to skin over the ceiling but not the walls, you must put up a strip of molding, such as picture molding, to hide the top edge of the cove.

1. Cut Narrow Cove Strips. Cut five or ten narrow strips of drywall about 1 to 1½ inches wide. You can do this quickly with a drywall-ripping tool, as shown, or by laying the sheet flat and cutting strips with a utility knife and straightedge. Do not use the strip taken from the tapered drywall edge, because it is thinner than the others.

2. Form the Cove. Use screws to attach the strips to the curved section, as shown. Leave ¼ to ½ inch between each strip. Use a 12-inch taping knife to apply a strong joint

line across the ceiling at each joist location, and snap the line to mark the joists on the ceiling.

4. Cut and Glue the Sheet. Cut the drywall to fit with the long edges perpendicular to the joists. If you must butt two sheets together, cut the sheet so that the end falls halfway across a joist. However, if you are sure the plaster is backed with wood lath, you can let the butt joints fall where they may. Before raising the

drywall, apply plenty of construction adhesive to the back of the sheet to keep it from sagging.

5. Hang the Sheet. Set the ladders directly under the area where you'll be working, and orient them so that you and your helper will face each other. One person should handle the T-brace; the other should handle the screw gun. Attach the drywall to the ceiling joists with screws in line with the joists. On a wood-lath backed ceil-

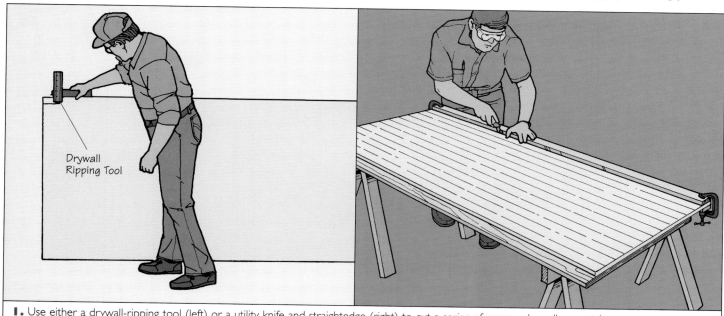

1. Use either a drywall-ripping tool (left) or a utility knife and straightedge (right) to cut a series of narrow drywall cove strips.

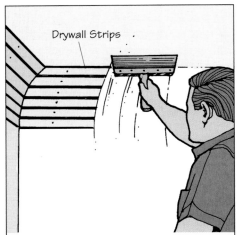

2. Attach the strips to the cove, leaving gaps of ¼ inch or so between them. Then fill between the strips and shape the cove with strong joint compound. It may take four or five coats to sculpt a smooth cove.

compound (perlited gypsum mixed with joint compound will work), and move the taping knife at right angles to the drywall strips. Fill the gaps between the strips, allow this coat to dry, and then apply a coat of joint compound over the entire cove. Let this coat dry; scrape off bumps and crumbs with the taping knife, and then apply another coat of compound. This is tedious work, which will take four or five coats—scraping and sanding after each coat—before you have a good, smooth surface.

REPAIRING CEILING DAMAGE

Ceiling repairs are similar to wall repairs, and the techniques described in "Repairing Drywall and Plaster," page 58 can be applied to ceilings. If the ceiling is in the top floor of your house, however, you may have access to an attic and will be able to use different techniques.

Repairing Water Damage.
A common problem in ceilings is water stains. Of course, you must be sure to fix the source of the leak. Then, as long as the affected ceiling drywall is still strong, you can let it dry out; prime it with a stain-killing primer (alcohol-based works best), and repaint.

Repairing Small Holes in Drywall.
Nailholes or screwholes can be patched with two coats of joint compound; but larger holes left over from, say, moving a ceiling light fixture, should be patched with wire backing and strong joint compound, such as perlited gypsum mixed with joint compound. From above, set a piece of wire mesh or wire lath overlapping the hole, and fix the corners

to the drywall with construction adhesive or strong joint compound. After a few hours, partially fill the hole from below with strong joint compound. Once it's dry, scrape it smooth with a putty knife and apply more compound. Build up the patch in layers until it's flush with the surrounding ceiling. Finish it with ready-mix joint compound or spackle, and then smooth and sand.

Repairing Large Holes in Drywall.
Holes larger than about 10 inches in diameter should be rebuilt with a new piece of drywall. From above, cut the damaged drywall back to the edge of the joists on either side of the damage, and use 2½-inch wood screws to attach 2x4s along each side of the opening, as shown. Cut a piece of drywall to fit, and use 1½-inch drywall screws to attach it to the 2x4s. Tape and finish.

Holes in Plaster

1. Install the Drywall Patch.
Remove any loose plaster by hand, or pry it with a putty knife. Cut a piece of drywall to fit into the area (it doesn't need to be a perfect fit). Plaster thickness varies, so you may have to use ⅜-inch or even ¼-inch

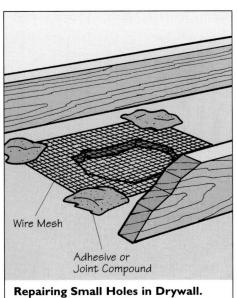

Repairing Small Holes in Drywall.
Press the corners of a piece of wire mesh into blobs of construction adhesive or joint compound. Then fill the hole from below, one layer at a time.

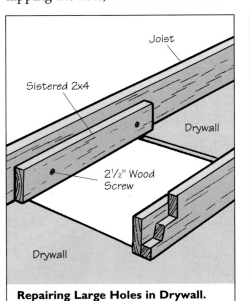

Repairing Large Holes in Drywall.
Cut back the damaged drywall to the joists, and "sister" 2x4s to the joists to provide nailing surfaces for the drywall patch that will follow.

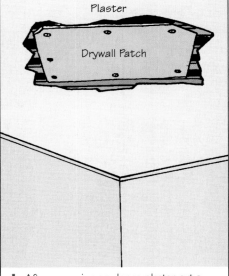

1. After removing any loose plaster, cut a piece of drywall the same thickness as the plaster to fit the hole. Attach the patch to the lath with 1½-inch drywall screws, mounted every 4 to 6 inches along the edges.

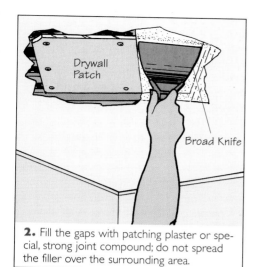

2. Fill the gaps with patching plaster or special, strong joint compound; do not spread the filler over the surrounding area.

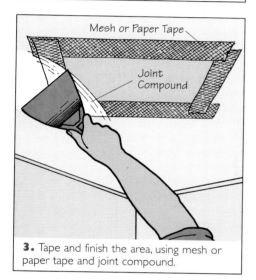

3. Tape and finish the area, using mesh or paper tape and joint compound.

rather than ½-inch drywall. Attach the patch to the lath, using 1¼-inch drywall screws every 4 to 6 inches along the edges.

2. Fill the Gaps. With strong joint compound or patching plaster, fill in the gaps between the patch and the good plaster. Do not attempt to feather out onto the good ceiling.

3. Tape and Finish. When the joint compound is dry or nearly dry, apply mesh or paper tape to the seams and cover with ready-mix joint compound, feathering out onto the good plaster. Let dry, sand, and repeat for one or two more coats. If the original plaster is textured rather than smooth, use a trowel or a sponge to match the existing texture as closely as possible.

SOUNDPROOFING CEILINGS

The principles of soundproofing a ceiling are the same as those for soundproofing a wall, but the number of possible interventions is more limited because of headroom issues. If you are building a new ceiling in a room where you'll need soundproofing, or you are trying to solve existing noise problems, use this section in conjunction with "Soundproofing Walls," page 48.

Keep in mind that sound travels through both the air and the house structure itself. For example, first-floor ceilings with living space above are subject to impact noise from such things as hard heels on a bare wood floor, whereas the sound of voices or television on the first floor can disturb people upstairs.

You can treat impact noises without touching the ceiling at all, by padding and carpeting the floor above. However, reducing the amount of airborne sound transmission requires ceiling modifications. A simple and effective soundproofing strategy that lowers the ceiling by only 2 or 3 inches is to insulate the ceiling and then hang the drywall from Z-channels; these are metal strips that hold the drywall away from the joists. Although it's best to insulate between exposed joists and fasten the Z-channels directly to the joists, you can install the channels on a finished ceiling, hang new drywall, and sandwich insulating board between the two ceiling surfaces.

Quieting Above the Ceiling. The most effective combination of materials for deadening impact sounds from a floor above is a layer of ½-inch insulating board nailed to the floor, followed by a layer of hardboard glued to the insulating board. This in turn is topped by a carpet pad glued to the hardboard, and then wall-to-wall carpeting is laid on top of that.

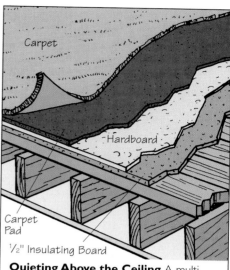

Quieting Above the Ceiling A multi-layer cushion will eliminate sharp raps on the floor above and deaden, but not eliminate, the sound of heavy footfalls.

This procedure will work only where it is practical to raise the level of the floor about an inch, and if you don't mind burying the original floor.

Soundproofing a Finished Ceiling

1. Locate the Ceiling Joists. Use an electronic stud finder, or probe with a hammer and nail to find the direction and spacing of the ceiling joists. Stud finders locate metal in hidden nails. Mark joist locations with pencils; then snap chalk lines across the marks (at right angles to the joists) about 6 inches out from either wall.

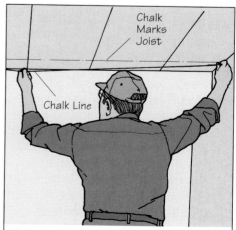

1. Probe to find the direction of the joists; then snap chalk lines across them about 6 inches from both walls.

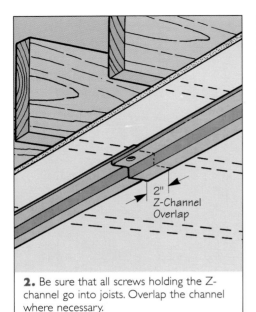

2. Be sure that all screws holding the Z-channel go into joists. Overlap the channel where necessary.

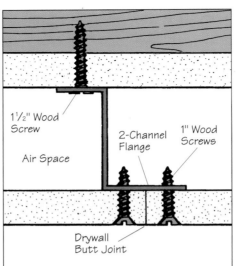

3. Attach drywall to the channels with 1-inch drywall screws, butting pieces centered on the flange.

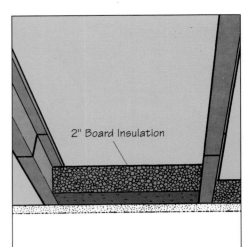

4. Insulate above the drywall as you complete each row, sliding in sections of 2-inch board insulation.

2. Attach the Z-Channels. Starting from one of the walls parallel to the two chalk lines you just snapped, snap more lines every 16 inches. Plan the drywall installation so that any sheet ending at a wall is supported by at least two Z-channels. Attach the Z-channels across joists with 1½-inch drywall screws driven into the joists with a screw gun. Orient each channel so that the middle of the bottom flange aligns with a chalk line. Make sure all the flanges face the same direction. Where channels won't reach from wall to wall, overlap the ends 2 inches and screw through the doubled channel into a joist.

3. Screw the Drywall to the Z-Channels. With a helper, raise the drywall sheets and attach them to the Z-channels with 1-inch drywall screws driven every 16 inches. (Use the techniques described in "Hanging a Drywall Ceiling," page 147.) Install the sheets with the long edges perpendicular to the Z-channels, and leave a ⅛-inch gap along the walls for paintable caulking. Where sheets of drywall butt together, center the joint on the Z-channel and attach the piece on the outer edge of the flange before attaching the one on the inner edge. This puts the least strain on the flanges.

4. Install the Insulation. After completing one row of drywall, slide 2-inch board insulation between the drywall and the ceiling above. Continue to install the drywall in this fashion. At the last strip, glue the insulation to the drywall between the lines where it will meet the channel.

Soundproofing a New Ceiling

1. Remove an Old Drywall Ceiling. Removing a ceiling to replace it with drywall is relatively

1. Cut pieces of drywall to get a good grip and remove manageable chunks. Be careful not to pull pieces down on your head. Wear protective goggles.

easy if the existing ceiling is drywall. Simply cut into the drywall (checking first for electrical wiring and other hazards as described in "Removing a Nonbearing Wall," page 24) and pull it down. Removing a plaster ceiling is almost more mess and trouble than it's worth; instead, simply install Z-channels and hang new drywall, as described above.

2. Insulate the Joist Bays. Staple fiberglass insulation between the exposed joists. The insulation should be thick enough to fill the joist bay.

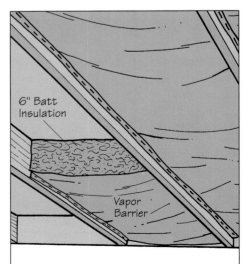

2. Push batts of 6-inch insulation between the joists, vapor barrier side down, and staple on both sides.

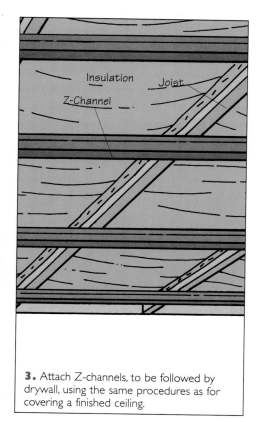

3. Attach Z-channels, to be followed by drywall, using the same procedures as for covering a finished ceiling.

3. Install the Z-Channels. Attach

Z-channels perpendicular to the joists, as described above, and cover with drywall.

INSTALLING A SUSPENDED CEILING

A suspended ceiling (sometimes called a dropped or exposed-grid ceiling) is a framework of metal channels that hangs beneath the joists on short lengths of wire. The metal channels support lightweight acoustical panels that form the finished surface of the ceiling. The beauty of this system is that it conceals obstructions, such as pipes and wiring, attached to the underside of the joists, yet it allows easy access for work there. Another advantage is that the ceiling is leveled as it is installed; the existing joists need not be level or even straight. A suspended ceiling also makes the job of installing ceiling lights easier: Simply remove an acoustical tile and replace it with a special drop-in florescent fixture.

Parts of a Suspended Ceiling

The metal framework of a suspended ceiling consists of main runners, cross runners, and wall molding. Main runners are the primary support members; they are fastened to the ceiling joists with lengths of lightweight hanger wire. Cross runners are light-gauge supports that fit at right angles between the main runners. Both main and cross runners are T-shaped when viewed from the end. Wall molding is an L-shaped metal channel that is attached to the walls. It supports ceiling panels around the perimeter of the room. Wall molding and main runners are sold in different lengths up to 12 feet; main runners can be locked end to end to reach greater distances. Cross runners are 2 feet or 4 feet long.

Sometimes called ceiling tiles, acoustical ceiling panels fit into the grid created by the runners. Panels can be 2-foot squares or 2-foot by 4-foot rectangles, and they come in three styles, each giving the ceiling a different look. Flush panels sit on top of the framework, leaving the runners completely exposed; raised panels have rabbeted edges that allow the panels to hang lower than the framework. Other panels have slotted edges, which allow the metal grid to be hidden completely.

Using Special Tools. Many of the tools needed for this project are basic: a hammer, chalkline, combination square, spirit level, hacksaw, plumb bob, and utility knife. But you'll also need a few special tools, including aviation snips. This tool easily cuts the light-gauge metals used in suspended-ceiling framework. Snips are available in right-hand, left-hand, and straight-cut models.

Use a water level to locate points around the room that are exactly at the same level. This simple, inexpensive tool, which can be purchased at hardware stores and home centers, consists of water contained in clear plastic tubing.

If you choose, you can use a rivet tool to join metal to metal. This inexpensive tool automatically inserts a fastener, called a rivet, and flattens the

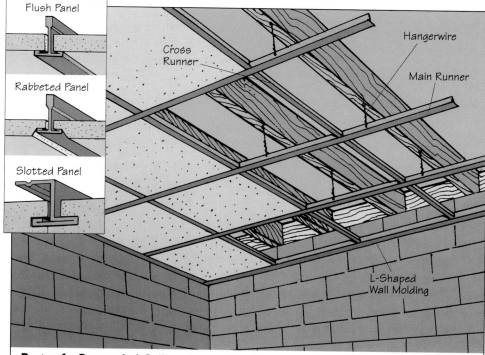

Parts of a Suspended Ceiling. Suspended ceilings are made up of the parts shown here. Runners are the primary support system for the ceiling. The look of the ceiling changes according to the types of panels and runners used.

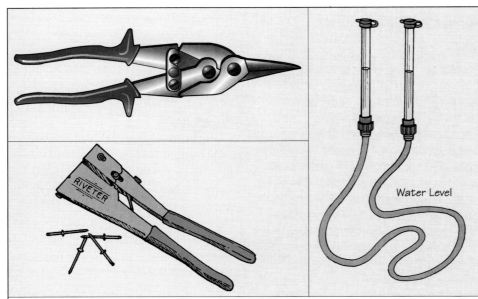

Using Special Tools. Some special tools you'll need include aviation snips for cutting the metal framework, a water level to locate points around the room that are exactly at the same level, and a rivet tool to join metal to metal.

Installing a Suspended Ceiling

1. Establish Benchmarks. In one corner of the room, make a pencil mark about 60 inches high on the wall. Then use the water level to transfer this mark to the other walls. When connected with chalklines, these benchmarks form a level reference point all around the room, and future measurements can be taken from it.

2. Determine the Ceiling Height. The standard ceiling height is 90 inches; it is also the minimum height for lighting in a suspended ceiling. The ceiling must be at least 3 inches from overhanging projections. Hang it completely below projections, or use drywall or wood paneling to box in the projections. Once the ceiling height has been determined, measure up from the benchmarks to locate the position of the wall molding. Snap a chalk line on the walls around the perimeter of the room. It is best to strike this line in the place where the top edge of the molding will be located; the chalk marks will not be visible after the wall molding is in place.

3. Install the Wall Molding. Nail molding to the walls, making sure each nail penetrates a stud. Use the aviation snips to cut wall molding to length. At inside corners, butt one end of the molding right to the wall; the other piece butts into the molding. At outside corners, it's best to

ends for a tight connection between, for example, wall molding and main runners, or wherever metal joins metal. Rivet tools are available at hardware stores.

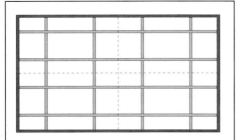

Planning the Job. Draw a plan to determine the number and size of runners and ceiling panels needed. If you must cut border tiles, center the layout.

Planning the Job. To help estimate the quantity of materials needed for the job, draw a plan view of the ceiling. For a better-looking job, lay out the ceiling panels to minimize the need for small pieces around the border. If the border tiles will be less than half the width of a field tile, adjust the layout one way or the other to eliminate this unsightly condition.

Although panels are available in 2-foot squares or 2-foot by 4-foot rectangles, use rectangular panels if florescent lighting will be placed in the ceiling, because standard lighting fixtures are 4 feet long. Also, 2-foot square panels require more cross runners, so the job is more time-consuming.

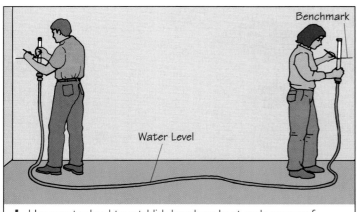

1. Use a water level to establish benchmarks at each corner of the room.

2. Measure up from the benchmarks to locate the ceiling height; then snap a chalk line between the marks.

miter the ends. Cut straight down the back and cut the bottom at 45 degrees. Butt lengths of wall molding where they meet midwall.

4. Establish Centerlines. Measure the length and width of the room, and divide these measurements in half to find the center point of each wall. Use layout strings to connect opposing midpoints, stretching them tightly between the wall molding. Check the intersection of the two strings to make sure they are square to each other. If not, adjust one or the other slightly until they are square. It is easier to adjust layout strings when they are attached to nails that can be wedged behind the wall molding, as shown below.

5. Install the Guidelines. Plan to install the first main runner parallel to the centerline and at a distance from the wall that is equal to the width of the border units. Stretch a guideline between the wall moldings where the first main runner will be located. Then stretch more lines representing the other main runners; space the lines either 2 feet or 4 feet apart, depending on the ceiling panels you will install. Use the guidelines to level the main runners.

6. Attach Hanger Wires. Start with the joist at either end of the ceiling. Install a screw eye (or fastener supplied by the ceiling manufacturer) into every fourth joist directly above the layout line. Twist a piece of hanger wire through each screw eye so that the wire hangs about 6 inches below the guideline. Cut a main runner to length, and hang it from the wire so that it is just barely above the guideline. Twist the wires to secure the runner in position.

7. Install Cross Runners. Slip the first cross runner in between the main runner and the wall molding (it locks

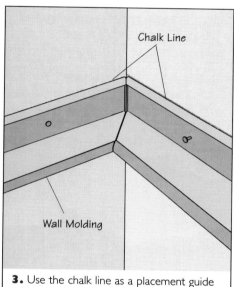

3. Use the chalk line as a placement guide to nail the wall molding in place.

4. Use a square to check the angle that is formed where the layout strings meet. Adjust the strings so that they make a 90-degree angle.

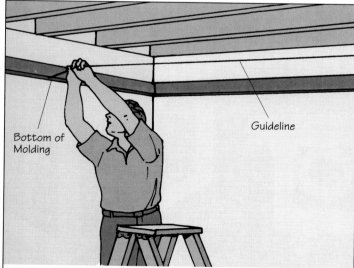

5. Stretch a guideline between opposite wall moldings; this line gives you a reference point for leveling the first main runner.

6. Attach screw eyes directly above the layout string, and loop hanger wire through each screw eye. Secure the main runner to the wire.

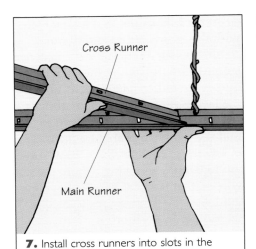

7. Install cross runners into slots in the main runner. Maintain the proper spacing according to the size of ceiling panel used.

8. After installing and wiring lighting panels, angle the ceiling panels through the grid and set them into place.

2. Attach the Channels and Ribs. Using pop rivets or self-drilling sheet-metal screws (such as those used for lightweight-steel framing), fasten a U-channel to the ceiling grid along the length of the obstruction. Then use pop rivets to attach the ribs to the U-channel.

3. Install the Panels. Connect the ribs with lengths of wall molding, and cut ceiling panels to fit the box as needed. Install the vertical panels first; they are locked in place when the horizontal panels are installed. Use hanger wire as needed to provide additional support for the box.

4. Work Around Posts. There are two ways to deal with posts penetrating a suspended ceiling. Either cut a

into the main runner's prepunched slots). Install the next main runner by using cross runners to gauge its spacing. Continue to work across the room until all the runners have been installed. Remove the guidelines.

8. Install Ceiling Panels. Wearing gloves to avoid smudging the panels, lift each ceiling panel into place by turning it at an angle and pushing it into the grid of runners. Use a utility knife and a straightedge to cut panels at the borders as needed. If you are installing raised panels, you will have to cut grooves, or rabbets, along any cut edges. Measure the depth of the rabbet and cut the edge of the panel. Measure the width of the rabbet and cut along the face of the panel. The exposed rabbet will be a different color from the panel, so consider spray-painting the rabbets you cut to match the panel color.

Working Around Obstructions

1. Make the Ribs. If a pipe or duct intrudes below the level of the ceiling, it can be boxed in with pieces of the grid system. You will need U-shaped channel molding and extra main runner and wall molding for this job. Include the box in original layout plans and leave the ceiling open for now. Use aviation snips to cut 90-degree notches in lengths

of main runner, then bend the runners at these points to form the ribs of the box.

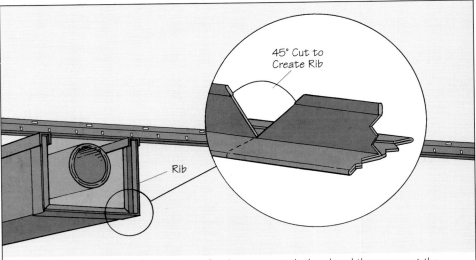

1. Cut 90-degree notches in the spine of main-runner stock; then bend the runner at the notches to form a U-shaped rib that surrounds the obstruction.

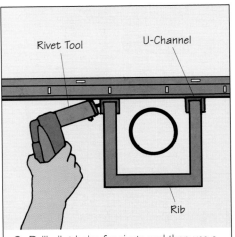

2. Drill pilot holes for rivets, and then use a rivet tool to attach the ribs to the U-channel.

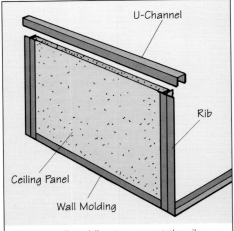

3. Use wall molding to connect the ribs and install the ceiling panels.

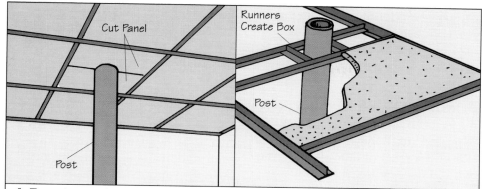

4. To work around a post, either cut a ceiling panel in half and cut each half to fit the post (left) or add runners and small pieces of ceiling panels to enclose it (right).

panel in half and shape the pieces to fit around the post, or use additional runners to box in the post. If the panel is cut in half, the seam between halves usually is self-supporting and unobtrusive.

FINISHING ATTIC CEILINGS

Compared with building an addition, finishing an attic is a relatively inexpensive way to add living space to a home. And compared with fixing up a basement, a renovated attic offers features many basements cannot, including access to natural light and natural ventilation. But an attic renovation also presents some insulation, ventilation, and framing challenges. Before you even begin to consider these, however, check the available ceiling height. Building codes require that 50 percent of the attic space have ceilings at least 7 feet 6 inches high; anything less, and you'll also have to apply for a variance when you apply for the building permit.

Unless yours is a perfect climate, insulation is a must for an attic ceiling. Otherwise, you will have an attic office or bedroom that is stifling on summer days and hard to keep warm in the winter. Typically, building codes require at least R-19 (6 inches of fiberglass insulation) in attic roofs, but you should check with your local building department for insulation requirements.

Adequate ventilation is essential for keeping the attic dry. The most effective type of ventilation combines soffit and ridge vents, allowing air to circulate between the rafters from the bottom to the top of the roof. Another type of ventilation, gable vents, are simply louvers located high in the walls near the roof peak. You must not block any vents when you do your attic renovation. In fact, it's a good idea to consult an architect before beginning work to be sure you will have proper ventilation.

Planning the Ceiling. There are two basic types of attic ceilings: a flat ceiling and a cathedral ceiling. The flat ceiling is built with ceiling joists spanning between the roof rafters. Typically, the flat ceiling meets a sec-

Planning the Ceiling. Attic spaces are finished with either flat ceilings or peaked cathedral ceilings. Use rafter vents to hold insulation away from the roof sheathing and allow air to circulate.

tion that follows the roof line, which in turn meets a knee wall. (For more on building knee walls, see "Framing-in an Attic," page 34.) You can use strings hung from nails to simulate such a ceiling to get a sense of what the space will look like as you plan the conversion. A flat ceiling is insulated between roof rafters and then between ceiling joists.

A cathedral ceiling gives a sense of greater space and eliminates the need for ceiling framing. Such a ceiling is built by insulating between the rafters and then attaching drywall to them. You will need to install plastic channel rafter vents to allow air to circulate between the rafters above the insulation. This results in some heat loss in the high part of the ceiling during winter, but during summer the room will be a bit less hot—especially if a window or exhaust fan is located near the peak.

Building a Flat Ceiling

1. Mark Rafters for Ceiling Height. Measure up from the floor at four corners of the attic and mark the ceiling height on the rafters. (Add 1½ inches for the thickness of the drywall and the finish flooring.) Stretch a line level from one mark to the other three, and check that they

1. Measure the height of the ceiling at one corner of the attic; then use a line level to transfer this height to the other corners. Snap chalk lines across the rafters to indicate the ceiling height.

are level with each other. Then snap chalk lines to mark the ceiling height on all the rafters.

2. Attach Temporary 2x4s. Use 10d nails to tack to the rafters straight 2x4s with their top edges even with the chalk lines. You will use the 2x4s as guides for installing level ceiling joists.

3. Cut the Ceiling Joists. Holding your tape measure against the roof sheathing, measure the distance across the temporary 2x4s. Subtract 2 inches, and transfer this measurement to the joist material. Ceiling joists are typically 2x6s, but you should use 2x8s if they will span more than 10 feet. Use a bevel gauge and a 2-foot level to copy the angle of the roof onto the 2x6, and then cut it with a circular saw. Test-fit the joist, and if it is correct, use it as a template for the other joists.

4. Install the Ceiling Joists. Rest the joists on top of the temporary 2x4s, and attach the joists to the same side of each pair of rafters by driving two 16d nails or 3-inch screws through the joist into the rafter; then drive two nails or screws through the joist from the other side of the rafter.

5. Insulate Walls, Floor, and Ceiling. Check with your local building department for the insulation requirements for your area, and buy fiberglass insulation with the appropriate R-value and appropriate width. Insulate the floor on the outside of the knee wall, taking care not to block any soffit vents. To allow air to circulate, staple plastic channel rafter vents to the underside of the roof sheathing between the rafters. Staple the insulation between knee-wall studs, rafters, and ceiling joists with the vapor barrier facing the living space, making a snug fit where the ends of batts or blankets meet.

Finishing Obtuse Angles. Once the drywall is in place, you can tape and finish it as described in "Taping and Finishing Drywall," page 44-47. Achieving straight, crisp seams

2. Temporarily install 2x4s with the top edge aligned with the chalk lines. When you install the ceiling joists, you can rest them on the 2x4s.

3. Measure the length of the ceiling joists to roof sheathing and cut them an inch or two shorter. Cut the ends at an angle to fit under the sheathing. To find this angle, use a level and a bevel gauge, as shown.

4. Rest the joists on the 2x4s and fasten the joists to the rafters, using four 16d nails or 3-inch screws on both sides of each joint.

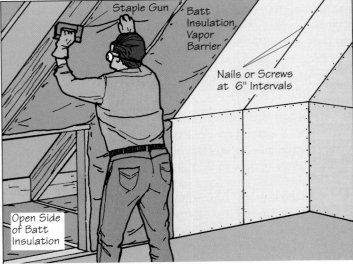

5. Install insulation for the knee wall, the sloped ceiling, and the flat ceiling. Make sure you do not inhibit necessary ventilation.

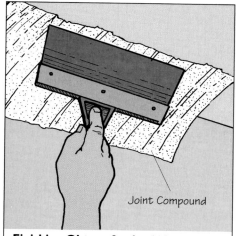

Finishing Obtuse Angles. Where knee walls meet sloped ceilings, mold a curve with successive layers of joint compound. Feather the edges after each coat.

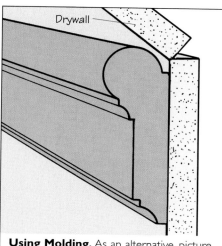

Using Molding. As an alternative, picture molding works especially well for covering up the obtuse angle where a knee wall meets a sloped ceiling.

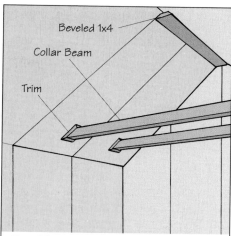

Considering Cathedral Ceilings. Cut drywall to fit around existing collar beams, and cover the seams with 1x2 trim. At the ceiling peak, install a beveled 1x4.

between walls and sloped ceilings is difficult, but you can hide these seams by sculpting them with joint compound. Spread on a fairly thick first coat of strong joint compound or patching plaster, with strokes perpendicular to the seam. Try to keep as regular a line as possible, feathering the edges and smoothing ridges between strokes. Let the seams dry; scrape and sand them, and then apply several layers of ready-mix joint compound, sanding after each application.

Using Molding. A much quicker and easier solution than sculpting seams is to install molding. Regular crown molding will not work because the walls and ceiling are not at right angles to each other. Experiment with several types of picture molding to see which you like.

Considering Cathedral Ceilings. The peaked roof in many attics presents the perfect opportunity to make a cathedral ceiling, where the ceiling surface—drywall or paneling—is attached directly to the underside of the rafters. Check with an architect to be sure you have adequate ventilation before you install insulation and drywall. Also, if your attic has collar beams supporting the roof, ask the architect whether you can move or even remove some of them. If the beams are high enough, you may

leave them in place and cut drywall to fit around them. To avoid a difficult taping job at the roof peak, cut a piece of 1x4 beveled on both sides to fit. Prime the 1x4 before nailing it in place. You can improve the appearance of the collar beams by cladding them with decorative wood, such as Douglas fir.

INSTALLING SKYLIGHTS

A good way to add natural light and a touch of drama to any room with an attic or pitched roof overhead is to install a skylight. Some of the work requires cutting through and removing the roof covering. For this reason, the difficulty of the project depends partly on the type of roof covering on your house. Cutting into a roof covered with slate, tile, or metal is not something most homeowners are prepared to attempt. These materials must be cut with special tools, and a skylight installed within such a roof must be waterproofed with special flashing. If your roof is made of slate, tile, or metal, contact roofing contractors for estimates or advice.

Another issue affecting the difficulty of the job is the size of the skylight. Small skylights that fit between exist-

ing rafters eliminate the need for special framing. To install larger skylights, you need to remove part of at least one rafter and then double the roof framing on either side of the skylight opening. Determine the rafter spacing and try to choose a skylight no wider than three rafters (you'll need to cut the center rafter). If you need to cut more than two rafters, consult an engineer for help in determining the proper sizing for headers.

Considering Types of Skylights. Skylights may be fixed, meaning they can't be opened, or operable, meaning they can be opened. Fixed skylights are generally less expensive, but operable skylights allow for air circulation (they come with screens to keep out bugs). Tempered glass is best because it is strong and minimizes danger if it breaks. Options include tinted glass to reduce glare, reflective (low-E) glass to limit heat gain, and frosted glass for privacy. In cold climates, you should choose a skylight with insulating glazing to minimize heat loss and reduce condensation problems.

Determining Skylight Height. The higher up on a ceiling you place a skylight, the better it ventilates the room. Keep it at least 12 inches from the ridge to provide room for framing and flashing. Placing the skylight lower on the ceiling sacrifices

Determining Skylight Height. A low skylight provides views and is easy to reach; a skylight higher on the ceiling ventilates the room more effectively and preserves privacy.

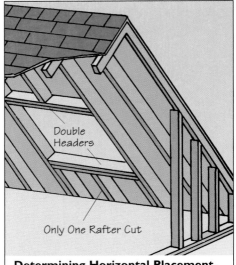

Double Headers

Only One Rafter Cut

Determining Horizontal Placement. When looking for a place to install the skylight, keep in mind that you want to minimize the need to cut rafters.

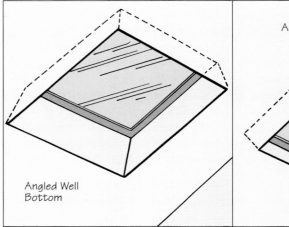

Angled Well Bottom

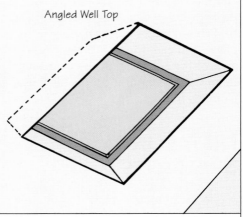

Angled Well Top

Building Skylight Wells. The rafters form the sides of a skylight well, but you can angle the bottom header, the top header, or both headers to let more light into the room.

some ventilation and perhaps privacy but may gain a view. Another reason for a somewhat lower placement is that it makes the skylight easy to reach. Depending on the weather, you may want to open and close a skylight frequently. Make sure that the skylight will not be in the way of cabinetry or furnishings you plan to install.

Determining Horizontal Placement. First, you must determine the size of the rough opening required for the particular brand and size skylight you plan to use. (The rough opening, sometimes abbreviated RO, is listed in the catalogs you'll

use to select your skylight.) The rough opening is measured between framing members. Decide approximately where you want the skylight, and then adjust the position of the rough opening to the right or left to minimize the need to cut rafters.

Building Skylight Wells. As you consider different places for the skylight, determine how it will be trimmed out in each instance. For a cathedral ceiling, where the ceiling surface is attached to the bottom of the roof rafters, you'll need to finish only the rough opening. For a flat ceiling with an attic above, you'll need to frame a skylight well. This

consists of an opening in the ceiling with walls framed between the ceiling opening and the skylight rough opening. You can build the walls at right angles to the ceiling framing, to put the ceiling opening directly below the skylight. Or for more light, you can angle the upper or lower portion of the well (or both portions) outward; this changes the position of the ceiling opening.

Installing a Skylight

Although you can build your own skylight by setting glazing onto a 2x4 or 2x6 curb, or by laying an inexpensive plastic dome over a hole in the roof, these types of skylights tend to leak. Factory-built skylights, on the other hand, are designed to be leak-free, and you don't need to build a curb for them. Manufacturers also offer flashing kits made especially for their skylights. A typical kit includes base flashing, head flashing, and either continuous side flashing or step flashing, all designed to fit snugly around the skylight curb. A factory-built skylight and its flashing are relatively easy for novices to install. Be sure to plan to complete the exterior installation in a single day. The interior can be completed at your convenience. Remember that the size of the rough opening you frame in the roof must suit the size of the skylight, so check the manufacturer's layout instructions before cutting into the roof.

The steps below describe how to install a skylight that requires the removal of part of one rafter. If your skylight fits between rafters, the installation is similar, but easier because you don't need to cut any rafters and you can use single headers instead of doubles unless the manufacturer specifies otherwise.

1. Locate the Roof Opening.
Lay out the rough opening on the underside of the roof sheathing. Drive a nail through the sheathing (and the roofing) at each corner of the rough opening. Then go on the roof, snap

1. Nail through the underside of the sheathing to mark the corners of the rough opening. Dotted lines show where the sheathing will be cut.

2. Snap a second set of chalk lines ¾ inch outside the first set; then use a circular saw to cut through only the shingles, along the outside chalk lines.

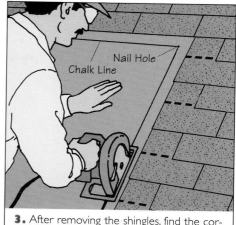

3. After removing the shingles, find the corners of the rough opening and snap chalk lines to outline it. Set the circular saw to cut through only the sheathing.

chalk lines outlining the skylight opening, and hit the nails back below the roof.

2. Remove the Shingles. The shingles should be cut back about ¾ inch from the skylight, so snap new chalk lines ¾ inch from the first ones, and then use a circular saw fitted with an old carbide blade to cut along the new chalk lines through only the shingles. Then use an ordinary garden spade to remove the shingles and the roofing paper. Later, when you install the flashing, you will need to remove some more shingles along the top and sides of the skylight.

3. Cut the Roof Opening. Snap chalk lines between the nailholes you made in Step 1 to mark the portion of the sheathing to be removed. Use a cat's paw to pull out the sheathing nails within the opening; and then, with a new blade in the circular saw, cut through only the roof sheathing. Remove the sheathing and sweep any sawdust and debris off the roof.

4. Cut the Roof Framing. Use a square to mark cutlines along the sides of the rafter to be cut. The top and bottom cuts will be 3 inches outside the rough opening to provide room for doubled top and bottom headers. To pick up the roof load of the severed rafter, nail braces across several adjacent rafters, as shown, and remove the braces only after the

4. Use a combination square to mark where you will cut the center rafter. Remember to add 3 inches for the headers to come at top and bottom.

headers are in place. Use a circular saw to cut the rafter partway through. Then use a hand saw to finish the cut.

5. Install the New Framing. Using the same-size 2-by lumber as the roof rafters, cut four header pieces to span the width of the skylight rough opening. At the top and bottom of the rough opening, toenail a header to the side rafters with 16d nails, making sure each header is square; then face-nail the headers to the ends of the cut rafter. Double the headers, toenailing each second piece to the side rafters and face nailing it to the

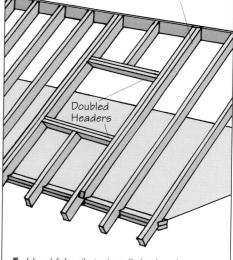

5. Use 16d nails to install the headers and to sister reinforcing rafters onto the existing ones.

first header. Next, sister the rafters on both sides of the rough opening, face-nailing the sister rafter to the existing one. The doubled rafters must span from the wall plate to the ridge.

6. Install the Skylight. Use a pry bar to loosen the shingles on both sides and along the top of the rough opening. Set the skylight in place, centering it over the opening. If you're installing an operable skylight, check it for square and make sure the unit works. Then attach the unit to the roof according to manufacturer instructions.

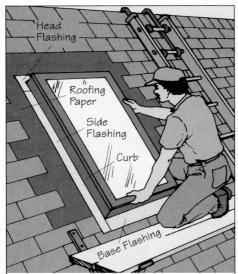

6. Set the skylight over the rough opening, square the unit, and attach it to the roof according to the manufacturer's instructions.

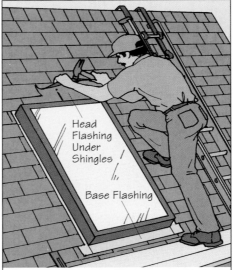

7. Install the base flashing over the shingles, and then slip the side flashing under each shingle course. Install the head flashing last, tucking its top flange under the shingles.

Finishing the Interior. One way to finish around a skylight is to trim the rough opening with drywall, and then cover the lip between the skylight frame and the drywall.

7. Install Flashing and Replace Shingles. The base flashing goes on first. Set it directly on the shingles, and nail it to the skylight with a single roofing nail at the top corner of the curb. Dab a bit of roofing cement over nailheads to seal them. Then install the side flashing by slipping it under each shingle course according to manufacturer instructions, as you work your way up the roof. Finally, install the head flashing. You may have to remove two courses of head shingles, but make sure the head flashing rests on the roof and that the next course of shingles overlaps the head flashing. No nailing is required.

Finishing the Interior. The bottom edge of a skylight frame is grooved to accept wood extension jambs, which provide more depth to the wood frame. You don't need to use extension jambs; you can simply trim the rough opening with drywall. You may need to use molding to hide the seam between the skylight and the drywall. Be sure to insulate the skylight opening, the ceiling opening, and the walls of the sky-light shaft before finishing the surfaces with drywall.

MAKING AND INSTALLING FALSE BEAMS

You can change the appearance of a room by adding simulated beams across a plain ceiling. If you have added a structural beam after removing a bearing wall to make a room larger, you can disguise the beam's presence by flanking it with a more attractive simulated beam.

You can buy molded-plastic false beams that you glue to the ceiling, or real wood pilasters with a distressed finish (gouged on the outside to look like adze marks) that you nail to the ceiling joists, or you can make your own false beams. Anyone comfortable with a hammer and saw can fashion false beams that look like true structural members. Wood false beams can be shaped and stained or painted for different visual effects. They can be scarred and stained for a rough-hewn look, or sanded and painted, or sanded to soften the edges and stained to resemble a timeworn piece of lumber. Be creative; for instance, a grid of beams crossing at right angles can add elegance to a high ceiling.

False beams are attached to 2x4 or 2x6 cleats nailed through the ceiling surface and into the joists. Before installing wood false beams you need to locate the ceiling joists; use a stud finder or probe for the joists with a hammer and 8d nail. Mark the joists at both ends, and snap chalk lines to show the joist locations on the ceiling.

Building and Installing False Beams

1. Plan the Design. Measure the ceiling and decide where to place the

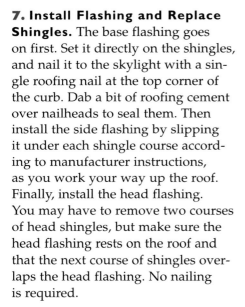

1. After marking the joists on the ceiling, you can mark false beams perpendicular to joists, as shown, and snap chalk lines.

beams. They look best when they're evenly spaced across the ceiling. You can install the beams at right angles to the joists or parallel to them. Snap chalk lines to show the beam layout, or simply decide to which joists you will attach beams if you will install them parallel to the joists.

2. Build the Beams. Build the beams from straight 1x4s or 1x6s with butted or mitered joints. Use 6d finish nails and glue to fasten the sides flush with the bottom. Set the nails. If one beam will not span the length of the room, stagger the butt end, as shown, so that it interlocks with the adjoining piece in an inconspicuous joint.

3. Finish the Beams. A false beam can be finished in a great variety of ways. You can paint it, stain it to look like any of several woods or to look aged, or give it a modern look with a clear finish. If you want a rough-hewn look, roughen the surface with a rasp before staining. Smooth the corners with sandpaper, a plane, or a rasp, depending on the effect you want. If you are painting, fill cracks and nailholes with wood putty before painting; if you are staining, fill cracks afterwards with putty matching the stain.

4. Install the Cleats. Use 16d nails to attach to the ceiling 2x4 or 2x6 cleats (the same width as the false beam) that are aligned with the chalk lines.

5. Fasten the Beams to the Cleats. Slip a beam onto a cleat and attach with 8d finish nails through the side of the false beam. Set and fill these nails and touch up as necessary.

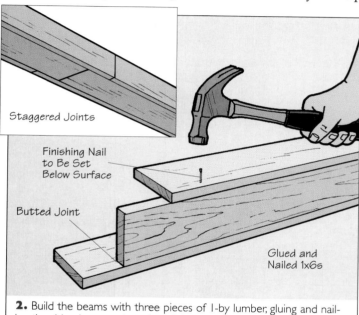

Staggered Joints

Finishing Nail to Be Set Below Surface

Butted Joint

Glued and Nailed 1x6s

2. Build the beams with three pieces of 1-by lumber, gluing and nailing the side pieces to the edge of the bottom piece. If you need to splice beams, stagger the ends, as shown.

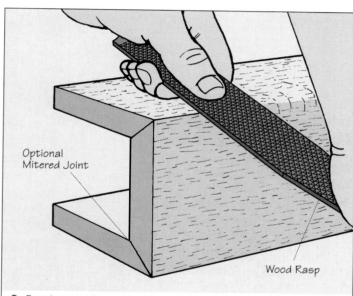

Optional Mitered Joint

Wood Rasp

3. Roughen and "stress" the beam with a wood rasp to give it a hand-tooled, rustic appearance. For a modern decor instead, fill cracks and sand the beam smooth; then apply the finish.

Chalk Lines Mark Joists

4. Use 16d nails to attach 2x4 or 2x6 cleats (depending on the width of the bottom of the beam) to the ceiling joists along the lines you snapped for the beams.

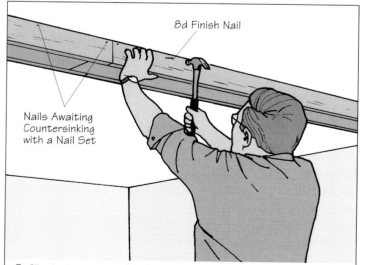

8d Finish Nail

Nails Awaiting Countersinking with a Nail Set

5. Slip the beam over the cleat and drive 8d finish nails through the sides of the beam into the cleat. To avoid bruising the wood with the hammer, finish the last 1/8 inch or so of nailing with a nail set.

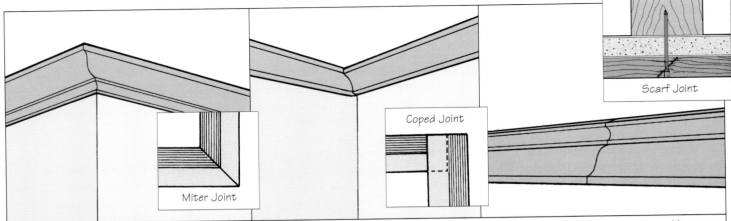

Installing Ceiling Molding. The three most common joints are miters, with ends beveled 45 degrees to fit an outside corner; copes, with one piece butted to the wall and the other cut to fit into the first; and scarfs, where two pieces are beveled in the same direction at 45 degrees and nailed end to end over a stud.

INSTALLING CEILING MOLDING

Ceiling molding—wide, decorative crown molding or narrow, curved cove molding—is great for dressing up the area where walls meet a ceiling, or for hiding joints between paneling and drywall. Installing ceiling molding is a bit more complicated than installing other moldings, but it's certainly within reach of most do-it-yourselfers. The first step is to mark some layout lines on the wall. Then you simply cut the molding to fit. You will need a helper to hold one end of the molding as you check the fit at the other.

Like other moldings, ceiling molding is available in many styles and grades. And, like base trim, ceiling molding is installed using a variety of joints: miters for outside corners, copes for inside corners, and scarfs for joining lengths of molding end to end. To cut these joints, you'll need a good miter box or power chop saw and a coping saw.

A mitered joint requires beveling the molding ends to fit over an outside corner. A coped joint consists of one piece butted against the wall and the other piece cut in a shape to fit over the first piece. You can make a cope by beveling the end of the molding at 45 degrees, and then cutting off the

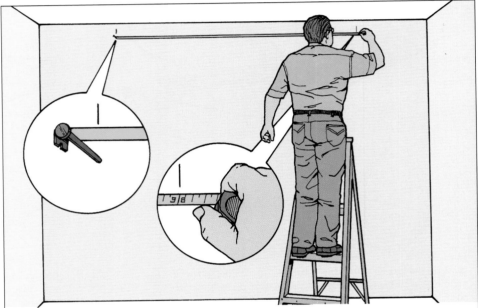

Measuring for Ceiling Molding. To measure a wall by yourself, hook your tape measure on a nail driven a certain distance from the wall, and measure to a mark made a certain distance from the opposite wall. Add the three distances.

pointed piece along the profile line. (For more information on coping, see "Coping Inside Corners," page 70.) If one length of molding won't span the entire wall, you'll have to splice two shorter pieces with a scarf joint that falls over a stud. (For more information on scarf joints, see page 69.)

Measuring for Ceiling Molding. Get a rough idea of the lengths of molding you'll need by measuring each wall and adding about a foot for waste. If you're measuring alone, use a nail to hold one end of the tape. Put the nail a set distance (for example,

2 feet) away from the wall, and then add this distance to the measurement when you hook your tape measure on the nail. Put the nail high on the wall so that the crown molding will cover the hole. Sometimes, it's tricky to get an exact measurement at the opposite wall because the tape won't fit tightly into the corner. Simply measure out from the wall a set distance—again, 2 feet is a convenient distance—mark this spot on the wall, and measure to this point. Add all the measurements to find the wall length.

Marking Layout Lines

1. Measure for Crown Molding. With a framing square representing the wall and the ceiling, hold a piece of crown molding as shown to determine how far below the ceiling its bottom edge will be. Call this distance "Molding Depth."

2. Draw Reference Line. After drawing a level reference mark on the wall two inches below Molding Depth, use a water level or line level to transfer the reference mark to other corners. Then simply snap chalk lines to connect all of the reference marks.

3. Find the Low Point. Measure up to the ceiling at various points in the room to find its low point. Make a mark at distance Molding Depth below this point.

4. Snap Molding Line. Measure up to the Molding Depth mark from your reference line. Do the same around the room's perimeter. Snap a second line at this height.

5. Install the Molding. The molding's bottom edge must line up with this second reference chalk line. Nail the top edge of the molding directly up into the ceiling joists, as shown. Any remaining small gaps can then be filled with drywall compound or paintable caulk.

Worst-Case Compromise. If the ceiling is badly out of level, it's better to install the molding parallel to the ceiling than to have no gap at one end and a big gap at the other. In this case, it's better to bend the molding to align with the ceiling. This will complicate the fitting of joints, however, so be prepared to adjust the cuts several times.

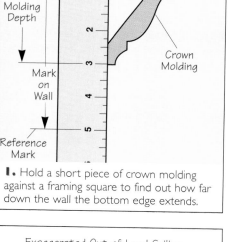

1. Hold a short piece of crown molding against a framing square to find out how far down the wall the bottom edge extends.

2. Use a water level to transfer the reference mark created in Step 1 to the other corners.

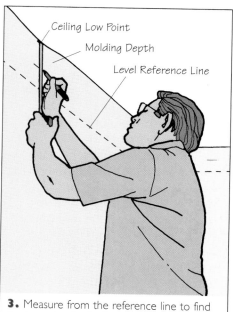

3. Measure from the reference line to find the lowest point in the ceiling, and mark "Molding Depth" at this point.

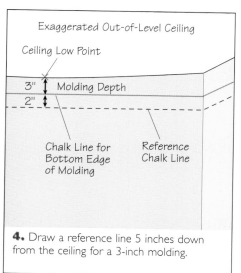

4. Draw a reference line 5 inches down from the ceiling for a 3-inch molding.

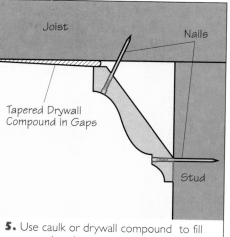

5. Use caulk or drywall compound to fill any gaps that the crown molding doesn't cover.

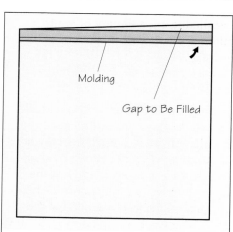

Worst-Case Compromise. If the ceiling is badly out of level, bend the molding to conform.

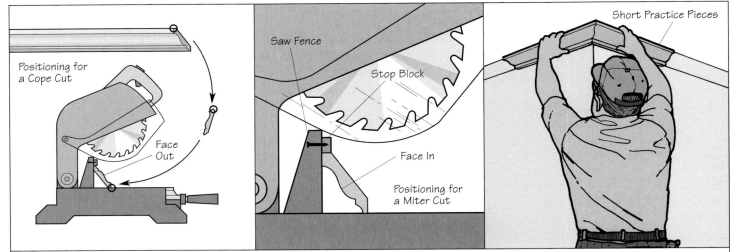

Cutting Ceiling Molding. Screw or clamp a hardwood stop block to the fence to position the crown at the proper angle. Place crown molding face out and upside down in the miter box to bevel the end for a cope; for a miter, place the molding so the front edge rests against the saw fence. Experiment with short pieces of crown, setting them in position at inside or outside corners to find the exact angle to cut.

Cutting Ceiling Molding. Unlike other types of molding, such as casing and baseboard, you can't just hold crown or cove molding flat against the back or bottom of a miter box; you must hold the molding at the angle it projects from the wall when installed. To make your job easier, draw a line on the miter box showing the height of the installed molding ("Molding Depth" from previous page). When you set the molding in the box, be sure to align it along the line. If you are using a chop saw, screw or clamp a hardwood stop to the back fence at Molding Depth. Then set the edge of the molding against the stop and cut. If you're cutting a miter, set the top edge of the molding (the ceiling edge) against the stop, with the back of the molding facing you, as shown. If you're cutting a cope, turn the bottom edge of the molding against the stop, with the front facing you, as shown.

Keep in mind that all walls are different, and corners are rarely exactly 90 degrees. So, before you cut the actual molding to length, cut some short lengths that you can use to test the joint for tightness. Start with 45-degree cuts, check the joint, and adjust the angle of the cut and the position of the molding in the miter box until you get a tight fit. Make a note of the angle you used, and then cut the actual pieces.

Installing the Molding

1. Find the Plates and Studs.
If the layout line is no more than about 2 1/4 inches below the ceiling, you won't need to find the studs; just make sure there's a top plate into which you can nail the ceiling molding. On the other hand, to find studs, use an electronic stud finder, or probe with a hammer and 8d finish nail to locate one or two studs near the end of the wall. Put the probe holes high on the wall, where the crown molding will cover them. Mark these studs with small pencil lines just below the layout line. When you install the molding, nail it at these studs first.

1. Crown or cove molding narrower than about 2 1/4 inches is nailed into the top plate. Wider molding is nailed into studs.

If studs are 16 inches on center, simply measure along the wall and drive nails every 16 inches to avoid making too many marks.

2. Install the First Piece Between Walls. After measuring the wall, square-cut both ends of a length of molding so that it fits nicely between opposing walls. The bottom edge of the molding should align with the layout line. Drill pilot holes and nail the crown to the studs or top plate with 8d finish nails.

3. Cope the Next Piece. Put the molding in the miter box so that you are looking at its front, with the edge that will go against the ceiling placed

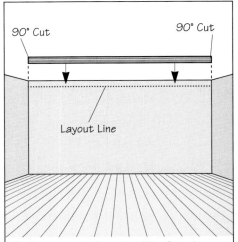

2. Square-cut both ends of the first piece and nail it in place with the bottom edge aligned with the layout line.

against the bottom of the miter box, as shown. Bevel the end at 45 degrees so that the back is longer than the front. Then use a coping saw to cut along the profile line created by the bevel. The profile line will become the front edge of the molding.

4. Check the Fit. Hold the coped piece of molding against the piece installed in the previous step to check the fit. Using a rasp or file, trim the back side of the molding, if necessary, to make a tight fit.

5. Cut the Other End of the Molding. If the other end will be part of an inside corner, simply cut the end square to butt against the opposite wall; the next piece of crown will be coped to fit. If the other end will be part of an outside corner, hold the molding in position and mark the back side along the wall. Then place the molding in the miter box so that you are looking at its back, with the top front edge of the molding resting against the saw fence, as shown. Bevel the end at 45 degrees for an

outside corner (the front of the molding will be longer than the back). Tack the piece of molding in place, using 8d finish nails. Do not set the nails yet; you may need to adjust the molding position when you install the next piece.

6. Finish Nailing Up the Molding. Once all the pieces are up, go back and complete the nailing. Put an 8d nail into each stud, or every 16 inches into the top plate. Set the nails and fill the holes. At outside

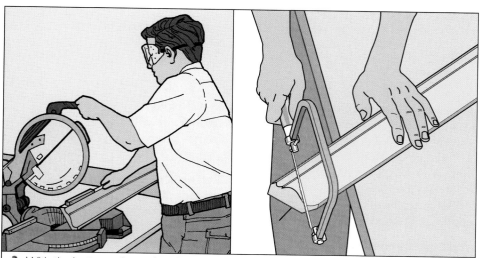

3. With the bottom edge against the stop block, begin the cope by beveling the end so that the back is longer than the front. Use a coping saw to cut along the profile edge of the molding's face. Angle the saw slightly so that the back is shorter than the face.

4. Hold the coped end against the first piece to check the fit. If it isn't tight, either use a rasp to shave parts that are too long, or else cut the molding again.

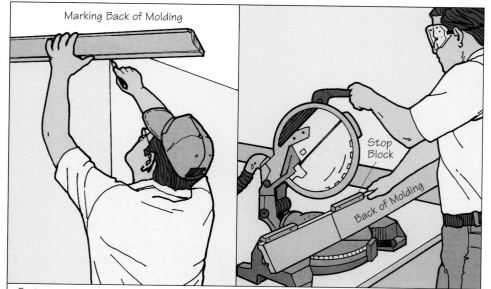

Marking Back of Molding

Stop Block

Back of Molding

5. At outside corners, hold the molding in position and mark the back side along the corner. Then place the molding in the miter box with the top edge against the fence, and bevel the end 45 degrees so that the front is longer than the back.

4d Finish Nail at Corner

6. After nailing the molding into the studs or top plate, tighten the outside corners by nailing them with a 4d finish nail. Drill a pilot hole and nail into the other piece.

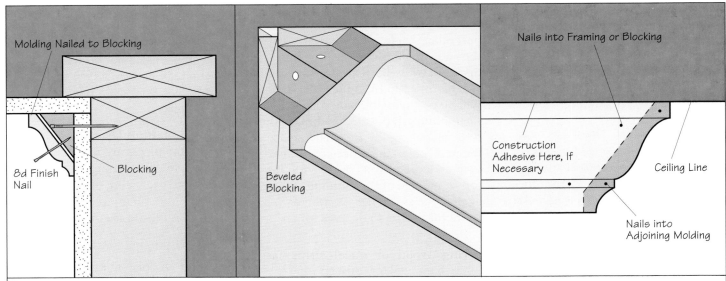

Using Blocking. If you can't find something to nail into, you can rip blocking at an angle on a table saw and nail or glue along the top of the wall. Then you would glue and nail the crown molding to the blocking.

corners, drill pilot holes and use 4d finish nails to nail the top edges of the molding together.

Using Blocking. In the unlikely event that you can't find the studs or top plate, and therefore have nothing to nail into, you can put some construction adhesive behind the molding (where it contacts the ceiling). Then nail it as best you can until the adhesive grips. If you have inadequate nailing, such as a single top plate, install blocking at the wall-ceiling joints, as shown, then nail and glue the crown molding to the blocking. Blocking can be made from solid wood or plywood.

Crown Molding Problems

Cutting crown molding is, in many respects, no different from cutting other profiled moldings. It does, however, present some special problems. For example, if any part of an installed crown molding dips below an imaginary line level, as shown, that crown will be impossible to cope. Avoid such profiles, or plan to miter the joints instead of coping them.

Walls parallel to the ceiling joists are often a problem because there's nothing to nail into. One solution is to install blocking at the wall-ceiling joint, as shown; then nail and glue the crown molding to the blocking. Blocking can be made from solid wood or plywood.

When there's no joist or blocking to nail into, you can put some construction adhesive behind the molding (where it contacts the ceiling). Then nail it as best you can until the adhesive grips.

Cutting Cove Molding. The procedure for cutting cove molding is the same as that used for cutting crown. The molding is placed in the miter box with the ceiling edge down so that it can be held firmly in place.

Crown Molding Problems. Molding contours can make cope cuts impossible below certain levels; either avoid such molding or miter it.

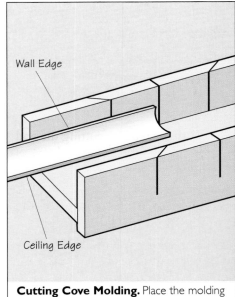

Cutting Cove Molding. Place the molding in the miter box, ceiling edge down, so that you can hold the molding firmly in place.

Beam A horizontal structural member that rests on posts or walls and supports the platform or roof above it.

Bearing wall A wall that provides structural support to framing above. Joists run at right angles to a bearing wall and rest on its top plate.

Building code Municipal rules regulating building practices and procedures. Local building permits are almost always required for new construction or major renovations. Inspections may be required to confirm adherence to code.

Casing Wood trim that covers the perimeter of finished windows and doors.

Cathedral ceiling A top-story ceiling that is peaked and commonly has exposed roof rafters.

Caulk An adhesive designed to seal cracks and joints against water, air, and noise. Usually sold in tubes, it is applied with a hand-squeeze gun.

Chalk line The mark left by a chalked line that was stretched taut between two points just above a flat surface before being pulled up in the center and allowed to snap back, leaving a straight chalked mark.

Cleat A small wood piece fastened to framing to strengthen a joint.

Collar beam A horizontal brace that ties facing pairs of rafters together.

Coped joint Made by cutting the end of a piece of molding to the shape of the molding it will fit against.

Corner bead Metal molding used at exterior corners of plastered and drywall-paneled walls.

Cove molding A molding with a concave face used as trim or finish for interior corners.

Crown molding Usually convex or ornate. Run where wall meets ceiling.

Double-hung window A window with upper and lower sashes that slide up and down.

Drywall Also known as gypsum board, wallboard, and plasterboard, this is a paper-covered sandwich of gypsum plaster. Inexpensive and easy to install as a wall surface.

Flashing Material, such as thin metal sheeting, used to prevent water from entering exterior joints of roofs, chimneys, skylights, dormers, and roof vents, as well as those of doors and windows.

Furring Wood or metal strips fastened to a wall or other surface to form an even base for the application of structural or finish materials, such as wallboard or flooring.

Girder A primary horizontal support for wood floor beams. In homes, girders are usually steel I-beams, solid timbers, or wood laminates.

Header A structural member that forms the top of a window, door, skylight, or other rough opening, while providing framing support and transferring loads.

Jamb The framework within a stud wall that supports a window or door.

Joint compound A premixed gypsum-based paste used to fill the seams between drywall panels and to patch imperfections.

Joist One in a series of parallel framing members that support a floor or ceiling load. Joists are supported by beams or bearing walls.

Knee wall A short attic wall, usually about 48 inches, extending from the floor to a slanted ceiling.

Lath Wood strips or metal mesh used as a foundation for plaster and stucco.

Molding Trim milled using a molder.

Mudsill Lumber piece installed on top of the foundation. Commonly referred to as a sill.

On center The distance between the centers of regularly spaced structural members, such as wall studs.

Penny (abbr. d) Unit of measurement for nail length, such as a 10d nail, which is 3 inches long.

Plate A horizontal member, at the top or bottom of a wall, to which the studs are fastened.

Prehung door A door delivered from the factory hung in its jamb framework.

Rafter Dimensional lumber that supports the sloping part of a roof.

Rim joist A joist that runs on the outside of the floor platform.

Saddle The board under a door that conceals the seam between adjoining rooms.

Sash The moving part of a window frame.

Shim A narrow wedge of wood driven between a fixed surface and a movable member to alter the position of the movable member.

Stud A vertical member in a frame wall, usually placed every 16 inches to facilitate covering with standard 48-inch-wide panels.

Subfloor The floor surface, usually plywood, that supports a finished floor.

Suspended ceiling A ceiling hung on wires from structural members.

Trim Decorative wood strips installed along edges of walls, floors, ceilings, doors, and windows.

Trimmer A vertical member nailed to a stud in a rough opening and supporting the header above.

Underlayment Sheet material—usually plywood—placed over a subfloor to provide a smooth, even surface for flooring.

Wainscot Paneling or other surface covering the lower third of a wall.

Wet sanding In drywall installation, the use of a damp sponge to reduce and smoothen the surface of hardened joint compound.

INDEX

METRIC CONVERSION TABLES

Lumber

Sizes: Metric cross sections are so close to their nearest U.S. sizes, as noted at right, that for most purposes they may be considered equivalents.

Lengths: Metric lengths are based on a 300mm module, which is slightly shorter in length than an U.S. foot. It will, therefore, be important to check your requirements accurately to the nearest inch and consult the table below to find the metric length required.

Areas: The metric area is a square meter. Use the following conversion factor when converting from U.S. data: 100 sq. feet = 9.29 sq. meters.

Metric Lengths

Meters	Equivalent Feet and Inches
1.8m	5' 10⅞"
2.1m	6' 10⅝"
2.4m	7' 10½"
2.7m	8' 10¼"
3.0m	9' 10⅛"
3.3m	10' 9⅞"
3.6m	11' 9¾"
3.9m	12' 9½"
4.2m	13' 9⅜"
4.5m	14' 9⅓"
4.8m	15' 9"
5.1m	16' 8¾"
5.4m	17' 8⅝"
5.7m	18' 8⅜"
6.0m	19' 8¼"
6.3m	20' 8"
6.6m	21' 7⅞"
6.9m	22' 7⅝"
7.2m	23' 7½"
7.5m	24' 7¼"
7.8m	25' 7⅛"

Metric Sizes (Shown before Nearest U.S. Equivalent)

Millimeters	Inches	Millimeters	Inches
16 x 75	⅝ x 3	44 x 150	1¾ x 6
16 x 100	⅝ x 4	44 x 175	1¾ x 7
16 x 125	⅝ x 5	44 x 200	1¾ x 8
16 x 150	⅝ x 6	44 x 225	1¾ x 9
19 x 75	¾ x 3	44 x 250	1¾ x 10
19 x 100	¾ x 4	44 x 300	1¾ x 12
19 x 125	¾ x 5	50 x 75	2 x 3
19 x 150	¾ x 6	50 x 100	2 x 4
22 x 75	⅞ x 3	50 x 125	2 x 5
22 x 100	⅞ x 4	50 x 150	2 x 6
22 x 125	⅞ x 5	50 x 175	2 x 7
22 x 150	⅞ x 6	50 x 200	2 x 8
25 x 75	1 x 3	50 x 225	2 x 9
25 x 100	1 x 4	50 x 250	2 x 10
25 x 125	1 x 5	50 x 300	2 x 12
25 x 150	1 x 6	63 x 100	2½ x 4
25 x 175	1 x 7	63 x 125	2½ x 5
25 x 200	1 x 8	63 x 150	2½ x 6
25 x 225	1 x 9	63 x 175	2½ x 7
25 x 250	1 x 10	63 x 200	2½ x 8
25 x 300	1 x 12	63 x 225	2½ x 9
32 x 75	1¼ x 3	75 x 100	3 x 4
32 x 100	1¼ x 4	75 x 125	3 x 5
32 x 125	1¼ x 5	75 x 150	3 x 6
32 x 150	1¼ x 6	75 x 175	3 x 7
32 x 175	1¼ x 7	75 x 200	3 x 8
32 x 200	1¼ x 8	75 x 225	3 x 9
32 x 225	1¼ x 9	75 x 250	3 x 10
32 x 250	1¼ x 10	75 x 300	3 x 12
32 x 300	1¼ x 12	100 x 100	4 x 4
38 x 75	1½ x 3	100 x 150	4 x 6
38 x 100	1½ x 4	100 x 200	4 x 8
38 x 125	1½ x 5	100 x 250	4 x 10
38 x 150	1½ x 6	100 x 300	4 x 12
38 x 175	1½ x 7	150 x 150	6 x 6
38 x 200	1½ x 8	150 x 200	6 x 8
38 x 225	1½ x 9	150 x 300	6 x 12
44 x 75	1¾ x 3	200 x 200	8 x 8
44 x 100	1¾ x 4	250 x 250	10 x 10
44 x 125	1¾ x 5	300 x 300	12 x 12

Dimensions are based on 1m = 3.28 feet, or 1 foot = 0.3048m

Dimensions are based on 1 inch = 25mm

For *all* of your home decorating and improvement projects, look for these and other fine Creative Homeowner Press books at your local home center or bookstore...

THE SMART APPROACH TO BATH DESIGN

Everything you need to know about designing a bathroom like a pro is explained. Advice about space, fixtures, and safety features accompany over 150 photos.

BOOK #: 287225   176 pp., 9"x10"

COLOR IN THE AMERICAN HOME

Find out how to make the most of color with ideas for coordinating color schemes. Learn how light affects the colors you choose. Over 150 photos.

BOOK #: 287264   176 pp., 9"x10"

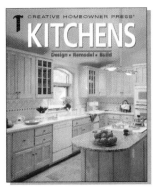

KITCHENS: Design, Remodel, Build

This is the reference book for modern kitchen design, with more than 100 full-color photos to help homeowners plan the layout. Step-by-step instructions illustrate basic plumbing and wiring techniques; how to finish walls and ceilings; and more.

BOOK #: 277065   192pp., 8½"x10⅞"

ADDING SPACE WITHOUT ADDING ON

Cramped for space? This book, which replaces our old book of the same title, shows you how to find space you may not know you had and convert it into useful living areas. 40 colorful photographs and 530 full-color drawings.

BOOK #: 277680   192pp., 8½"x10⅞"

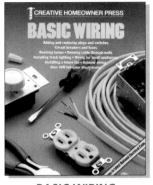

BASIC WIRING
(Third Edition, Conforms to latest National Electrical Code)

Included are 350 large, clear, full-color illustrations and no-nonsense step-by-step instructions. Shows how to replace receptacles and switches; repair a lamp; install ceiling and attic fans; and more.

BOOK #: 277048   160pp., 8½"x11"

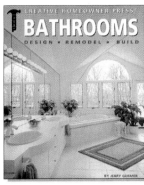

BATHROOMS

Shows how to plan, construct, and finish a bathroom. Remodel floors; rebuild walls and ceilings; and install windows, skylights, and plumbing fixtures. Specific tools and materials are given for each project.

BOOK #: 277053   192pp., 8½"x10⅞"

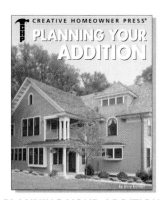

PLANNING YOUR ADDITION

Planning an addition to your home involves a daunting number of choices, from choosing a contractor to selecting bathroom tile. Using 280 color drawings and photographs, architect/author Jerry Germer helps you make the right decision.

BOOK #: 277004   192pp., 8½"x10⅞"

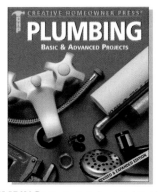

PLUMBING: Basic & Advanced Projects

Take the guesswork out of plumbing repair and installation for old and new systems. Projects include replacing faucets, unclogging drains, installing a tub, replacing a water heater, and much more. 500 illustrations and diagrams.

BOOK #: 277620   176pp., 8½"x10⅞"

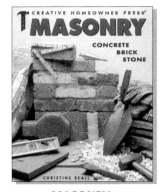

MASONRY

Concrete, brick, and stone choices are detailed with step-by-step instructions and over 35 color photographs and 460 illustrations. Projects include a brick or stone garden wall, steps and patios, a concrete-block retaining wall, a concrete sidewalk.

BOOK #: 277106   176pp., 8½"x10⅞"

For more information, and to order direct, call 800-631-7795; in New Jersey 201-934-7100

Please visit our website at http://www.chp-publisher.com